DISCA
From Nashville Public Library

D0968729

Nashville
Public Library
Foundation

*This book
made possible
through generous gifts
to the
Nashville Public Library
Foundation Book Fund*

UP THE ROAD

CYCLING'S MODERN ERA FROM LEMOND TO ARMSTRONG

Samuel Abt

Photographs by Graham Watson

Boulder, Colorado

Up the Road: Cycling's Modern Era from LeMond to Armstrong
© 2005 Samuel Abt
Photos © Graham Watson

All rights reserved. No part of this book may be reproduced, stored in a retrieval system, or transmitted, in any form or by any means, electronic or photocopy or otherwise, without the prior written permission of the publisher.

Printed in the United States of America.

10 9 8 7 6 5 4 3 2

Distributed in the United States and Canada by Publishers Group West.

Library of Congress Cataloging-in-Publication Data
Abt, Samuel.
  Up the road : cycling's modern era from LeMond to Armstrong / Samuel Abt.
    p. cm.
  Includes index.
  ISBN 1-931382-78-6 (hardback : alk. paper)
  1. Bicycle racing. 2. Cyclists. I. Title.

GV1049.A288 2005
796.6'2—dc22

                                          2005024723

VeloPress®
1830 North 55th Street
Boulder, Colorado 80301–2700 USA
303/440-0601 ◆ Fax 303/444-6788 ◆ E-mail velopress@insideinc.com

To purchase additional copies of this book or other VeloPress® books, call 800/234-8356 or visit us on the Web at velopress.com.

Cover photos by Graham Watson
Cover and interior design by Margaret McCullough
Part One opening photo by Cor Vos (Phil Anderson and Sean Kelly, 1984)
Part Two opening photo by Graham Watson (The Festina Affair, 1998)
Part Three opening photo by Graham Watson (Tour de France, 2005)

One more time,
this book is for my children,
Claire, Phoebe, and John

As the sun makes it new
Day by day make it new
Yet again make it new

—Ezra Pound

CONTENTS

Contents

ACKNOWLEDGMENTS

Once, when there were no more than three or four English-speaking reporters covering professional bicycle racing and I was the only American, it was easy to acknowledge those who helped me at races. Now, I am troubled by the fear that I will forget somebody among the dozens of English speakers in the sport. Nevertheless, here goes: Thanks for the friendship and support of Sal Zanca, George Vecsey, John Wilcockson, Rupert Guinness, Sal Ruibal, Ian Austen, Andy Hood, Barbara Bell, Becky Rast, Bonnie DeSimone, Bob Ford, Dale Robertson, Alasdair Fotheringham, William Fotheringham, Stephen Ferrand, Jeremy Whittle, Ellis Bacon, Daniel Friebe, and especially James Startt, a pillar of sincerity, constant good humor, and talent.

I also thank the many fine editors who have worked with me at the *International Herald Tribune* and *The New York Times,* where many of these pieces first appeared. Equal thanks to two excellent editors at VeloPress, Renee Jardine and Jade Hays.

My gratitude, finally, to John Abt for his research and technical help with this book, not to mention his encouragement, and to Anne-Sophie Bolon, queen of software, hardware, and everywhere in between, for her continuing computer assistance.

Part One

THE FOREIGN LEGION ARRIVES

ON THE INSIDE

1988

They appear at every race, a handful of cheery old men who try to be helpful. Does the organizer need an extra driver for sponsors' guests or reporters? Is some team short a gofer? The old men, always smiling and soft-spoken, step right in. Nothing is too menial if it allows them to maintain ties to the small world of professional cycling.

At the Créteil-Chaville race in the fall of 1987, one of the old men asked if anybody had heard about a reception later in the week that Peugeot was sponsoring. Most of us already had invitations, since our names and newspapers appear on the official lists. The old men don't make it onto those lists any longer. The teams they rode for are long gone, a pale memory of the days when riders wore a spare tire on their backs and a cabbage leaf under their caps on a blazing summer day.

But if the old men don't exist on the official guest lists, they still hear things and always manage to show up at social occasions, milling outside the door. That was where I found the Créteil-Chaville old man a few days later. We greeted each other and walked together up to the woman checking invitations; I explained that he was an honored ancien, an old-timer, of the sport. Gaily, she waved us both in—someday we'll all be old and reliant on kindness—and we separated in the crowd of other twinkly old men, riders, officials, journalists, photographers, and commercial sponsors.

As usual, it was a dull evening and, as usual, nobody would have missed it.

On the sidewalk stood fans and rubberneck tourists, the outsiders. We were the insiders. Not to be there was not to belong.

It's a long winter between Créteil-Chaville, also known as the Race of the Dead Leaves, in France, and the Ruta del Sol, the Road of the Sun, in Spain, where the next season traditionally starts. Young or old, a man needs a sense of community to see him safe through the winter.

Or through the spring, summer, and fall.

I wish I could say, as many do, that what first attracted me to racing was its athletic splendor. I can't, though. Of course, I appreciate the grace of a Stephen Roche riding a time trial, the snarl of a Bernard Hinault steaming away from the pack, the sheer physical drive of Greg LeMond climbing in the Alps or Sean Kelly elbowing his way into position for a sprint. I respect, admire, the way a Pascal Simon will continue riding with the agony of a broken collarbone in the Tour de France because he is wearing the yellow jersey, and I grieve with Phil Anderson when he comes up empty in the mountains but refuses to quit, even when his teammates have to push him uphill.

I marvel when Luis Herrera wins the feared climb at Alpe d'Huez and is able to regain his breath and begin answering questions a minute or two later. I am dazzled when Laurent Fignon shifts gears, bends his back, and accelerates—positively zips—away from Angel Arroyo on a 15-degree grade on the roof of the world in Switzerland.

"It's the hardest job there is," LeMond says, and who can quarrel with that?

And yet that's only partly the sport's attraction for me. Like the Créteil-Chaville old man, I seem to need the feeling of being inside. It's a small world, agreed, but our own.

That's elitist, of course. The average person cannot circulate as freely among the riders as anybody with a press accreditation can do, chatting with the LeMonds and Hinaults. To the outsider, one bicycle race is like another: a bunch of men pushing pedals. At its worst, television portrays the sport just that way in overhead views of a spun-out pack, tight shots of knotted backs and churning legs, middle-distance views of the final sprint to the finish line. The sameness is stultifying.

This kind of mundane presentation does little to refute the notion that bicycle racing is simply a hyped-up version of a ride to the corner store. "Everybody rides a bicycle when he's a kid and so he thinks it's the easiest thing in the world to do," Hinault complained to me once. "Or maybe they still ride on the weekend with their kids or go to the grocery on a bicycle. That's enough to convince them that they understand racing. Sometimes they might even get rained on before they make it home, so they know just how it is for us with 150 kilometers to go in the rain or snow. If everybody has done it, it can't be very hard, can it?"

The trick is to put the sport into a context, to know not necessarily the riders but their stories, to follow the newspapers and the gossip available to all, to understand that this is a personal world inviting all fans to enter. Not to make myths of athletes, not to exhibit an underlying distrust of the sport's pure appeal by turning dramatic situations into personal anecdotes, but to help forge the sport's dimensions of an epic. A seemingly meaningless victory or defeat may have a history all its own. If the spectator doesn't know that history, he is nothing more than the objective television camera. Worse—he misses the fun.

Look at a summer day in 1986 in the Pyrenees, the morning after Hinault built up a five-minute lead on LeMond with a long breakaway. In the parking lot before the stage, LeMond was downhearted about his chances, but Steve Bauer, his friend and teammate at the time, pointed out that LeMond had not raced that hard the day before but that Hinault had. Who knew what would happen the second day in the mountains? asked Bauer.

I went off, preceding the race, in a car with two Canadian friends, riding through sweet-smelling hay meadows and the high peaks of the race, following it on the Tour's radio. Late in the morning, we parked atop a pass amid dirty ice fields and thousands of spectators and watched the riders struggle up in a long, broken line behind us as Hinault broke away on the first descent, just as he had the day before.

Off we went after him, shadowing him for many miles through hairpin turns wet with runoff from glaciers and through villages packed with people waiting to cheer France's hero.

Suddenly the car began to wheeze, its overheated radiator a victim of the thin mountain air, and then simply quit.

Apologizing to my hosts, I jumped out and stood by the side of the road to flag down another press car. A pair of Spanish journalists picked me up and we continued the chase after Hinault as he began the final climb. At that point, the Spaniards' car flatted and again I jumped out, with more apologies, to seek another lift.

This time it was three cheering Colombian reporters who picked me up. They were cheering for Herrera, who was overtaking the faltering Hinault on the climb to Superbagnères. National pride rode with Herrera, the first Colombian to win a Tour de France stage but a bust since that 1984 triumph. "Olé, Lucho," the reporters cried out the windows, but Herrera sputtered and began falling back as LeMond, Alexi Grewal—since his Olympic victory another lost soul—and Andy Hampsten pulled up to him and then passed. The Colombians moaned and cursed.

In the town of Luchon, we drove to the press headquarters and watched the final hour on large-screen television, the better to begin writing our stories in time for deadline.

On the screen we watched LeMond win the stage and recover the five minutes he had lost the day before to Hinault. We saw the crushed Hinault straggle in and pull on the yellow jersey that he had nearly won for good and that we all realized he would not wear much longer. The entire race had changed, and what a fine story it made to write and discuss!

Throughout that day, not a person in the world had known where I was except for those on the inside with me. It was a fine, free feeling of escape and yet of belonging. For a few hours, I was on a breakaway myself.

"In French, the language of cycling," I once wrote, "a breakaway is an échappée, an offshoot of the verb meaning to escape. Escape, get away from it all, break away: the language of travel agents. Immune to responsibility or bills or telephone calls, beyond the reach of preachy wives or unjust bosses, the breakaway is riding for every envious man watching him and cheering that the escape will never end."

Does it sound magical, the community of cycling? As Walt Whitman wrote, "Not I, nor anyone else can travel that road for you, / You must travel it for yourself."

A LITTLE ENGLISH ON THE TOUR

1981

There were plenty of Frenchmen, Belgians, Dutchmen, Spaniards, and Germans, and even the odd Luxembourgeois, Swede, Swiss, and Portuguese in the 1981 Tour de France. But a main attraction was the Anglo-Saxon group, five riders who put some English on an otherwise unexciting competition.

As the riders ended their twenty-four-day slog on the Champs-Elysées in Paris, Bernard Hinault was more than fourteen minutes ahead in overall elapsed time. It was his third victory in four years, and he had been preparing his victory speech for weeks.

Because Hinault's triumph was almost certain from the outset, much interest focused on the five riders whose native tongue was English. Known inevitably as the Foreign Legion, they were Phil Anderson, a 23-year-old Australian; Jonathan Boyer, 25, an American; Graham Jones, 24, and Paul Sherwen, 25, both Englishmen, and Sean Kelly, 25, an Irishman.

Anderson ranked highest in the group. He finished tenth among the 121 who completed what 150 started in Nice. For nearly two weeks he was second behind Hinault, then a bad day in the Alps dropped him back.

Jones, who like Anderson rode for the Peugeot team, ranked 20th. Boyer, Hinault's teammate for Renault, ranked 32nd, and Kelly, riding for Splendor, ranked 48th. Sherwen, who rode for La Redoute, was eliminated with a week to go by a series of mechanical failures.

This was not the first time Anglo-Saxons—as the French lump together those who speak English—participated in the Tour. What made it different this year was that the English-speaking riders not only did so well as a group, but also showed promise to do better in the future.

Two of the widely acknowledged future stars of the sport are Greg LeMond, a 21-year-old American, and Stephen Roche, a 20-year-old Irishman. Both were judged by their team directors to be too young now for the long grind, although both were expected to start next year.

Boyer was the first American to ride in the Tour. Before his debut the month before, he said, "It's not a question of enough first-class athletes; we have plenty back home. It's a problem of finding sponsors."

Boyer, who was born in Utah and reared in California, spends a good part of the year at his home near Annecy in eastern France. Despite the star-spangled jersey he wears as unofficial U.S. champion, he is often mistaken for a Frenchman because his nickname, Jock, causes his name to appear as "Jacques Boyer," as if he were a youngster from Normandy.

He is considered something of a novelty on the circuit because he is both a vegetarian who carries a supply of California dates and a businessman who spent part of the previous season trying to sell other riders a brand of sticky tape that aids their grip on the handlebars.

"They just kind of look at me as an oddity sometimes," he said. "They wonder why I'm racing. They have the idea that America is a big and easy place to live, which it is. They wonder why I'm cycling, which is the hardest sport."

One answer was given by Roche, who astonished the cycling world by winning the Tour of Corsica, the Paris-Nice race, and the Tour of the Indre and Loire in his first season as a pro in France.

"Before I became a cyclist," he explained, "I worked in a factory. I liked my work well enough but I had dirty hands, dirty hair, I worked fixed hours, sometimes on Saturdays and Sundays. I'm trying to escape that life. Bicycling is hard work but in a few years you can guarantee the rest of your life."

The same sort of answer comes from Anderson. "The only way to make money in Australian sports is through golf, rugby, tennis, or yachting," he said. "In Europe, even if I don't make my fortune, I think I can earn enough to live well and make a name in Australia. When I'm done here, I hope to return home and capitalize on my reputation."

Such thinking is readily understood in a sport that has long been regarded by Europeans as a way of escaping from the family farm.

Maurice de Muer, the team director for Anderson, Roche, and Jones, said, "They develop a sense of responsibility when they leave their countries to seek their fortunes here. The only choices they have then are to do well or go home. So they're happy with everything—the way they live, the equipment, the crowded racing schedule.

"Anderson was so eager to make good, he even cut his long hair."

A DRIVER'S STORY

1982

The last time he saw Paris, Alain Meslet's heart was neither young nor gay, but troubled. He had just publicly confessed to throwing bicycle races and using illegal drugs, and then, on July 19, 1981, there he was riding in the Tour de France, completing the traditional last laps on the Champs-Elysées and finishing 41st overall.

At the end of the afternoon, while hundreds of thousands of Frenchmen were cheering Bernard Hinault's victory, Meslet, then 31 years old, retired. His six-year career as a professional ended on the broad and elegant avenue where he had known his only real glory: In 1977 he won the final stage in Paris, crossing the finish line with arms upraised and the sly smile of somebody who has surprised even himself.

The final day's winner is always eclipsed by the finish of the long haul and the anointing of the overall champion; even the daily victory ceremony in which the stage winner is given a bouquet is usually overlooked as some French dignitary presents a Sèvres porcelain vase to the overall winner. So Meslet's victory was unsung. But it mattered to him.

"I used to make between 1,500 francs and 1,800 francs [then $300 to $350] in each of the criteriums," local races staged throughout the country day and night for weeks after the Tour de France. "In 1977, I reached 2,500 francs, which wasn't bad."

Money means a lot to Meslet. As a professional rider with four teams, he sometimes was willing to do anything to make money, as he admitted just before the Tour ended. And then he slipped away, opening a bicycle shop in his native Brittany—"turning a page," as he put it.

Meslet will be back in Paris when the 69th Tour de France completes its 2,188-mile journey (about 3,500 kilometers) from Basel, Switzerland. This time, instead of by bicycle, Meslet will arrive by car, driving for the newspaper *Le Télégramme* of Brest, a city in Brittany near his home in the village of Evron.

Brittany is big cycling territory, so *Le Télégramme* devotes pages every day to the race and sends along two reporters to cover its every moment. Meslet chauffeurs them, picking his way with horn and occasionally brakes through the 140-odd riders remaining of the 169 who started in Basel. He shadows the pack from town to town, moving through the riders to reach advance observation posts or restaurants, staying at their heels while the reporters observe and make notes. When the riders reach the day's finish, the reporters scramble from the car and trust Meslet to park it and prepare it for the next day's chase.

With more than 300 reporters following the Tour by car, not to mention up to half a dozen vehicles for each of fifteen teams plus innumerable cars for officials, there is plenty of employment available for drivers. No special training is needed, since job requirements exactly fit the average French motorist: disregard for speed limits, contempt for others on the road, and heartfelt trust in immortality. Many of the drivers have been involved with the Tour de France before as riders and now sit behind the wheel as a way of staying in touch.

Jean-Claude Theillère, for example, was a professional racer for eight years and rode in the Tour for four years as a teammate of Jacques Anquetil, five times a winner of the race in the late 1950s and 1960s. Theillière, who now owns a printing shop in Clermont-Ferrand, has been a driver for the press for three years.

"I applied six years ago," he says, "and then one day they called and said I had the job. They pay me, of course, or else I would spend July at the seashore, but it's still nice to be back with the Tour de France."

He never won a stage but, like Meslet, he once had a day to remember: In 1966, Theillière won the French championship. He keeps the blue, white, and red jersey—"silk, you know"—in a closet at home and shows it occasionally to friends. "It's a nice souvenir," Theillière says.

Meslet does not have a similar souvenir, but he came close. "My biggest regret was the championship of France in 1976 at Montauban," he has said. He finished second because, he admits, he threw the race for money.

Meslet revealed this just before he retired, in an interview with the respected Noël Couëdel in the French daily sports newspaper, *L'Equipe*. The interview caused no stir because the next day Hinault won his third Tour de France and for weeks everybody was discussing little else but the man in the yellow jersey.

Since then Meslet has generally dropped out of sight. In Brittany he runs a small store: "I sell bicycles and sports clothes, my family has an apartment upstairs." His presence in this year's race seems to have caused no adverse comment.

"I still have a lot of friends among the riders," he insists. "Nobody is nasty to me because of what I said." He got his chauffeur's job, he says, when *Le Télégramme* phoned and invited him to work. "Of course I said yes. I like the Tour de France and meant it no harm. I said what had to be said, what I needed to say."

"What you're saying," Couëdel asked him the year before, "you're saying out of rancor?"

"Not at all," Meslet contended. "I'm happy to say it because young riders don't pay attention."

"You quit cycling happy?" Couëdel pressed.

"Oh yes, very. Without cycling, I would have wound up working in a factory."

Nobody has publicly challenged what Meslet said, so it can be inferred that he spoke truthfully. He insists that he also spoke for many other riders, so his remarks presumably offer some insight into the world of professional bicycle racing.

Discussing the 1976 championships, Meslet said: "I was racing with [Guy] Sibille, who was smarter than me. He offered me a lot of money to let him win. I was starting to build a house and I was making 2,500 francs a month, so I was taking a big risk building a house. I accepted the offer of money.

"I'm sorry to have sold out. . . . Instead of the [50,000 francs] I got, I could have made four times that by winning the championship, between the criteriums and a salary increase. I made a mistake."

"Sibille got the best of you," Couëdel said, "but later you did the same to others."

"Naturally," Meslet replied. "You have to be cold-blooded and not worry about making friends. I've sold races, but that happens often enough. Last year, for example, I sold my services to anybody who wanted them. I was racing well on the Côte d'Azur and in the Tour of the Tarn but you've got to be a realist. Those are only second-rank races; I wasn't selling the championship of France.

"I wasn't winning enough and I needed money. Cycling is a nice way to make your living, but it can be deceiving. The sport I like is track and field. It's healthy, it's pleasant to watch, and it hasn't been ruined by money."

Then Meslet turned to the use of drugs. During the professional season from February to October, riders are exposed to wind, rain, and even snow as they log up to 150 miles a day, often in the mountains. They feel tired and they get sick, and often they are treated with some of the many drugs banned by the sport's officials. Riders are occasionally caught by urinalysis and then penalized—Angel Arroyo was stripped of his victory in the Tour of Spain and Eric McKenzie of his victory in the Championship of Zurich.

"In 1976," Couëdel said, "you were astonished that nobody noticed you had gained a lot of weight during the Tour de France."

"That's right, I remember," Meslet answered. "I trusted the way we were prepared for the race. But in the first stage, I finished in the last five. Something had gone wrong. That night I felt like my skin was cracking. I looked in the mirror and got scared. I was swelling up as I watched.

"I know I was to blame, too, because I accepted all that stuff, including vitamin potions with the labels scratched off. I needed money. I was young. I was dazzled by good results.

"And then I understood that health was worth more than all that. In 1977 I took care of myself. It's better to be a minor racer than to burn up inside. Cortisone, there's the enemy.

"What I've got to say is simply this: Pay attention to your health. Don't take cortisone, it stays in the body. All that saved me is that I was stupid for only a short time."

At the end of the interview, Couëdel noted, "People are going to say that, in this interview, you and I give a bad impression of cycling."

"Perhaps," Meslet said. "But you have to understand that everything I've said, a lot of riders think but hesitate to say. I assure you that many riders think like me. But nobody talks about it. When they're asked, they tell lies. What I've said is the truth."

So Meslet continues to insist. "Nobody holds it against me," he said one morning this month, waiting for the race to start. "There were no reprisals after the interview and here I am, back with the Tour de France." The bicycle racers set off and Meslet excused himself. It was time to slip behind the wheel of the car and follow the pack to Paris.

THEIR DAY IN THE SUN

1983

Nearly a year late, the Tour de France arrived Sunday in the village of Fontaine au Piré, fulfilling its 1,217 inhabitants' dream of becoming the smallest community ever to be host to the world's premier bicycle race.

The records show, village officials said proudly, that since the race began in 1903 no smaller town had ever been the finish of a daily stage. This was a boast that Fontaine au Piré, 125 miles northeast of Paris, almost couldn't make.

On July 7, 1982, the Tour was also scheduled to finish a stage there. But an unemployment protest by one thousand steelworkers in Denain, 25 miles up the road, stopped the riders and forced the day's stage to be canceled. By the time the steelworkers dispersed, the riders were gone by car to Lille and the next day's stage.

In Fontaine au Piré, meanwhile, the crowds waited and waited. By the time Tour officials arrived to confirm the impossible rumors—the first cancellation in the Tour's history—village officials had decided to try again. As one of them said then, "We'll try every year until they finally make it here."

Finally they did, in a team time trial from Soissons, 60 miles away. The Coop Mercier team finished fastest, in 2 hours, 18 minutes, and 59 seconds, or 17 seconds ahead of Peugeot and 44 seconds ahead of third-placed Aernoudt in the field of fourteen teams with ten riders each.

All the teams were welcomed by tens of thousands of spectators who came from nearby villages and towns to fill Fontaine au Piré's few streets. On a hot and sunny day, the road from Soissons was lined with people out for a picnic and a diversion. Here it was a gathering of the faithful.

Finally, in midafternoon, a rumble reached the crowd in the main square, the Place Jean Jaurès: "Ils arrivent, ils arrivent"—"They're coming, they're coming."

As the first riders from the first team to leave Soissons, the Colombians, turned left on the Rue Salengro and entered the final straightaway on the main street, Rue Gambetta, a roar went up and the applause began.

Hours later, Rue Gambetta was still mobbed. The last racer had long since been slapped on the back and the last bicycle carefully packed away from admiring hands, but nobody was quite ready to go home yet. It was clearly the most memorable day for Fontaine au Piré since it was pillaged by Austrian troops on August 15, 1793, and a far sight more joyful.

The village had been working for its afternoon for the last five years. "Nobody took us seriously," said the mayor, Jean-Marie Lemaire, the previous year, when explaining why Fontaine au Piré had tried and would try again.

What inspired this village was the same goal that moves other communities along the route—a place in the sun, international television coverage and newspaper datelines, a day of being just as important as Paris, the overall finish line.

Paris, however, is rich. "Around here," said the mayor, "nobody is rich."

When he and a delegation first presented their bid, "Tour de France organizers smiled. They showed me all it would take. . .money, equipment, all the enormous demands the Tour makes. Everybody smiled. But Fontaine au Piré remained a candidate."

When it was awarded the stage finish in 1982, the town went to work to prepare for the arrival. Roads were resurfaced, sidewalks repaired, a dressing room with showers for the cyclists was built, houses were repainted.

To raise funds, the village turned to cottage industries, producing T-shirts, hats, pennants, and all sorts of gadgets. In this farming and textile region, everybody worked at night, after their regular jobs, except for pensioners and schoolchildren, who worked during the day. All 439 families pitched in, the mayor reported.

And so, alerted by fifty thousand brochures distributed in the north of France, a huge crowd had turned out the previous year. Flowers awaited each team of racers and the town hall was decorated with the flag of every nation represented in the Tour. There was champagne on ice, but the riders were stopped 25 miles away by the steelworkers, who had been told the night before that their plant would be closing.

Unemployment is no better in France now than it was then, but nobody wanted to make trouble again for this village. The riders passed without incident through St. Gobain, where the glass factories have laid off workers, and through Originy, where the cement works have been quiet.

It was calm all along the route, in fact, until the Tour de France reached Fontaine au Piré, where the joy and excitement threatened to keep exploding all night.

SHE BLAZED A TRAIL

1984

Betsy King started the Bordeaux-Paris bicycle race two hours before everybody else and finished last, more than an hour after the winner. It was a great triumph, and she promised to let no one forget it soon.

"I'm doing this to say, 'Hey, man, we count, too. Women are important,'" King, a native of Farmington, Connecticut, said before the race. Covering 586 kilometers, or 350 miles, Bordeaux-Paris is believed to be the world's longest one-day bicycle race. It is also France's oldest, begun in 1891 and run this year for the eighty-first time. Never before had a woman entered.

"I look forward to this as much as you look forward to getting your wisdom teeth out," King said in Bordeaux, the southwestern wine center. "But it has to be done. A lot of people think women can't ride a race like this. So somebody's got to do it to show them a woman won't die."

Although she was far behind when the field finished at Fontenay Sous Bois, an eastern suburb of Paris, few of the thousands of spectators left before her arrival, some eighteen hours after she had begun. A wave of applause swept up the final hill with King as she followed a pace-setting motor bicycle, trying hard, and utterly failing, to conceal her satisfaction with the cries of "Bravo, Betsy!"

At the finish, one of the first persons she thanked was Gerard Labarthe, her trainer, who had set the pace for her.

Most races do not specifically exclude women, but classic professional races are rarely open to amateurs, and there are no female pros. Bordeaux-Paris is an exception, allowing licensed pros and amateurs. That was the opening for the 32-year-old King, who had been riding as an amateur for French clubs for three years but had never thought of entering a pro male race.

"I am above all a woman, but I am not above all a feminist," she said.

Yet she had chafed against the French and International Cycling Federation rules that limit women's competition: no more than one race a day, and that race not to exceed 80 kilometers; no competition against men except on Sundays and holidays, and such competition not to exceed 120 kilometers.

She was also disturbed by what she described as men's unwillingness to lose to a woman. "I win races with 90 people in them every Sunday, but the people are all women," she said. "When I race against men, they will block the course, they'll help each other just to stop me.

"I know I can win against men. I'm really nasty when I'm riding, and the Lord gave me a good body. I have a lot of power." She pulled up the left leg of her Renault team sweatpants and showed her calf. "That's muscle, more muscle than a woman is supposed to have," she said. Standing 5 feet 3 inches, she weighs 115 pounds.

When Labarthe, the trainer for her club at Antony-Bercy, outside Paris, suggested that she enter Bordeaux-Paris, she was ready if not quite willing. "He really likes this race and really cares about women's cycling," King said.

Her intention to compete was made public over the winter, when she was in the United States visiting her hometown, where her father, Edgar King, is a probate judge and the town clerk, she said. Betsy King, named Marjorie Elizabeth at birth, attended Farmington High School, Mount St. Joseph's Academy, and the Austin School in nearby Hartford. She said she had gone "to about five colleges, finally the University of Connecticut, and studied cell biology but never got a degree."

After the visit home, she attended the Olympic Training Center in Colorado Springs in January, then continued her bicycle team training in Arizona and Texas before returning to France in April.

When she learned that she would be allowed in the race, she recalled, "I couldn't back out then; all I could think was, 'Here I go off to the sacrifice.'"

Bronchitis delayed her training until May 9. Then, she said, she started riding hundreds of kilometers a day, alone or behind a motor bicycle, which is used for the final 358 kilometers of the race. (There is a rest stop of three-quarters of an hour just before this point.) She logged 1,000 kilometers in the week before Bordeaux-Paris.

She competed not as an official entry but in an unspecified and singular category, starting two hours before the men, at 12:30 a.m. It was not until 2:30 p.m., in the upper Loire Valley, that Marcel Tinazzi, the eventual winner, overtook her. In the next few hours, she was passed by all sixteen remaining riders of the twenty who had started.

As King rode, she was loudly cheered, especially by those who had not expected a woman. "It was like all of France was pushing me," she said. "There were lots of people yelling, 'Allez Betsy!' This, and finishing, meant a lot.

"Suddenly a lot of women riders are saying to me, 'I didn't know we could do Bordeaux-Paris. Next year I'll ride it, too.'

"I've made my point."

THE ROAD NOT TAKEN

1985

They were waiting for Alexi Grewal in Nokere and had even reserved brassard No. 1 for him in the bicycle race. They explained that No. 1 seemed right for the gold-medal winner in the road race at the Los Angeles Olympic Games.

What they didn't say in the Belgian village of six hundred inhabitants was how unexpected it was to have the Olympic winner announce his intention of being at the twenty-third annual Nokere kermesse, or village race.

One of hundreds held every year in Belgium and worth only 100,000 Belgian francs (about $1,600) in prizes, the race was just a local affair. But not much happens in Nokere most of the year, and race day is a holiday.

So, toward noon, farmers with wives and children began to gather behind barricades on Nokerdorp Straat, the main—and almost only— street, passing the two hours left to race time by eating hamburgers, salted herrings, simmered snails, and other staffs of life in this part of Flanders.

In a corner of the Café Schuttershof, where the riders signed in, a few old people nursed a beer in hopes of seeing such celebrities as Grewal or Lucien Van Impe, now 36 but in 1976 the winner of the Tour de France, or any of the unknown hopefuls who rank 12th or 15th on European professional teams. The teams are allowed to enter no more than ten men in most major competitions, so a kermesse is an opportunity to give experience to a lesser rider.

Or to Grewal. Nine months earlier, one hundred thousand, two hundred thousand, half a million people lined a freeway outside Los Angeles to cheer him, and millions more around the world watched on television as he won the 190-kilometer race by a bicycle length. Now Grewal rides unheeded except for the occasional motorist traveling on back roads through the Ardennes in the Netherlands. As it turned out, even the race in Nokere was more public attention than he wanted now.

The 24-year-old American had been recovering from suspected hepatitis for five weeks and had not ridden in competition since he finished the weeklong Tirreno-Adriatico race in Italy in March. It was his second professional race. "I was making incredible efforts just to finish each day's stage," Grewal explained later by telephone from his apartment in Geleen, the Netherlands. "It's a hard race but not that hard. That's when I knew I was sick."

Lately he had been feeling better, he said in another phone conversation. "My legs are a lot fuller, a lot denser. That's a pretty good sign. The doctors say my blood is back to 57, but I don't know what the number means. Normal is 40 and not long ago my number was up to 71, so 57 isn't too bad. Whatever it means."

He was still looking forward then to the Nokere race, a 13-lap, 147-kilometer circuit of farmland in resolutely flat Belgium. "My legs need to start talking," Grewal explained. "If you back up who you are with your legs, then you earn the respect of your teammates."

He signed in the fall with the Panasonic-Raleigh team, which is based in the Netherlands and is one of the strongest teams in European competition.

"I have a lot of obligations here," Grewal admitted. First on his calendar is the Tour of Spain, the Vuelta, which begins in Valladolid and continues for twenty days.

When his schedule was made up during the winter, his two major races were the Tours of Spain and Switzerland, followed perhaps by the Tour de France.

But before all the national tours came the race in Nokere (hang a right in Kruishoutem), where chickens peck in yards on the main street. "It's just a small race," Grewal said. "If I don't do well there, I won't do well anywhere."

Alexi Grewal did not do well in Nokere—did not even show up—because he decided the night before that, after all, the race was not worth the effort. "It was a two-hour ride by car just to get there and if you get a flat tire on the first lap, that's it," he said on the phone afterward. He rejected a suggestion that he might have been gun-shy about resuming competition, pointing out that he would fly Monday from Brussels for the Tour of Spain.

"I needed a really hard training ride today," he continued. "I went out for seven and a half hours in the Ardennes. It was a killer training ride."

Grewal has been going on hard training rides every three days during his convalescence, while acknowledging that "if you ride with hepatitis, you can permanently damage your liver." His weight has dropped a few pounds from his usual 155 pounds on a 6-foot-2-inch frame.

"Since Tirreno-Adriatico, I've missed only a week's training," he said. "But my longest ride for a long time was four hours, about 80 kilometers, not really a lot." In fact that distance is standard training for an amateur rider, a world away from his status now. He found that out when Panasonic welcomed him to the professional ranks by revising something as basic as the way he sat on a bicycle.

"They changed my position the first time I met with them, in November," he said at the team's presentation lunch in Brussels. "They moved me down and back."

Grewal was a star attraction at the presentation, explaining to European journalists that his name was pronounced GREY-wall; that he was indeed part Indian, but "I'm not an Apache, my father was a Sikh"; that despite his reputation as a climber in the Tour of Colorado, "I'm an all-arounder more than a pure climber; I'm an overrated climber"; and that, despite his reputation as a rebellious loner, he could be diplomatic.

During lunch he showed how diplomatic: "I'm pretty much unproven," he told a questioner, "an unknown commodity, maybe even with a bad reputation. I have much to learn, but I don't think it's a handicap."

Did he worry about going from Olympic champion to being a new member of a successful team? "Everybody can beat me at first; it's not going to bother me. I expect to start at the bottom. A beginner can't expect much.

"Like many athletes, I often know when I start I cannot win, but when you start a race you know you can win and don't, that's the worst. I can't say which, because I don't know exactly when I'll have form and I don't know when I'll have luck, but if I do have luck, opportunity, and form, then I expect to win the race. When's that going to be? Next week or two years from now, that's what I don't know."

In Nokere, eighty-five riders set out on the first of the eleven circuits toward Kruishoutem and the two toward Wortegem. Badly needing the experience of sprinting and elbowing in a pack on the corners, Grewal decided instead to go for one more solitary ride before the Tour of Spain. "Three weeks ago I couldn't go out for more than an hour and a half without feeling exhausted," he said. "Now I'm up to seven and a half hours. That's real progress even though I'm beat."

"Who's taking care of you?" Grewal was asked on the phone. "Three people," he answered. "Me, myself, and I."

LOOKING FOR A FEW ANSWERS

1986

The 209 other riders in the Tour de France set off on a bicycle race, but Alexi Grewal says he is making a journey into himself.

Two years after he won the gold medal in the road race at the Olympic Games in Los Angeles, Grewal no longer yearns for victory or even competition. "I didn't mind the glory one bit," he said in an interview. "Then when I got it again, I found it empty. It just made me want more."

Two weeks ago he was ready to quit professional racing. "What am I doing this for?" he remembered asking as he rode in the Tour d'Armorique, a tune-up in Brittany for the Tour de France. A month shy of his 26th birthday, Grewal could not answer his own question.

"Physically I felt fine, but I had this weird feeling, this questioning," he explained as he fiddled with his bicycle before the start of the Tour de France. To everybody else it is the world's most important bicycle race, but to Grewal that wasn't enough. "I realized it was just a big race instead of something I can really grow with," he said. "I realized it wasn't going to bring me peace of mind."

Victory had nothing to do with it, he insisted, as he measured the height and angle of his saddle. "It didn't really matter how well I did on my bike. That wasn't going to make me happy.

"So I decided to drop out of the Tour d'Armorique on the next-to-last day. Ten minutes after the stage was over, I went to a telephone booth at the side of the road near Rennes and called some people in the United States— my mom, my best friend, my father. I didn't even have enough money to talk, so I phoned them and told them to call me back." His parents, who are divorced, both live in Aspen, Colorado, Grewal's hometown.

"And we talked and talked. I was a little bit afraid to just drop cycling, and in the end they convinced me to try again, that I was kind of obligated to the people who have supported me.

"And here I am. I'll do the Tour de France and I know I'll find out whether I should keep racing. If I don't enjoy it, that's the end of racing."

For physical reasons, Grewal was close to dropping racing in 1985. After he won the Olympic medal he signed with the Panasonic team in the Netherlands and was touted as the climber the team lacked. A few races in early spring of 1985 left him sick and weak, his usual 155 pounds down to 143.

He had to withdraw from the 1985 Tour of Spain, his first major race as a professional, in the second week. Team doctors ordered a liver biopsy, which was said to indicate hepatitis. At first it was feared that his racing days were over.

"I went home to the States and was cured in four days," Grewal said as he fitted tires to his bicycle frame. "Back home the doctors diagnosed my trouble as malaria and fixed me right up." How had he contracted malaria? "From a mosquito," he deadpanned.

In any case, he celebrated his return by winning what he called the Tour of Crested Butte, Colorado, a three-day race, that September.

Grewal's career has often been marked by problems. He suffers from asthma and was winning the 1984 Coors Classic in Colorado when he was expelled and suspended because an herbal-compound pill he had taken for asthma was found to contain a substance illegal in cycling. The ruling was reversed quickly on appeal and he went on to ride soon afterward in the Olympics.

As Grewal tells it, his problems are not solely physical. He admits, for example, that he quit high school in 1978 just weeks short of graduation. "I was wasting my time. All I learned was that I didn't want to go." His parents, he said, did not object strenuously. "My parents were getting a divorce and trying to survive in Aspen. That kept them busy."

The illness in Europe changed his thinking, he said. "Getting back to form has been an obsession to me, and when I finally got my form I was dissatisfied. I was so obsessed with good results that the rest of my life was suffering. It was almost impossible to do anything else."

Grewal appears to enjoy his reputation as an eccentric loner, though not everybody agrees with the description. One person who speaks highly of him is Bernard Thévenet, a 37-year-old Frenchman who won the Tour de France twice in the 1970s and now coaches the RMO team. Grewal rode with RMO in late spring of 1986 on a release from his American team, 7-Eleven.

"He was well integrated into our team," Thévenet said. "He worked well with us, helped one of our riders win the climber's jersey in the Midi Libre race. Grewal doesn't speak much French and that was a barrier but he got along well with us.

"I think his reputation as a pig-headed kid is unfair. He's a nice boy."

Grewal rode three races with RMO, a minor French team then in its first year of operation. "I rode with RMO because it was the only team that would take me," he admitted. "I was tenth in the Midi Libre, won the mountains prize in the Tour of Luxembourg, and then dropped out of the Tour d'Armorique.

"In a way this is just a job," he said, speaking of his role with 7-Eleven, the first U.S. team to ride in the Tour. "I'm not really close to anybody on the team. They're all pretty good guys, but I just don't get close to them. I haven't had much fun with them."

He continued, "The only time I've had a lot of fun was when I went out in the wilderness with my brothers," Ranjit, 22, and Rishi, 19. The three went into the Mount Zirkle Wilderness near Steamboat Springs, Colorado, the previous October and spent five days riding mountain bicycles, living in one tent, "and cooking whenever we felt like eating, which wasn't much."

Grewal said he thought often about returning to the wilderness, any wilderness, perhaps enrolling in an Outward Bound program or another survival school, "one in the desert, another in the mountains.

"I'll know in a few weeks whether I'll be going," he said. "It depends on this race. Some people have goals in the Tour de France of winning a stage. My goal is to find out whether I'm not tortured if I'm doing bad, not dissatisfied if I'm doing well."

CORONATION DAY

1985

Finally it was coronation day for the man the French referred to as King Kelly, and not only because his first name, Sean, is so difficult for them to pronounce. King Kelly he became in March 1984, when the professional season began in earnest on the Continent, and King Kelly he was affirmed in October, when the season wound down. Now, as Europe's coldest winter in years waited outside, Kelly stood at center stage of a ballroom in a Paris hotel while blue laser beams traced his name in 6-foot-high letters on a curtain behind him.

He was being honored as champion of the Super Prestige competition, which is sponsored each year by a French aperitif, Pernod.

The bicycling fraternity regards this title, based on the year's accumulated results in a series of major races, as the unofficial world championship. "Oh yes," Kelly said when asked if he concurred in the judgment. "Most definitely I do."

He was wearing a rainbow sash and holding the golden sunburst trophy that accompanied his check for 50,000 French francs, roughly $5,000. "I'm going to invest the money in something sound," he joked with an American reporter, "something like dollars."

The 28-year-old Kelly was in fine humor then, patiently posing for just one more photograph and then just one more after that, kissing Miss France on the cheeks and shaking hands with Bernard Hinault, who had won the Prestige award for French riders only. With a late-season spurt to victory in the Grand Prix des Nations, the pros' major individual time trial, in southern France in September, and the Tour of Lombardy in Italy almost a month later, Hinault also vaulted into second place in the Super Prestige competition. But he still trailed far behind the Irishman at season's end, 305 points to 450, as did the 1983 winner, Greg LeMond, who finished seventh with 125 points.

As the disparity in points indicates, the night belonged to Kelly. His achievements for the year were well known to the audience, hundreds of cycling team officials, reporters, and hangers-on, but the announcers read them anyway: first in Paris-Nice and the Criterium International de la

Route, two of the spring's major stage races. Then came the classics: first in Paris-Roubaix, the toughest and most respected of the one-day races, first in Liège-Bastogne-Liège, second in Milan-San Remo, second in the Tour of Flanders.

Next came the national tours, with Kelly gaining a fourth place in the Tour of Switzerland and a fifth place in the Tour de France. Afterward there were the fall classics: second in the Grand Prix des Nations, first in Blois-Chaville in France, and third in Paris-Brussels—a ranking Kelly lost on a doping conviction, the first positive drug test in his eight-year career as a professional.

Including those that didn't count toward the Super-Prestige title, Kelly's record for the year came to thirty-three victories, far and away the most by any rider. In addition to the Super Prestige award, he was ranked an easy first in the computer standings of the authoritative *Vélo* magazine in France.

"Yes, I'm at my summit," Kelly said in fluent French at the ceremony, agreeing with the announcer as the audience applauded lustily. Even Hinault, who was winning his fourteenth Pernod award, looked on approvingly. He also shared in the joke when Kelly was asked how he was spending the off-season in Ireland. "I've been doing some hunting," he replied. "For badger?" the announcer asked with a smile, since Hinault's nickname is Le Blaireau, the Badger. "Not right now," Kelly replied. "For now it's pheasants."

As the laser beams winked overhead and the crowd strained to hear his soft words, Kelly paid tribute to his Skil-Sem teammates and his long-time team manager, Jean de Gribaldy, who signed him after he spent half a season with the Metz-Woippy amateur team in eastern France. Kelly felt he owed his loyalty to de Gribaldy: "It was three years before I started producing as a professional and he stayed with me. Now it's my turn to stay with him."

The huge salary Kelly is said to be getting from Skil for the 1985 season, estimated at $250,000, also may have had something to do with his rejection of offers from Italian teams.

Plus, Kelly has hinted, Italy seems such a long way from home, either the apartment he keeps near Brussels during the racing season or the farm where he was born in Carrick-On-Suir in Ireland. Those who have been there know it as a working farm of about forty acres with dirt floors in the house, the sort of farm that Irishmen say spawns men of the people, like Kelly.

The Irish like to tell Kelly stories. How the obstetrician told his mother, "Mrs. Kelly, your baby has the finest muscle tone of any baby I've delivered." How the young Kelly belonged to a cycling club that couldn't sponsor a race because it did not have the money to buy medals for the winners and how, hearing this news, Kelly rode home, packed a sack, returned to his club, and, pouring the medals and trophies on the table, asked, "Here, will these do for Sunday?"

The Irish will tell of Kelly's race with a schoolboy team, ages 13 and 14, against a junior team, ages 15 to 17, with all the difference in strength and skill that the age difference implies. Kelly was the only schoolboy able to keep up with the juniors. Five minutes into the race, he pulled up and waited for his teammates because he was just a lad, and a lonely one, too. Maybe, just maybe, it was the last time he ever lost his nerve.

Joining one of Ireland's top amateur teams, he was asked if he would work for the leader, and he replied, "Sure I'll work for him, provided he'll keep up with me."

The likeable Kelly is too quiet to tell them himself, but the stories go on and on. How he was selected for Ireland's cycling team at the 1976 Olympic Games in Montreal but first raced in South Africa, smart enough to use a false name but dumb enough to think he could continue to evade the sport's blacklist for competing in South Africa. How he was suspended and went instead to France, where he joined the team in Metz, getting 250 francs a month for the food he cooked in a furniture exhibition hall and living in a curtained-off corner there. He won eighteen of twenty-five races for his club, then went home for the winter. De Gribaldy flew over to Ireland in his private plane and, negotiating with Kelly in the mud of the farmyard, offered him a professional contract that Kelly was only too pleased to accept if de Gribaldy would only double the money involved, which the Frenchman was clever enough to do.

For all this, Kelly's development as a professional was slow, as he admitted at the Pernod ceremony. When he swept the spring races in 1984, he was able to say truthfully that he might be 28 years old but he felt much younger since he had spent his first three years as a professional not doing much more than watching and learning. By 1982, he had five stage victories and the green points jersey in the Tour de France, and by the next year, when he won the Tour of Switzerland, he seemed to have mastered the mountains. When a knee injury kept Hinault out of the Tour de France in 1983, Kelly should have been a strong favorite, but he seemed uncertain whether to go for the yellow jersey or the green and disperse his energies by collecting points in the road sprints and intermediate climbs.

Probably not even Kelly can say whether this apparent indecision affected him when he put on the yellow jersey for the first time in 1983 in Pau at the foot of the Pyrenees. But the next day he had a bad stage in the mountains, losing enough minutes that the yellow jersey was soon out of sight. He took over the green jersey and wore it the rest of the way to Paris.

In 1984, after his great start, he announced that the green jersey no longer interested him. He should have been a strong favorite for the yellow jersey again, but the doubts remained about his ability in the highest mountains. "Sometimes he climbs so darn well you can't understand why he gets dropped in the Tour," LeMond said. "But he does."

In 1985 Kelly will be riding in at least the Tours of Spain and France, with the third grand Tour—Italy's Giro—a strong possibility. "It'll be a challenge, riding in the three Tours," Kelly admitted, but his reputation as a workhorse is unmatched. In 1984 he raced 155 days, a schedule he plans to reduce to 130 days; by contrast, LeMond raced 70 days in 1984 and hopes to increase the number to 110.

Although Kelly nearly always starts as a favorite these days, de Gribaldy was not overly optimistic about his rider's chances in the Tour de France, a view Kelly shared. "I'll be riding it again," he said, "but I'll still be at the same disadvantage—the high mountains."

Otherwise, he said, he was hoping for another fine showing to follow his explosion into the superstar class.

CARRYING ON

1985

There were thunderous, epic days in the 1985 Tour de France, and there were quiet days, too. The glorious days: Bernard Hinault falling in the last kilometer at St. Etienne and finishing the stage with blood washing his face and his yellow jersey; Luis Herrera, a winner the day before, carefully dawdling off the wheel of Fabio Parra a fellow Columbian and a teammate, on the climb to Lans en Vercor, and letting him claim the victory; Greg LeMond triumphant in the time trial near Limoges, the first stage victory by an American; Rudy

Matthijs leading the final rush up the Champs-Elysées to win his third sprint of the 1985 Tour and being ignored as the band broke into the Marseillaise to celebrate Hinault's record-tying fifth victory in the race.

But this was one of the quiet days, the weather hot and sunny, the landscape hilly as the riders moved west of Burgundy toward the Alps, 204 kilometers from Epinal to Pontarlier. The climactic Strasbourg time trial, in which Hinault reclaimed the leader's jersey for good, was two days behind; the climb to Morzine, where Herrera and Hinault conspired to humble the 159 other riders, was still a day ahead. None of the big names would figure in this tenth stage of the twenty-one-stage event; the day's famous men were Dietrich Thurau and Paul Sherwen.

Didi Thurau was a few months short of his 31st birthday and was by then riding for Hitachi-Splendor, the fifth or sixth team of his erratic career. Champion of West Germany in 1975 and 1976 and a revelation of the Tour of Spain in 1976, he burst into the Tour de France in 1977 by winning the leader's jersey in the prologue and holding it for more than two weeks as a burned-out Eddy Merckx struggled to overtake him. In the end, Bernard Thévenet overtook them both, but the 22-year-old Thurau, winner of four Tour stages and the fifth-place finisher overall, had captured the spotlight.

"A sort of demigod on a bicycle, beautiful to watch," sang one French cycling magazine, "tall and slender, supple and strong, he must know that time is on his side."

A celebrity back home in Frankfurt after the Tour and a second-place finish in the world road race championship, Thurau discovered a vast appetite for money and spent the off-season wholesaling himself at supermarket openings and promotional fairs. Appearance fees were fine, but the real money, Thurau knew, was in six-day races, especially in West Germany, where he was the only native star. He spent a fatiguing winter competing in these lucrative races on European tracks.

His results fell off the next season, when he left the strong Raleigh team for a weaker but better-paying Dutch one. In 1979 he won the Liège-Bastogne-Liège classic and another stage in the Tour de France, but the glory days were over. The Netherlands, Italy, Belgium-Thurau moved around, his career going nowhere but his reputation still strong.

By 1981, when the Tour de France started in Nice, Thurau, only a spectator, was to be seen drinking champagne while allowing himself to be wooed by the organizers of yet another new team that never materialized.

Then it was back to Italy for a few more seasons and finally in 1985 a summons from Hitachi.

Thurau had a mediocre spring. In the Tour he was no longer the golden boy of 1977 but an *équipier deluxe,* a high-priced support rider. Hitachi had a good race but Thurau a commonplace one, culminating in a one-minute penalty at the Strasbourg individual time trial for pacing himself on the wheel of Charly Mottet.

A bitter Thurau, 26th overall and 17th in the time trial, complained that the official who reported him, Raymond Trine of Belgium, held a grudge.

It was Trine, Thurau said, who had reported him positive in a drug test at the German championship in 1980, and it was Trine who had unsettled him at the start of the 1985 Tour by minutely inspecting his bicycle before the prologue and questioning the legality of its design (there was a stylized mud guard under the saddle that officials suspected was an aerodynamic aid). The drug test, on a second opinion, had been negative, Thurau continued, and the prologue bicycle had finally been cleared.

And now Trine had recommended the penalty for pacing, but only against Thurau, not against Mottet. "If I deserve a minute's penalty in the time trial, Mottet deserves one too," Thurau said. "If he doesn't, I don't."

That morning, just before the pack set out, Thurau crossed paths with Trine and boiled over, seizing the Belgian by the throat. "He grabbed me from the back, started to choke me, and warned that the next time, I would land in the hospital," Trine said later. Immediately ejected from the race, Thurau left unnoticed.

This was one of the quiet days.

"It was a normal day," said Paul Sherwen, "for everyone but me." Then a 29-year-old domestique for the Redoute team, the Englishman was riding in his seventh Tour de France. He had finished three: in 1978, he was 70th, in 1982 he was 111th, and in 1984 he was 116th. He had a few other laurels. In 1981 he won the Grand Prix du Hainault Occidental and in 1983 The Grand Prix de San Sébastián. In 1983 he also won the first stage of the Four Days of Dunkirk and finished the race second overall. In 1982 he was fourth in the Paris-Bourges classic and eighth in the Belgian classic Het Volk.

Sherwen was alongside his teammate Jérôme Simon as the pack left Epinal. The riders were bunched and the road was narrow, and someone must have grazed Simon's bicycle, for he began to wobble. "I grabbed Jérôme by the jersey and tried to hold him on," Sherwen recalled weeks later. "In trying to help him, we touched wheels and I fell on the side of the road and hit a crash barrier." That was after 1 kilometer of the 204-kilometer stage.

"I was quite stunned and in a lot of pain," Sherwen continued in his chatty, flat way. "I landed on my head as well as my back, but it was the back that hurt."

He remounted, thinking that, "I wouldn't have any difficulty catching the bunch up. Often a rider gets back on because the others slow down for him, but the pace was quite fast—the day's average was 40 kilometers an hour."

By the time Sherwen was rolling again, the pack was nearly fifteen minutes ahead except for two teammates, Alain Bondue and Régis Simon, Jérôme's older brother. They shepherded Sherwen on his slow way toward the Alps.

"After 30 kilometers I told them to leave me," he continued. "I had so much pain in my back I had trouble following them and I thought there was no reason they should stay and throw away their race on an invalid. I told them to leave me but they wouldn't go, so I had to tell them two or three times."

After 80 kilometers, Bondue—"one of my best friends," Sherwen called him—and Simon finally obeyed. Sherwen was alone.

Months later, the elder Simon recalled the moment: "Oh Lord, was he in pain and exhausted. I never thought he'd finish. Really he was in shock and his neck hurt so much. When he told us to leave him the first time, we refused. Paul, Bondue, me, we're all good friends and we didn't want to just leave him there alone. But he really chewed us out and told us to look out for ourselves.

"The second time, we still didn't want to go, but decided that we had to respect the man. If that's what he wanted, we had to respect him. We went off thinking that was the end for him."

"A lot of times I felt like getting off," Sherwen remembered, "but I kept thinking it was probably my last Tour de France and that was no way to end it. 'Carry on, carry on,' I kept saying to myself. 'What a futile effort,' I kept thinking, but what I was saying was 'Carry on.'"

Once before, in 1981, Sherwen was eliminated from the Tour de France on time differential. He recalled it exactly: "I was 50 seconds outside the limit on the Mulhouse stage."

This time he finished 63 minutes behind the winner, Jorgen Pedersen of the Carrera-Inoxpran team, and half an hour behind Régis Simon, the next-to-last rider.

By the time Sherwen crossed the line, the viewing stands there were being dismantled. "I saw the cars coming down," he said, realizing that he was so far behind that race officials had given up on him and reopened the road to traffic.

Waiting at the line was his team manager, Raphaël Geminiani, who rode in twelve Tours de France himself. Geminiani hugged Sherwen and wrapped a jacket around him.

"Paul, this is your yellow jersey," Geminiani said. Sherwen wept. By the rules he should have been put out of the race but the judges decided otherwise. "I thought they might be rather clement," he admitted.

"There are four reasons to avoid eliminating a rider—the general speed of the stage, the point where the accident occurred, the effort the rider made to finish, and the amount of traffic blocking the road. They cited all four reasons to put me back in the Tour.

"But first I went straight to hospital for X-rays. They showed extremely large bruising of the head and shoulders. I was back in the race by the next morning's start but I had a pretty rough two or three days afterward. Luckily, I was in good condition before the Tour started. And I finished, didn't I?"

Sherwen made it to Paris, 141st of the 144 riders left, 3 hours, 28 minutes, 13 seconds behind Hinault.

He wanted it understood that he did not exaggerate the meaning of that quiet day. "People say it was a fantastic feat but for me it was nothing exceptional. I think it was part of what the Tour de France is all about—Eugène Christophe and how he repaired his bicycle by working the forge himself and got back into the race [in 1913]. All those little stories that make the race what it is."

THE VIEW FROM THE TERRACE

1986

Nelson Vails wishes to assure his family, friends, disco partners, and other fans that he has not gone Hollywood.

Ignore the Joe Cool sunglasses perched atop his head at breakfast. Forget his role in the recent movie *Quicksilver*. Pay no attention to his home in the Surfside subdivision of Sunset Beach, California. Please overlook his devotion to the boogie board when the surf's up.

Deep down, Vails said, there's no place like home, and that means New York. The problem is that New York is too wonderful a town for Vails, the former Manhattan bicycle messenger who won a silver medal in the bicycle sprint championship at the 1984 Olympic Games in Los Angeles.

After that unexpected success, Vails moved to Southern California, with mixed results. "For the last two years I haven't worked as hard as I did prior to the Games," he admitted between races in the Paris area. "Part of it is the convenience of being an American. Like the East German riders—you win it once, you're going to have to win it again or else you get your visa taken away."

For an American, he continued, the racer's life offers different perils. "My living habits have grown, my habits period have grown. Once you have a million, you always want a million. I'm living in California, California is beaches, so you have to have a house on the beach. I bought a car to compete with the rest of the cars in California. Because of cycling, my living habits have changed. It's a big incentive to do well. I want more, I want it all for myself." He paused, then added, "But that's not saying I won't share it.

"I can't live in New York and be a successful bike rider," he said. "Not enough clubs have the bodybuilding facilities I need."

As a sprinter, Vails works long hours building overall body strength for his short, intense races and the "balancing" that often precedes them as opponents stand motionless on their bicycles, jockeying for position and psychological advantage.

Also, Vails confessed, New York offers too many distractions. "Too much is happening there, diversions. I'm the type of person that can afford to have a good time all the time and New York is a place that can provide a good time. Bunch of all-night places to go dance, things to do, and people to do them with."

Clearly, the 25-year-old Vails likes attention. "That's what makes me go—the attention. Attention is a pretty good motivation.

"It's not like I'm doing it for myself," he insisted. "I'm doing it for everyone else, whoever shows up. It's like I pay $20 to see this guy and he didn't even do anything.

"You take your date or whatever and go to see this guy Nelson Vails race—'He's really good, let's watch him'—and then you go all the way out, you drive, you go out to watch me race and then I don't even do anything.

"If I don't win any races, I won't get the attention."

As "the baby of ten brothers and sisters," Vails got a lot of attention, he said, when he was growing up on 115th Street in Harlem, where his family still lives. "I grew up as a good kid," he said. "People think that because I grew up in Harlem I was a rough kid and always got myself in trouble, but I wasn't like that. Harlem—the name throws people off."

At 15, Vails went to Manhattan's garment district to find his first job, pushing racks of clothes along Seventh Avenue from subcontractor to manufacturer to showroom. That lasted a few months. "Then I got a job inside at a company—right time, right place—as a shipping clerk." He stayed from 1976 to 1980, when he became a bicycle messenger in Manhattan.

Not just any messenger, he pointed out. "There were 150 guys and I was one of the top 10 messengers."

Quality was measured by how much of the customer's fee was paid to the rider. "I was a 60 percent rider," Vails explained, "making $400 a week. If you're good, you're good."

More specifically, he added, "I was quick in delivering the messages, able to handle the load in pressure. Instead of giving you one or two, I could handle eight at a time." He imitated a dispatcher: "'Pick up here, pick up here, pick up here, pick up here, pick up here, tell me when you're done.'

"I delivered everything from a set of keys to a $100,000 check. I delivered to Cartier's, I delivered to Rolls-Royce, I carried blueprints to the World Trade Center."

During the two years that he worked "off and on" as a messenger, Vails began racing competitively in Central Park, among other places. He attracted a sponsor and soon was racing as part of the U.S. national team, winning the gold medal in the kilometer race at the Pan-American Games in 1983.

The next year, in Los Angeles, he placed second in the match sprint to another American, Mark Gorski, as the traditional track champions, the East Germans and Russians, boycotted the Olympics. In 1985 Vails finished second, with Les Barczewski, in the 2,000-meter tandem race in the world cycling championships.

His immediate goal is the world championships to be held in August 1986 in Colorado Springs, and he was in France for a series of races leading to the Goodwill Games in Moscow. At the Colorado championships, he said, he hopes to win in both the individual sprint and the tandem. He rated his chances as "better than most people's." Why? "That's just the way it is."

A fuller explanation came from a U.S. team coach. "Nelson's really on an even keel—no temper, no anger," Carl Leusenkamp said. "He gets nervous, but never in a way that hurts him. If there are some rough guys in a race, Nelson will just say, 'I got two skin suits. If this one gets scuffed, I'll just put on the other.'"

Another tribute to Vails came from his teammate and tandem partner, Barczewski. "From the start you could see his natural power and his undeniable burning to be the best. He showed it not just in a race but every day in the weight room—that burning look in his eyes. He was pretty raw but you could see the spark.

"I wasn't worried about this kid," continued Barczewski, seven times a U.S. champion. "I told him all my secrets. He learns so quickly—tell him once and he learns it."

Still, as Vails admitted, victories have not been plentiful since Los Angeles. "I must be doing something wrong because I'm not where I want to be right now. But it's probably not my time. I probably have a lot more maturity to do but it's not like I have to sit down and wait for it to grow on me. You have to work hard on it.

"My discipline isn't that good," he conceded.

"I've become a person with no time, especially for my family. Every chance I get, I go back East to see my family. A lot of the time when I'm in New York it's just for business with no time to hang out. I know if I stay I won't get the time I need for training."

In Southern California, he continued, he can train the year around. "It's warm. That's why I chose to live there, because it's warm." He rides "every day if I can. I go out early in the morning an hour, an hour and a half, then have the rest of the day to relax.

"I'm on the beach, I share, I rented a house with another guy, another girl, a photographer, an electrician. He surfs, she suns, I boogie board.

"New York is not the place for me to be right now. After cycling I can maybe afford a place overlooking Central Park. If you want to say that's a goal, that's a goal.

"To sit outside on my terrace and have the New York City skyline, it's a big thing. Being a messenger, I've been in houses like that, waiting in somebody's lounge. There are plenty of places like that.

"Doorman and elevator: That's the lifestyle I want to live. I don't care for a garage with a lawn and a lawnmower, back yard. You can have all that on the terrace if you're in an apartment in New York. Get a big palm tree plant and stick it outside on the terrace."

TAKING CARE OF THE BOYS

1987

Entering the hotel restaurant for lunch, Shelley Verses carefully chose a seat backing onto the aisle. "This way I can keep an eye on the boys and get up quickly if they need anything," she explained. She has ten "boys," all of them members of the Toshiba professional bicycle racing team.

Verses is one of the team's eight soigneurs, the French word for people who truck baggage for the riders, offer them first aid, prepare and deliver their sandwiches and high-energy food during races, ease their way at hotels, and massage them.

Massage—as Hamlet, prince of Denmark, said in a somewhat different context, "Ay, there's the rub." Here the rub is that in what has been a man's world, Shelley Verses is a pioneer, the first full-time woman soigneur for a European team in memory.

Toshiba, a twenty-five-rider French team that raced in 1986 under the name of La Vie Claire, is one of bicycling's top formations and is led by Greg LeMond, the American who won the 1986 Tour de France.

"They didn't look at my sex when they hired me," Verses explained. "They knew my work."

In the town of Compiègne for the Paris-Roubaix race, a team spokesman seconded this: "She has an excellent reputation as a soigneur."

"She rubs legs like nobody else," said Alex Stieda, 26, a Canadian rider with the American-based 7-Eleven team, for which Verses served as soigneur for two years. "She has very strong hands and can rub deep. She's excellent, the best I've known."

And yet, and yet. The 26-year-old Verses is vivacious and attractive, the All-American Golden Girl—adjectives and nouns never heretofore applied to a soigneur.

"Ninety-nine percent of soigneurs are just backdrop," confirmed Roy Knickman, a 21-year-old American rider for Toshiba. "Nobody could ever call Shelley that. She just stands out in any crowd.

"But," he continued, "she was hired because she's a hard worker. It's nothing to do with male or female.

"I like her especially because I can talk English with her but all the riders agree that she's a skilled soigneur."

Lying on his back on a massage table as Verses rubbed a mixture of sunflower oil and Nivea cream into his legs, the Swiss rider Nikki Ruttimann, 25, agreed with Knickman. "She's a very good soigneur," he said. "And it's good to have a woman because it helps your morale. It's nice to have a woman to talk to."

There is another body of opinion, one strong enough to have cost Verses a job.

Paul Köchli, the coach of the Toshiba team, tried to hire her late in 1986 but, Verses said, "I was intimidated by the offer and the team, and said no." Then Peter Post, the manager of the Panasonic team, which is based in the Netherlands, called her at home in Santa Barbara, California, and offered a job. "It was less money but the team seemed more American because they all speak English." She came to Panasonic's notice when she served as soigneur to the team's star rider, Phil Anderson, an Australian, during the world championships in Colorado in September 1986.

"Two weeks after I signed with Post," she recalled, "he called and said the riders' wives were protesting, making all kinds of trouble about a woman massaging their husbands. He said he was afraid he was ahead of his time in signing a woman. I explained to Post that it was degrading to me as a woman to be treated that way by a mafia of the riders' wives.

"Hey, I grew up on Title 9," she exclaimed, referring to the U.S. ban on sex discrimination in educational institutions that receive federal funds. "I felt I had broken the ice, but I hadn't. I felt discriminated against.

"They offered to pay me for the whole year. 'Just stay home in

California,' they said. They thought they were dangling chocolate in front of a kid, never considering that I was a professional. I didn't want to stay in Santa Barbara for the season. I wanted to work. So two days later, I called Köchli, and here I am."

Despite Köchli's attitude, Verses noted that some Toshiba riders' wives preferred not to have her massage their husbands. "That's OK," she said, "because there are plenty of riders to go around."

For most races, the team uses three soigneurs, who massage the same riders each day of a race, even ones as long as the three-week Tour de France.

The major object is to remove toxins from the muscles and thus aid a rider's recuperation from the day's trials. A secondary goal to relaxing the rider physically is to soothe him emotionally. "If he wants to talk about the race, I'll talk with him," Verses said. "But if he doesn't, I don't. Some days it's psychotherapy, some days silence. Sometimes laughs, sometimes not.

"One real problem is how shy a rider can be before he gets to know you. I say to them, 'Take off your underwear.' They look sort of funny and say, 'You want me to take off my underwear?' And then I say, 'You want your butt massaged, take it off.' You've got to do it, you know, because of saddle sores."

She combats the sores with a variety of salves, unguents, and lotions ("I've been studying homeopathy and essential oils for three or four years") including what she refers to as her "hippie remedies, my gypsy things." One gypsy thing is a paste whose ingredients include beeswax, slippery elm, bloodroot, and myrrh gum. She buys the paste in Boulder, Colorado, from, she said, a woman named Feather.

The other tools of her trade—adhesive tape, alcohol, cotton swabs, scissors, bandages—fill four big boxes, with just enough room left to fit in an atomizer of Rive Gauche perfume.

A native of Stamford, Connecticut, Verses attended Springfield College in Springfield, Massachusetts, on a field-hockey scholarship for two years before deciding in 1980 to transfer to the University of California at Santa Barbara.

But the school had no field hockey team, so she helped pay her bills as a physical education and physiology major by being a sports trainer ("football, basketball, volleyball, baseball, as the seasons changed") and by helping dissect cadavers for a human anatomy course. "From muscles, it wasn't too far to massage," she said.

"I tried to sign up at the Santa Barbara School of Massage but they didn't teach sports massage. In those days, massage meant just basic relaxation. I had to give 100 hours' massage to get my license and I just told all the athletes I knew, 'You want a massage, come over to my house.'

"Some bike racers got me interested in going to races with them because I didn't know that a soigneur does so much else beside massage. I thought riders just ate before a race, not hours before, and I didn't know they ate during a race and that somebody had to prepare their food and hold out a bag at the side of the road when they go by. But I learned."

By 1983 she had learned enough to attract a job offer from the coach of the U.S. Olympic cycling team. First she worked at the Olympic Training Center in Colorado Springs and then in Los Angeles at the Olympic Games. "I massaged the men's and women's road teams and the time trialers and the alternates, everybody, and I was doing it for free, for $20 now and then and having to hang out signs, 'Wash and wax your car, $10.' I just wanted to get the credentials to work.

"And some of the riders who were also members of the 7-Eleven team said to me, 'Drop the Feds and come with us. We'll pay you.' So I did."

When 7-Eleven competed in the Tour of Italy in 1985, Verses was added to the team at the last minute. "It was taboo—no women. But they were unhappy with European soigneurs and decided to take me.

"The first week it was real bad," she admitted. "I didn't know how to market, how to order meals, even where to find ice. I watched the Italian soigneurs and I learned. Every night I stayed up late, studying an English-Italian dictionary. It became a challenge to me to do as well as the European soigneurs, to blow their minds.

"Some nights I was so tired, when everything was done I would lie down on the massage table to rest and then wake up and it was morning. But I never let anyone know, because that would be a sign I was a girl."

STICKS AND STONES

1987

Stephen Roche is Irish, so undoubtedly he has kissed the Blarney stone, if not eaten it whole. How else to explain his statement after he won this year's Giro d'Italia: "This Giro was not a simple individual victory, it was a victory for the team."

Perhaps he misspoke—his Italian is rickety in the best of times and these were the worst.

Even by the quirky standards of the Giro, the seventieth edition was a spectacle. The point of the race, understand, is that an Italian should win and thus satisfy the *tifosi*, as the sometime lynch mob of Italian cycling fans is known. *Tifosi* thoughts turn surly when a foreign rider breezes home first, as Eddy Merckx did five times and Bernard Hinault three. The Giro, second in prestige only to the Tour de France, has in fact been won by foreigners just seventeen times since its start in 1909, and those count as seventeen stabs in the Italian heart.

So, to help along a paisano, the *tifosi* have been known to douse a foreign racer with vinegar instead of water. They form human chains to push a national hero like Francesco Moser up a hill, and they threaten to spread nails along a foreigner's course in a time trial. But no, they do not go that far, contenting themselves instead with spitting on him, hurling insults and the occasional rock.

The race organizers do their bit for national pride. In 1984, when Moser was making his eleventh attempt to win his first Giro, he held a slim lead the night before a daunting mountain stage. Knowing that Moser is no climber, the organizers evaporated the mountain by announcing that it was snowbound, although a check by foreign reporters found it clear. By a change of route, other mountains in other years have been leveled.

Finally, the Italian television chain, the RAI, pitches in. Its helicopters have been known to fly low behind an Italian rider in a time trial, pushing him along on the cushion of air flung off its rotors. (When Bernard Hinault was trying unsuccessfully to overtake Moser in 1985, the Frenchman's employer, Bernard Tapie, threatened to send up his private plane to intercept the RAI helicopter that was trailing Moser during a crucial time-trial stage.)

But enough tame stuff. The main contest in this year's Giro was between the two leaders of the Carrera team, with one of them (Roberto Visentini, the winner of the 1986 Giro) pledging publicly to attack the other (Roche) at any opportunity and making the shocking admission that he had tried to spill another teammate (whom the Italian saw as being allied with Roche) on purpose during a final sprint in one of the stages.

After a string of tantrums by Visentini, Roche needed two police motorcyclists as permanent outriders and had to go on television again and again to plead for *tifosi* understanding. The race was still days from its finish when Roche's employer threatened to keep him out of the Tour de France as punishment for his eventual victory. In turn, he let word be spread that he would be changing teams next year.

"I've been petrified with fear for the last few days," Roche said toward the end. "People want to hit me and I've had to protect myself behind other riders to avoid the fans' blows and their spit. My nerves are shot. I've gone through hell."

The feud and the way it tore apart the Carrera team were reminiscent of Greg LeMond's running battle with Hinault in the 1986 Tour de France. The difference was that both La Vie Claire riders had enough class not to try to inflame their fans. LeMond admitted after the decisive Alpe d'Huez climb that he had been terrified by the thought of a French fan knocking him off his bicycle, but Hinault had the wisdom to tell the American to stay with him all the way up the mountain; their seeming reconciliation, with LeMond throwing his arm around Hinault's shoulder just before the finish and then granting the Frenchman the victory, did wonders for injured national pride.

Carrera, which journalists voted the best team in the sport in 1986, was not up to such tact. Now it stands to lose its two leaders, with Roche moving on and Visentini planning to retire after the 1988 season.

Visentini took the parting from Roche in stride. "Some reports say he has already signed with another team," the Italian announced. "That doesn't matter. The important thing is that where I race, he doesn't. Otherwise something really serious could happen."

What could Visentini mean? Something more serious than purposely trying to knock a Belgian teammate, Eddy Schepers, off his bicycle during an already dangerous final sprint? "Of course I tried to put him in the ditch," Visentini said of Schepers. "But that was the least I could do after what he did to me during the Sappada stage."

Schepers's crime, and Roche's too, on the Sappada stage, more than halfway through the 3,912-kilometer Giro, was to join in a mountain attack that far outdistanced Visentini and cost him the pink jersey. Roche, who had worn the jersey early in the race before losing it to Visentini in a time trial, insisted that he had not attacked a struggling co-leader but had tried to put the pressure on Carrera's rivals.

"Besides," the Irishman continued, "when I was wearing the pink jersey he did nothing to help me. I see no reason to sacrifice myself for him. No, truly, I owed him nothing."

That stage cost Visentini more than six minutes and dropped him into seventh place overall, three minutes behind his co-leader. "Visentini Betrayed By Roche," the headlines in the Italian press said. Visentini said the same. "He ought to be sent home," he charged. "He knew that the rider in the pink jersey was the only captain of the team and that he could not attack. When someone does me dirt, I wipe them out of my life, the way I've done with Schepers and Roche. As far as I'm concerned, they no longer exist. From now on, they're enemies and I'll attack them at the first chance.

"The cycling world disgusts me," Visentini continued, "and I'll be very happy to leave it after next season. Nothing in the world will make me stay, not a million dollars."

In truth, money is not that important to the 30-year-old Visentini, who comes from a wealthy family of undertakers and drives sports cars. He has long been considered a playboy—a dilettante, really—with fragile nerves that often crack in big races. The 1986 Giro is his sole major victory.

Roche, too, has a record of problems, but his have been physical. In 1981, when he turned professional with the Peugeot team in France at the age of 21, Roche showed that he was a future star by winning the Paris-Nice stage race. The next year was a washout as he began experiencing a weakness that was later diagnosed as a lack of minerals in his blood. By 1985 he was back on track, finishing third in the Tour de France, second in Paris-Nice, and winning the Criterium International for the Redoute team in France. That winter, riding in the Six Days of Paris track race, he fell and tore up a knee. He joined Carrera but could not post a victory for his new team until this spring. The triumph in the Giro, by a final 3 minutes, 40 seconds, was his first in a major Tour.

When Visentini quit the Giro after a fall in the last few days, he left the final word to Roche: "I'm happy I learned my trade in France," the Irishman told a group of Italian journalists before leaving their country for a rest and then the Tour de France. "In Italy, riders are far too coddled. They're treated like princes and they don't know how to suffer. I don't think I could have stood up to the strain and suffering and won the Giro if I had never ridden for anybody but Carrera.

"Visentini and I are truly different and what happened was inevitable. He wanted to win the Giro at any price, without making any concessions. He insisted that we had to defend his jersey, but I too wanted to win the Giro. I think, finally, that he has no interest in our team. He is too much an Italian for that. Outside the Giro, nothing interests him.

"He's a good fellow, Visentini, but he's not a man."

THE LONG GOOD-BYE

1987

His legs and his pride tell Joop Zoetemelk that 41 is the age to retire from bicycle racing, and he is obeying, reluctantly. The rest of his life will begin some day soon, but not quite yet. "Can you see me behind a counter selling sporting goods?" he asks plaintively.

The first of his absolutely, positively final farewells was celebrated in Germigny l'Evêque, some 50 kilometers east of Paris. Hundreds of his fans ignored a cold, steady rain to attend a cyclo-cross race in his honor in the French village where the Dutch-born Zoetemelk has lived for fifteen years.

Like the man himself, the farewells will be international. Asian fans will get their last—and first—look at Zoetemelk when he zips around downtown Tokyo in a race intended to boost bicycling in Japan. Closer to home, another last race will be staged in the Paris suburb of Montreuil. And anyone who still has not shaken Zoetemelk's hand good-bye can find a chance at the six-day indoor race in Maastricht, the Netherlands. Finally, there will be an adieu cyclo-cross in the Netherlands.

In fact, all of 1987 has amounted to a farewell tour for the veteran racer. He spent the season making the rounds in France, Belgium, and the Netherlands, choosing his races carefully to avoid the tough ones. Despite his fabled dedication to training and the spartan life, Zoetemelk has reached a point where he can no longer keep up with the pack, which averages fifteen years younger than he.

How difficult has it been to let go? "When I was younger," Zoetemelk has said, "I thought it would be easy to live without a bicycle. And now I'm terrified of stopping. I think that as long as I have the strength to do well, I'll stay. It's as simple as that."

Or not so simple. For the first time since 1974, when he was seriously injured, Zoetemelk did not ride this year in the Tour de France. "The day the Tour de France goes off without me," Zoetemelk said a few years ago, "that's when I'll feel old." His absence ended his record of sixteen appearances and finishes in the race.

Nice guys finish second—Zoetemelk did that six times, also a record, in the Tour de France. He won just once, in 1980, when Bernard Hinault had to yield the leader's yellow jersey because of tendinitis in a knee.

Zoetemelk's misfortune was to bridge the eras between Eddy Merckx, who won the Tour five times starting in 1969, and Hinault, who won five times beginning in 1978. The Dutchman was second in 1970, 1971, 1976, 1978, 1979, and 1982.

Still, his victories were impressive—the 1968 Olympic gold medal in the team time trial; Dutch road champion in 1971 and 1973; a handful of classics; the Vuelta a España in 1979; the world road race championship in 1985, when he was 38 and by three years the oldest professional champion ever.

Typically, when he crossed the finish line to win the rainbow jersey as world champion, he started to raise his arms in the traditional claim of victory before quickly pulling them down. "The moment I crossed the line and raised my arms, I wondered, 'Is there anyone ahead that I didn't see break away?'" Caution was always Zoetemelk's watchword.

As a boy in the village of Rijpewering, near Leiden, he learned the adage, "Do not praise the day before evening comes." Endurance and patience are the keys to Zoetemelk's personality, according to a Dutch psychologist. "He is the kind of person who knew all along that the snail would win in Aesop's fable," the psychologist wrote in a bicycling magazine.

Zoetemelk's father, a farmer, offered the magazine *Miroir du Cyclisme* another view of his son's personality: "He wasn't even 12 years old, and I asked him to dig a hole with a shovel in the garden, and told him I'd say when it was deep enough. I forgot all about it, and when I got home that evening the hole was so deep we had to lift him out because he couldn't have climbed out alone. It can seem stupid, but for me it was a sign of his character."

He showed his character again this year, when he threatened to sue international cycling authorities if they did not waive the rule that nobody over 40 could compete. The waiver was granted.

Character did not explain it all. In 1974 he rounded a corner in the Midi Libre race in France and collided at high speed with a car parked where it shouldn't have been. His skull was fractured and the injury led to spinal meningitis, which nearly killed him. After eight months of physical inactivity, the doctors said he had recovered but would need at least five years to regain his strength. Instead he started the next season with a victory in his first major race, Paris-Nice.

"That fall broke my career," Zoetemelk said a decade later, still at the top.

His seriousness as a racer was acclaimed. "Joop doesn't have any secret except to remain faithful to the most simple and most healthy principles," said his team manager, Jan Raas. "He's always led a calm life. Nothing bothers him. He sacrifices everything to racing, but to him it isn't a sacrifice."

The sacrifices over, Zoetemelk has no specific plans for his future. He and his wife own a hotel in the city of Meaux, near his village, but he doubts he will become involved in running it. Nor does he foresee a career in sports broadcasting. For now he will remain with his Super Confex team as a public relations representative, traveling to races, spreading goodwill, and continuing to make his farewells.

CINDERELLA STORY

1988

The night before the 1988 Tour de France began in Brittany, Nathan Dahlberg was home in Ghent, Belgium, a thousand kilometers away, cooking dinner. Then he heard a knock at the door.

"I was just standing around, making my meal," Dahlberg remembered. "Nothing fancy, just rice and bean sprouts with a bit of tomato, a bit of cucumber.

"I had ridden a race that day and I was hungry as well as tired. It was 9 o'clock at night and I wondered who was knocking."

As always in fairy tales, it was opportunity. The Belgian who stood at the door told Dahlberg that the 7-Eleven team had telephoned from France to say that a rider had just been injured and that Dahlberg was needed to replace him.

A 7-Eleven support rider, Bob Roll, had collided with a spectator while warming up. Roll hurt his head and a knee in the crash and would be unable to join the nine-man team when it started riding the next morning.

If Dahlberg could make it to the line on time, he would ride instead; if not, the team would race with eight men.

Occasionally a team will have to call up a Tour de France replacement for an injured rider, but never before had a team turned at the last minute to a first-year professional who was not even on its roster and who had just completed a 185-kilometer race that day (finishing 24th).

The first thing he did, Dahlberg said, was eat his dinner.

"I had just ridden a race and I was famished." He left the dishes in the sink and set off with the Belgian in an old car to drive to Brittany.

"We drove all night," Dahlberg continued, "setting out at 9:30 and getting to the 7-Eleven hotel at 5:30 the next morning. I got about three hours' sleep in the car and about an hour's sleep in the hotel once we got there."

At 9 a.m. he was signing in for the first stage of the Tour de France. In hours, the 23-year-old New Zealander had jumped from the small-time Belgian circuit to the world's major bicycle race.

"It just must be destiny," said Mike Neel, the 7-Eleven directeur sportif, with a laugh. Neel was the man who called a friend in Ghent and asked him to alert Dahlberg, who had no phone in his room.

Neel filled in the gaps in Dahlberg's promotion. A sensitive man with a growing reputation as a director, Neel made it plain why he chose the New Zealander.

"Nathan rode for 7-Eleven last year as an amateur in a race in California and he finished sixth, so we had some awareness of him," Neel said. "We wanted him to ride for us in the Tour of Sicily this year after he turned professional, but it didn't work out.

"But he did ride for us in the Tour of Flanders and a little in Spain and some other races and he did a real good job. I always wanted Nathan to be able to ride with the team because I believe he has a lot of talent.

"Also because he was a little bit of an underprivileged rider, coming from so far away and he has no money, no support." A faraway look filled Neel's eyes as he spoke.

Now 37, Neel was one of the rare Americans who rode the professional circuit in Europe without much distinction a decade ago, long before Greg LeMond won the Tour de France in 1986 and made American riders credible.

"I had the same experiences, yes," Neel acknowledged.

"He lives in a cold-water flat in Belgium and you should see the one I used to live in. I thought, 'This guy deserves it.'

"A lot of people out there don't get the chance. We had two other replacements on our roster and I could have brought in one of them, but it was Nathan I wanted."

And how was Dahlberg doing as the three-week race continued its clockwise journey around France?

"I'm riding all right," he said. "That first day was rough but now I'm getting my rhythm, getting my sleep.

"It's another world, this one. In Belgium you come home from a race, rub your legs a bit, wash your gear, spend your time trying to survive. Here it's all done for you."

He gestured to a team masseur who was rubbing warming ointment into his legs just before the race began a daily stage. Nearby a mechanic was checking Dahlberg's freshly washed and polished bicycle.

"I'm really enjoying it. It's almost a bit of a holiday—I'm just riding my bike," he said.

A native of Wanganui, New Zealand, Dahlberg said he "got addicted to cycling" at age 16 when he went out for the sport in high school. Three years later, in 1984, he came to Europe to compete.

"If you think you're any good, you've got to come to Europe to find out." After spending three years with amateur clubs in Belgium and France, he turned professional.

"I had my ups and downs the first three years," he said, "but I won seven races in Belgium." As a professional, his best finish in a major race was a 40th place in the Grand Prix of Frankfurt, which he characterized as "not that good a performance, but for me it was good."

He said he looked forward to the daunting mountain stages in the Tour de France.

"Normally I say I can climb better than anything else," he said. "I'm more a strong rider than a quick one and I'm pretty self-motivated, so that should keep me going."

As a support rider, he mainly chases after dangerous enemy break-aways, does such small chores as passing on messages from the team car, and allows his leaders to draft off his wheel and save their energy.

His personal Tour goals are simple: "I'd just like to survive, do as well as I can, help my team leaders, and get a contract with 7-Eleven."

To ride in the Tour, he signed a team contract for this year, with an option for the next two years based on his performance.

"The more I do for the team, the better it is for me," he said. "The better the team leaders do thanks to me, the better I do."

He stood low in the overall time classification weekend, but neither Dahlberg nor Neel cared about that. He is not expected to win for the team but to work for it.

"It's a Cinderella story," Neel said. "Here he's had a chance and here he's one of our best team workers."

A TIMELESS ONE-DAY VICTORY

1989

Dirk Demol still feels like Cinderella at the ball even though he understands that his time is running out. When the glass coach turns back into a pumpkin, he will not make a fuss.

"No regrets," Demol says. "It's been a wonderful year, wonderful."

He peppers his speech with words like "wonderful," "great," "happy," and "glad." Life has been good to Demol, a man who makes few demands on it, since April 1988 when he unexpectedly won the celebrated Paris-Roubaix race.

That was one of the biggest upsets in the recent history of the sport: A rider who had won only a handful of local races in Belgium finishing first in one of the greatest of all classics. To the list of such champions as Eddy Merckx, Bernard Hinault, Francesco Moser, Fausto Coppi, and Sean Kelly was added Dirk Demol, who vaulted from domestique, the rider who relays instructions from the team car or distributes water bottles and raincoats, to celebrity.

"Everybody knows me now," he says happily.

The victory finished the days when he made ends meet by contesting every bonus sprint for the extra $10 or $20 they offered or looked forward to the occasional triumph because the president of his fan club would reward Demol with 1,000 Belgian francs ($25) and a free meal.

Immediately after Paris-Roubaix, his salary of about $12,000 a year was nearly doubled by the ADR team based in Belgium.

From a world ranking of 461st he leaped to 70th, a number that became financially valuable as teams moved to the World Cup system based on rider standings. When the Lotto team lured him away from ADR in the winter of 1988, his salary soared again.

"I'm living a dream," Demol said shortly after the Paris-Roubaix. "When I got home after a team banquet and a reception by my fan club, I watched the race again on a videocassette recorder just to make sure that it really was me who won."

The yearlong drama is nearly over. The long and grinding Paris-Roubaix race, 265 kilometers including 56.5 kilometers of cobblestones, will be run again, and Demol's chances of another victory are regarded as, at best, minimal.

Three factors are working against him, Demol admits.

One is that he has suffered for nearly two months with tendinitis in his left foot. He did not even start in the Tour of Flanders, the classic that passed not far from his modest home between Hulste and Harelbeke.

"We're hoping that he will be ready for Paris-Roubaix, but we're worried about his condition," said the Lotto directeur sportif, Jean-Luc Vandenbroucke, before the Tour of Flanders set off.

Another factor is that Demol will be taken seriously this time and will not again be allowed to join an early breakaway without a few favorites on his wheel.

Finally, and most harshly, riders of Demol's limited ability do not often win two classics in their careers.

"No matter," Demol replies. "I will win two classics if possible but, if not, I find it great that I won one. So many riders never win even one."

The 29-year-old Belgian ranked high among that great majority until 1988. Demol began racing as a professional in 1982 and registered victories only in kermesses, as minor one-day races around and around a circuit are called in Belgium and the Netherlands. In semi-classics, as slightly more important races are called, he sometimes finished in the leading group; in classics, he was never close.

Overall his record was bleak. In 1982 he won a kermesse at Herne, in 1983 at Wielsbeke and Courtrai, in 1984 at Courtrai and Izegem. In 1985 he won not at all and became so discouraged that he considered quitting.

"But that would have meant going back to the carpet factory where I started working at 14. The pay was the same as I made as a rider, so I finally decided to keep riding."

In 1986 he won a kermesse at Rummen and in 1987 at both Grammont and Desselgem. The following year he had just a second place at the kermesse in Wellegem until the Paris-Roubaix race. Although his results tailed off afterward, Demol still brims with assurance.

"Before Paris-Roubaix, I always thought 'I can't win,'" he said. "I'd go to a race and see some of the riders and I'd say, 'He's here and he's here, no way I can beat them.' I never thought of winning. In my mind, it wasn't possible.

"My kind of races were semi-classics and all I hoped for was to finish in the first fifteen. Now I know I can win.

"And even if I don't win anything important again, I'm happy. The victory in Paris-Roubaix, it's for all my life."

TOURING TRUMP

1989

Donald Trump is growing tired of all the jokes about the name of his bicycle race, the Tour de Trump.

Until the ten-day, 837-mile inaugural Tour de Trump started in Albany, New York, races had always—not even usually or mostly—traveled around the object of the preposition. Thus the Tour de France, the Giro d'Italia, and the Vuelta a España.

At no time, however, will the Tour de Trump circumnavigate a Trump, least of all Donald, the 42-year-old developer.

Instead the race will move from upstate New York to Manhattan, then hang a left and pass through parts of Pennsylvania, Virginia, and Maryland before winding up May 14 on the boardwalk of Atlantic City, New Jersey. On that last day, the Tour de Trump will come closest to a namesake when the start and finish lines face the Trump Plaza Hotel and Casino.

No matter, Donald Trump said in an interview sandwiched into a day full of news conferences, television appearances, and autographing sessions. Adding his name to the race, he explained, had made it successful.

"This race has already turned out to be a tremendous success if you look at the coverage," he said. "Normally you'd have a bicycle race and there would be nobody here."

Outside his gunmetal-gray stretch limousine, a large and enthusiastic crowd stood in the Empire State Plaza to watch the race's opening ceremonies.

"I really feel that when I attach my name to something, I have to make that something successful," Trump continued. "My name is probably my greatest asset and I have some nice assets."

Or, as he said wryly at a news conference earlier when asked why the race hadn't been called the Tour of America: "We could, if we wanted to have a less successful race, if we wanted to downscale it."

The truth is that the Tour de Trump did get off to a fine start, attracting 114 riders in 19 teams from 12 countries. Among the major racers competing are Greg LeMond and Andy Hampsten, American winners of the Tour de France and the Giro d'Italia, respectively; Steven Rooks of the Netherlands, who was second in the previous Tour de France; Slava Ekimov, the Soviet Olympic pursuit champion; and Eric Vanderaerden, the strong Belgian sprinter. They will compete for $250,000 in overall prizes, including $50,000 to the winner.

Another sign of the race's importance is the seven and a half hours of television coverage it will get in the United States, where the Tour de France rates four hours. The National Broadcasting Co. is a sponsor of the Tour de Trump and will show four hours of live racing.

"We have the greatest teams in the world, we have the greatest cyclists in the world," Trump said of the race. "A couple of people that wanted to come and didn't come, they're very regretful now because they didn't have any idea how big it was going to be.

"This has never really happened in this country," he said. "This country has a lot of bicycle races and they don't mean very much. This race obviously seems to mean a lot."

With an option to promote the race two more years, Trump was enthusiastic about its growth prospects.

"It can go longer, it can go further," he said. "We can have it starting in New York and going out to San Francisco, throughout the country.

"We can go down to Philadelphia and major cities along the Eastern seaboard—Washington, Baltimore—there are very few places in the world that can top that in terms of population."

At other moments, he has compared the Tour de Trump favorably to the Tour de France, but now he backed off.

"I have great respect for the Tour de France," he said. "I have to say that up front. To make the Tour de Trump as good as the Tour de France, just to make it almost as good as the Tour de France, would be a tremendous honor for me."

The coming edition of the Tour de France will be its seventy-sixth and the Tour de Trump had not yet spun a wheel. Was it peculiarly American or peculiarly Trump to be comparing the two?

With no hesitation, he answered, "I think it's peculiar to me."

Why?

"Because I like to have big successes early. I do."

In apartment buildings, gambling casinos, and yachts, in the private helicopter in which he rotored to and from Albany for the day, Trump likes things to be big.

"I have a tendency to overdo sometimes," he admitted while discussing the organization of the race. "We have a bigger production staff than a lot of people would have. I'd rather have a few extra security people than too few where you have problems. I'd rather have too many cars and good circulation than not enough, where things don't work out.

"I think we've done it first class. I'd rather have it overdone than underdone, at least in the initial year," he continued.

"I'm not guided totally by the dollar, despite what a lot of people would think. I really am guided more by what I think is good, what can happen. And I think, ultimately, that's one of the reasons I have become successful: The fact that I don't necessarily just go by the pure bottom line."

He insisted that the Tour de Trump was a case in point.

"It started as a fun event," he said, recalling the moment when the promoters who became his partners proposed the race. "They came in and said 'the Tour de Trump' and I wasn't even sure if they were serious. I literally fell off my seat when I heard the name. Then all of a sudden it started growing."

Before it did, Trump was a bicycling fan in only a small way, watching the Tour de France on television, he said. He does not have the time to cycle personally.

"I play baseball, I play golf, but I don't get the time to play anything now," he said. "The problem I have is time.

"I'd love to ice skate on the Wollman rink, which I run and I built for New York City, but I haven't been on the rink in four years. I have not ice skated there ever and yet I built it for the city. It's really a question of time. I guess I'd rather be doing what I'm doing than be doing the other."

MADAME DIRECTOR

1989

Nothing was going right for the Eurocar professional bicycle riders in the Tour de Trump, and the team's manager had finally had enough.

After four of Eurocar's six riders finished far behind on the stage from Gettysburg, Pennsylvania, to Winchester, Virginia, a team meeting was called.

"We definitely had a big, loud discussion," the manager admitted. "I just said I thought they could be riding a lot better. I told them they had to muster their forces and get their morale back together and try to salvage something, just get themselves back together."

Had the riders been told this in a loud way?

"Most of the time I am pretty low key," the manager said, "but because I have sort of a high-pitched voice and I'm kind of diminutive—I'm not a big person—I end up in a lot of these meetings speaking in a raised voice. Not screaming but being pretty vocal and vehement. Sometimes I get really angry."

Did it work?

"Yeah," said Robin Morton, the Eurocar manager and the only woman leading a professional bicycle team. "Yeah," she repeated with a broad smile, "it worked."

The next day, on the stage from Front Royal, Virginia, to Charlottesville, Eurocar riders finished as high as 16th and 20th in the 99-man field. The day after that, at the end of a stage from Charlottesville to Richmond, the team had a rider place ninth and two others place 15th and 20th.

"They listen, they definitely listen," Morton said. But attentiveness is no substitute for talent, and Eurocar resumed its downward slide as the Tour de Trump made its way to the finish line in Atlantic City, New Jersey. In the final standings, it ranked last among the five professional teams and 17th among the total of nineteen teams, professionals and amateurs.

"This race has been terrible for us," Morton admitted. Before the start in Albany, New York, burglars broke into the team's van and stole three bicycles and ten sets of wheels. Once the race was under way, the team was plagued by tire blowouts. Then its best rider, Roberto Gaggioli, fell far behind.

Morton is not one to make excuses, especially for a low-budget team with no stars.

"This is a really little team—fourteen riders—but soon we'll have fifteen, because a Dutch rider will turn pro and join us. But we're little budgetwise—about half a million dollars a year for everything, including salaries, and of that $100,000 to race in the United States." Major European professional teams have budgets that begin at about $3 million a year.

Although she spent the race as managers do, driving the support car that stays near the riders, Morton noted that her job usually does not correspond to what Europeans call a directeur sportif.

"I'm more the business manager of the team," she said. "My job is mainly to be a liaison with the sponsor, to organize the program for the team in America, and to take care of the organizational part of running the riders." The only other woman in professional bicycling with a similar job is Agnès Pierret, the manager of the Helvetia-La Suisse team in Switzerland.

Eurocar, based in Switzerland, divides its time between the United States and Europe, where this year it will race a heavily Italian schedule plus the Tour of Switzerland. Morton sometimes helps the team's directeur sportif, Domenico Cavallo, in European races but is on her own in the United States. She defined her role as limited.

"I don't tell them what to do tactically in a race," she said. "Maybe sometimes, but what I mostly do is tell them what is going on in the race on a given day. None of the riders are neo-pros, all of them know how to ride a race and if they don't know what to do, we're in trouble. They basically decide their own tactics. So we don't have as many strategy sessions as sort of pep talks.

"I don't presume to tell them how to ride the race. I was never a racer but I've been around it now for eight years. So, up to a point, I can tell them what I think needs to be done. They would not take it too kindly, I'm sure, if I said 'You have to do this, you have to do this, you have to do that.'"

That, she insisted, is not because she is a woman.

"No," she said firmly. "It's just because I'm not a racer, I've never raced." Her sex, she continued, is rarely an issue.

"There's no objection, none at all, to me in America. The sport is pretty open here, with women riders, women organizers, women in the bicycling federation, women masseuses with all the big American teams.

"In Europe I really haven't encountered too many difficulties. European team officials don't view me, so to speak, as their equal, but most of the time I haven't encountered any problems."

Those that she has encountered center on her place behind the wheel in the long caravan of support cars that follow the riders and offer advice, information, and bottles of water.

"When I first went to Italy in 1984, the other team directors actually had to vote on whether they were going to let me in the caravan at all. This was in the south of Italy. They actually had to take a vote. I got the OK.

"In France, it was much the same thing. I've driven the team car in the Dauphiné Libéré, the Midi Libre, and the Tour de l'Aude, but the first time was the Dauphiné. We went to a meeting of directeurs sportifs and they all had to take a vote too. I thought it would be much more difficult in France but they all voted yes, and afterward we all drank champagne and everybody thought it was great."

Relations with riders are even less of a problem, she said.

"I've been married thirteen years and, at 35, I'm much older than most of the riders, ten years maybe than a lot of the guys. I've never encountered problems with the riders on my teams in any way at all."

Nor with their wives, Morton added. "No problem at all, to my knowledge. I mean nobody has ever said anything to me—I don't think there's a problem."

With another laugh, she added, "I don't know if I've been fortunate or I'm just not cognizant of what's going on."

Morton entered the racing world through her husband, Glenn, the manager of the computer department for the Federal Reserve Bank in Philadelphia. He raced on the East Coast for the Philadelphia Bicycle Club and she began helping to find sponsors.

At that period she had studied art and art history at a community college in Pennsylvania, at the Tyler School of Art at Temple University, and at the Barnes Foundation, the private treasure house of art on the Main Line. (Her favorite painters are the Flemish masters and, Morton said, she looks forward to races in Belgium so she can visit museums "when I have time, except that I don't have a lot of it when I'm with the team.") She was painting, too, but helped pay the bills by working as a graphic artist for an architect.

Then John Eustice, an American who had been riding in Europe, returned home in 1982 and began riding with Morton's husband.

"I met John and he told me he was interested in putting an American team together," Morton said. "So we did."

Eustice, who rides for Eurocar, and Morton also have a bicycle-importing company in Philadelphia, Velo Marketing, which keeps them busy during the winter.

"When I first started working with John and the team, back in 1983, I was holding down my job with the architect," Morton remembered. "But so much of my time started being taken up, that he said, 'You have to make a decision.'

"Luckily my husband has been really supportive, and he said, 'Well, go for it, let's see what happens.'"

With that, Morton had to leave. There were bicycles to be looked after, rooms to be sorted out, riders to be encouraged, and the map of the next stage to be studied. A manager's work is never done.

UPHILL WITH LEMOND

1989

There are good days and bad days, Greg LeMond was saying in Florence, and for the previous two years the bad days had been far more plentiful. Now he was hoping for the rare good day.

"Today or never in this Giro," he said just before the time trial that closed the 3,655-kilometer Giro d'Italia.

Once again, LeMond had entered a long bicycle race with high hopes and once again he had been disappointed. Since he was accidentally shot while hunting in April 1987, the first American to win the Tour de France had not finished first in a major race.

"I'm in the tunnel where you don't see the end," LeMond said as he sat in his team car and awaited his turn against the clock. "I'm doing better but I'm a long way from being with the very best.

"Who knows? It could click around maybe in the Tour, maybe at the world championships. But it takes much longer than I thought."

The problem, he explained, is his body. For an athlete who takes great pride in his ability to suffer and recover in a race, LeMond is realizing that he no longer has total control over his body.

"It's so weird how your body works," he said. "It's difficult to imagine, some days where I've been so very bad, that I can be better. But one day I had my worst day and the next day it was one of my best days."

As fans pressed in for autographs, LeMond complied but kept talking. He was gloomy, not self-pitying, as he likened the recovery from his shooting to a new start in his professional career.

"Part of my curve now is that I have no knowledge of what my body will do because it's all so new to me," he said. "I have the experience, but my body. . . ." His voice trailed off.

The route to the top is a long one, he continued.

"When I was real good in 1985 and '86, it took me four or five years to get there and I had some very bad moments prior to that level," he said, recalling his victory in the 1986 Tour de France and his second place finish the year before.

"So you have to expect that kind of problem for maybe another year or two, maybe even three years." In three years, LeMond will be 31 years old, just short of the age where most professionals retire.

His comeback has also been slowed by troubles not always physical, LeMond acknowledged.

"Sometimes, it's mental," he explained. "With me, I have a bad day, I have no hope, no motivation. But when I was young, because I was always striving to get to a point, I never thought twice about it. 'Oh, I had a bad day, tomorrow I'll have a better day.' Now it's 'I had a bad day, God, am I going to come back?'"

With only the time trial ahead in the 72nd Giro, LeMond ranked 47th, more than fifty-five minutes behind the leader, in the field of 141 remaining riders.

He needed a boost, he said, something for his morale.

"I just want to test myself in this race today," he said cautiously. "I don't think I can win but I want to do a good placing. It would mean so much."

Moving with the force that marked his best years, LeMond then went out and rode a dominating time trial. Within 6 kilometers he caught the rider who started a minute and a half before him. In 15 more kilometers, he overtook and passed the rider who started three minutes before him.

His back bent into his work, his line around curves tight and efficient, LeMond pedaled 54 kilometers past Tuscan villages and fields, down the right bank of the Arno River in Florence, past the Ponte Vecchio and thousands of cheering fans, across the river, and up to the line that marked the finish of his latest ordeal.

He did not quite manage to surpass the previous fastest time, 1 hour, 5 minutes, 34 seconds by Lech Piasecki, a time-trial specialist, but LeMond's clocking of 1 hour, 6 minutes, 37 seconds was more than a minute ahead of the third-place finisher. All smiles, LeMond coasted off with the memory of at least one more good day.

JUST SAY NO

1989

Andy Hampsten would like to win the Tour de France for most of the usual reasons, including fame and fortune, and for a special purpose: to speak out against the use of drugs in a sport bedeviled by them.

"If I do win, it would be a good example for me to say, 'Anyone can do it without drugs,'" the 27-year-old American rider said in an interview. He is concerned particularly about the image that professional bicycling presents to youth.

"Young people who want to get into the sport, they hear—or have the idea—that it's full of drugs and they lose interest," Hampsten said. "Or they think they have to use drugs to do it, and when they're very young, they're already damaging their bodies."

The leader of the 7-Eleven team, Hampsten ranks fifth in the Tour de France and, as a strong climber, remains among the favorites in the race. In 1988 he won the Giro d'Italia and he has also won the Tour of Switzerland twice.

He is outspoken in his condemnation of drugs, mainly steroids and stimulants but also cortisone.

"Bike racing is a hard sport," he said. "The reason it fascinates people is because it's a brutally hard sport. It's supposed to be hard. So if you're just taking pills to take the pain away, it's not much of a sport, is it?"

Hampsten is equally critical of the medical program in the Tour de France.

"When we do our medical tests at the start, they should look for everything," he suggested. "Now, there are no urine samples, no drug testing.

"Tell people a year in advance that you're going to test for drugs and, if they fail, they're out of the race."

Still, he had some good words for the daily drug tests for the winner, two riders selected at random, and the overall leader at the start of the stage.

"I think cycling was the first sport to have drug testing," Hampsten said. "We're doing something about it. I'm disgusted that in my sport there is a drug problem, but at least we're confronting it."

Confining his comments to interviews and public statements,

Hampsten explained that he was not part of any organization that fights doping. "I'm not a politician," he said when asked if he was planning a broader campaign.

"I simply don't think drugs have any place in the sport," he added. "Obviously they change the sport. They change the lives of people who use them and they make it harder for people who don't use them to keep up.

"I think people ride better without drugs than with drugs. That's a different attitude than some European riders have, different from the tradition at least.

"So, yes, I think it would prove a lot," Hampsten said of the prospects of his victory. "I think it would show young riders, especially, that in the long run, drugs are not going to help you."

Hampsten was in the forefront of those few riders who condemned Pedro Delgado a year earlier when he was found to have tested positive for a drug that masks steroids. Because the drug was not yet illegal in professional bicycling, Delgado was allowed to continue as the leader, and eventual winner, of the Tour de France.

Although the race has since tightened its drug tests, no rider has yet tested positive. The Delgado case was the most publicized of three positive findings in 1988 among the Tour's 198 riders; the year before, two riders were found positive by the daily tests.

"I can't say other riders use drugs," Hampsten continued. "Some do, obviously, since they're caught doing it. But I don't know if it's just them or if 90 percent of the pack uses them."

Most general estimates put the use of steroids and stimulants much lower than that. Yet in France alone, more than thirty riders at all levels were found to have used banned substances in 1987.

Part of the reason, as Hampsten hinted, is the overall attitude of European riders to drug use.

A typical remark comes from Teun Van Vliet, 27, a bright and talented rider with the Panasonic team, based in his native Netherlands. Van Vliet said he had never tested positive for drugs.

Asked about the Delgado drugs scandal, he corrected his questioner: "I'm sorry, but it wasn't a drug scandal because it wasn't on the list" of banned drugs.

"So there was no drug result—he was really negative, not positive."

What if an opponent did test positive for a banned drug? Here Van Vliet drew a common distinction.

"It depends on what kind of medicine he used," he said, avoiding the word "drugs."

"Sometimes you need some medicine because you need it, because you're a little bit ill or you're really ill.

"It's your profession so you have to do it," he continued. "Somebody who's working in an office and who's ill, he sees the doctor and the doctor says, 'I'll give you something but you can't go to the office because you're positive'—that's crazy.

"When you look at the world—Europe, America—all the people using drugs, everybody drinking alcohol, everybody doing something, it's not really a problem of the sports world, it's the world itself."

He was not speaking with Hampsten, but the American had already offered a response.

"I think I'm a fairly talented rider who can go pretty far without drugs," he judged. "Some people might argue that if I used drugs, I could ride better."

How would he answer them?

"I don't have to," Hampsten said. "To me, it doesn't mean a thing.

"If someone tells me, 'You would have won this race if you'd taken these pills,' it's not even within my realm of options.

"It's like saying, 'If you wiggle your ears and wish, you'll be on top of this mountain.'" He laughed at the thought of climbing the Alps that way.

THAT TIME TRIAL

1989

In 26 minutes, 57 seconds, Greg LeMond won the Tour de France for the second time in 1989. His margin of victory over Laurent Fignon was eight seconds, the smallest ever.

The race had already covered 3,225.5 kilometers in three weeks when LeMond set off on the last stage, a 24.5-kilometer time trial from Versailles into Paris. He was 50 seconds behind the overall leader, the Frenchman Fignon.

Few besides LeMond, a 28-year-old American, believed he had a chance to make up that time.

"It's still possible," he said the day before, but most observers doubted him.

As a half million people watching on the Champs-Elysées burst into a roar of cheers, LeMond proved all the doubters wrong.

"I just went all out," he said. "I thought I could win but I knew I needed something special."

Asked what he thought about during the race, he explained, "I didn't think; I just rode."

Ride, he did. LeMond won the time trial easily, finishing 33 seconds ahead of Thierry Marie, a Frenchman, who was timed in 27 minutes, 30 seconds. LeMond needed all his speed and power as Fignon came in third, 58 seconds behind LeMond.

The American's time translated into a speed of 54.5 kilometers an hour, the fastest for a time trial in Tour de France history by nearly 5 kilometers an hour.

The eight-second margin of victory is the smallest, by 30 seconds, in the history of the Tour, which began in 1903 and has been interrupted only by the two world wars.

The previous record of 38 seconds separating the first two finishers was established in 1968 in similar circumstances: Jan Janssen, a Dutchman, trailed Herman van Springel, a Belgian, by 16 seconds and beat him by 54 in a time trial into Paris.

LeMond waited in the finish area for the arrival of Fignon, who set off two minutes after him. As the seconds went by, LeMond said later, "All I could think was how terrible it would be to lose by one second."

When it became clear that Fignon was not going to win, LeMond began pumping the air with his fists. He broke into a huge grin and punched one uppercut after another as Fignon raced down the broad avenue and the public address announcer shouted that his time was more than the necessary fifty seconds behind.

In finishing one-two, LeMond and Fignon made remarkable comebacks.

LeMond was accidentally shot while hunting wild turkey in California in April 1987, nine months after he became the only American to have won the Tour de France. He had not won a major race since the shooting. After finishing 39th in the Giro d'Italia only a month ago, he said before the Tour de France began in Luxembourg that his goals were a stage victory and a finish among the first fifteen or even twenty.

Fignon, soon to turn 29, won the Tour de France in 1983 and 1984 but then developed tendinitis in his left heel. After surgery in 1985, he had only occasional successes until he won the same Giro that LeMond did so poorly in.

"I think maybe I've come up a bit since the Giro and some of the others have come down a bit," LeMond had said a few days ago.

Gasping for breath and draining a bottle of mineral water, Fignon at first offered no excuse for his defeat. "I rode the hardest I could," he said. "Obviously it wasn't good enough."

Later, he complained of saddle sores. "I could hardly sit in the saddle it was so painful," he said. "I've been having this trouble for three days. I didn't even think I would be able to start today it was so bad."

He has never beaten LeMond in a time trial in any of the three Tours de France they have competed in. Those were in 1984, when they were both on the Renault team, and Fignon won and LeMond finished third; 1986, when LeMond rode for La Vie Claire and won as Fignon dropped out; and the current race, when LeMond won two of three time trials, not including the prologue.

The two riders dominated this 76th Tour de France, with LeMond wearing the yellow jersey of the overall leader eight times and Fignon nine.

The American's final jersey was the one he was awarded on the victory podium Sunday, as the fifty-five men of the Band of the Eighth Regiment of the French Signal Corps broke into "The Star-Spangled Banner."

"We've practiced it, of course," said the band's leader, Major Roger Baquie, before the finish. He smiled the sort of smile that implied he would be leading "La Marseillaise" instead in a few hours.

Taking a quick lead in the time splits of the race, LeMond ruined that musical interlude.

After 11.5 of the 24.5 kilometers, he led Fignon by 21 seconds. That mounted to 24 seconds after 14 kilometers, 29 seconds after 18, and 32 seconds after 23, when LeMond turned left at the Louvre and passed into the Rue de Rivoli.

He rode the way a person swims the crawl, keeping his head down low over his handlebars and regularly lifting it to gulp air.

Wearing an aerodynamic helmet and leaning on extensions on his handlebars used by triathletes for better streamlining, he held his tuck from the moment of the start on the avenue leading from the Palace of Versailles.

Through the dreary suburbs of southwestern Paris he came, holding to his sure line and riding powerfully. Then he was onto the Champs-Elysées, heading uphill into a slight headwind and changing his gears before he looped back just before the Arc de Triomphe and sped toward the finish line.

No tie between Fignon and LeMond was possible because the race Sunday was timed down to hundredths of a second. If that had failed to resolve the situation, the riders' placings in all twenty-one daily stages would have been added. And, if that had not worked, the Tour de France would have been decided by the outcome in the previous day's skylarking stage: LeMond 40th, Fignon 50th.

THE EAGLE OF VIZILLE

1989

"I am Eagle," exulted the cosmonaut Gherman Titov from space in 1961, and the world understood. Eagle: soaring high above the rest.

Féderico Bahamontes was an eagle too: the Eagle of Toledo. The Spanish bicycle rider was so swift a climber that legend says he once made it to the top of a mountain in the Pyrenees and was able to halt and eat an ice cream before the other riders joined him.

Bahamontes won the king-of-the-mountains jersey in six Tours de France. In 1959 he won the Tour itself, and his yellow jersey still hangs in tribute in the rafters of the cathedral of Toledo.

The nickname of Eagle is not easily given to professional riders, but Thierry Claveyrolat carries it. Somewhat mockingly, the French press often calls him the Eagle of Vizille, his home town in the French Alps.

In recent years the Tour de France has zipped through the village, leaving a trace more dust on its handful of homes and the pizzeria that Claveyrolat has tended during the off-season. Each time, he has tried to excel in that mountainous stage before his neighbors, but the Tour de France has too many better climbers than the 30-year-old Eagle of Vizille.

He shines in smaller-bore races, not the grand Tours or the one-day classics of spring and fall, where the highest honors of professional bicycling are gained. Claveyrolat stands 5 feet 6 inches and weighs 120 pounds, and his main accomplishments during seven seasons as a professional match his frame: four stages won in the Dauphiné Libéré since 1986, best climber in the Midi Libre in 1987, a stage won in the Tour of Catalonia in 1989.

A rider for the modest RMO team since it was founded in 1986, Claveyrolat was considered its leader for three years, until big money was spent to upgrade the roster. Among those hired was Charly Mottet, who ranks No. 2 on the computerized list of the world's top 600 professionals.

Claveyrolat, who ranks No. 36, had no trouble accepting his demotion. Happy to win a stage and finish third in the 1989 Dauphiné Libéré, he was just as happy to help Mottet win the race.

"In bicycling," he says, "whoever is not capable of being a leader has to be a team worker. That description fits me, and I'm not ashamed to admit it."

Then, for a few hours this summer, the Eagle of Vizille spread his wings.

"For a while I thought I would become the world champion," Claveyrolat said as he waited for the start of the Paris-Tours classic. "I thought of it, I really thought it would happen," he said of the rainbow-striped jersey the world champion wears. When he thinks about it now, his face puckers.

"I'm very happy with my season but, of course, disappointed with what happened at the world championships."

He was remembering the 12.3-kilometer course in Chambéry that the field covered twenty-one times. On the eighth lap, nine riders attacked. They built a lead of 4 minutes, 50 seconds by the eleventh lap, when four of the group, including Claveyrolat and Dimitri Konichev of the Soviet Union, jumped off.

By the nineteenth lap, Claveyrolat and Konichev had been joined by Steven Rooks of the Netherlands but had left the two others behind. Although their lead was down to 1:28, there were barely 25 kilometers left to race.

Their lead was 11 seconds at the bell lap as nine men rode in pursuit, including Greg LeMond of the United States, Laurent Fignon of France, and Sean Kelly of Ireland. Fignon attacked on the final climb, chasing Claveyrolat, his teammate for this one day, when national teams replace the sponsored teams that racers work for the rest of the year.

By going after the leaders, Fignon pulled two rivals, LeMond and Kelly, along with him, which is why teammates are not supposed to attack each other.

"It would have been better to believe in Claveyrolat," said Mottet, another member of the French team. "Laurent told me he felt very strong on the last lap but I think, in fact, that he wasn't as strong as he thought."

Paced by Fignon, the threesome caught the leaders. At the red triangle that marks the final kilometer, Fignon tried for the last time to get away and was countered by LeMond. With 200 yards to go, the American decided it was time to sprint, and Fignon and Claveyrolat were left behind as the four others tore for the line. LeMond crossed first, followed by Konichev, Kelly, and Rooks. Claveyrolat was fifth and Fignon sixth.

"If somebody had told me before the start, 'You'll be in front for 180 kilometers and finally finish fifth,' I would have been awfully happy," Claveyrolat admitted.

"But, because of the circumstances, I feel terrible. It would have been understandable if the Spaniards or the Italians had ridden after me, but not my own team."

He blames both Fignon and Bernard Hinault, the great star of French racing before his retirement in 1986, who was the French team's coach.

"Both of them together—Hinault for never bothering to come up in the car to find out how strong I was and Fignon for attacking on the last climb without being strong enough to win.

"It's a shame. The world championships are held in France once every ten years, and we didn't have the right to ride this way and not produce a winner.

"Winning would have been everything," Claveyrolat continued. "For me it would have been more than a dream.

"But there's no point still thinking about it. All it is now is a motivation for better things to come. There's next year and the Dauphiné Libéré and the Tour de France and all the other races. There are still a few races left this year.

"I'll never forget the world championship at Chambéry, but it's time now to think of other things."

Those other things could not include Paris-Tours, which was too flat and windy for the small climber. He finished 84th. The Eagle of Vizille would have to wait for another day to rise, to glide, to soar again.

WHEN AUTUMN COMES

1989

Out in the countryside of France, the fields are brown and barren, their corn long harvested and the stalks chopped down for fodder. Until the stubble is plowed under when winter wheat is planted, the landscape is bleak and the air full of despair.

For professional bicycle riders, April is not the cruelest month. Far from it. In April, hopes for a successful season are as green as the shoots just then starting to push through the fields that the riders pass in their early races. The cruelest month is really October, when the nine-month racing season ends and the riders finally know what they have failed to accomplish.

The one-day classics of spring—the Tour of Flanders, Paris-Roubaix, Milan-San Remo, Liège-Bastogne-Liège—roll past trees in bud, and now those same trees give a name to the final fall classics in France and Italy. "The Race of the Dead Leaves," they call Paris-Tours and the Tour of Lombardy. The leaves have fallen from long avenues of plane trees in every small town.

Laurent Fignon knows the mood. On the first day of spring, he won Milan-San Remo and stood in the warm sun of the Italian Riviera to proclaim that this time he was well and truly back on top. The winner of two Tours de France by the time he was 24, Fignon then developed tendinitis in his left heel and gave away a year to surgery and recuperation. After that, nothing went right.

He lost confidence in his climbing and time-trial ability; managed to finish only one Tour de France before 1989; and found victory in even minor races elusive, with the exception of Milan-San Remo.

Fignon's performances in 1989 justified the comeback talk. The 29-year-old Frenchman won the Giro d'Italia and finished second in the Tour de France by just eight seconds, as Greg LeMond overcame a 50-second deficit on the final day. Fignon came back to win the Tour of Holland by 1 second and finished sixth in the world championships as LeMond unleashed a strong sprint to capture the title.

"He's my bête noire," Fignon said, before going on to win the Trophée Barrachi and the Grand Prix des Nations.

The surge put him atop the computerized list of the world's top 600 professional racers. Just as the list and Fignon's No. 1 ranking were made public, the French Cycling Federation announced that Fignon had tested positive for drugs in the Grand Prix of the Liberation. Traces of amphetamines had been found in the urine sample he was required to give after his Super U team finished second.

A similar positive drug result stripped him of his 1987 victory in the Grand Prix of Wallonia, a minor spring race. Since two years had elapsed between offenses, he was treated as a first-time offender and given a three-month suspended sentence. A second offense within two years calls for a six-month ban from competition and a third offense calls for a year's ban.

Fignon had little to say about the public announcement of his positive drug test.

"It's in the hands of my lawyer and I have nothing to add to that."

When the Super U team cars arrived in the Paris suburb of Chaville for the start of the Paris-Tours classic, 283 kilometers long, Fignon refused to answer questions. He got on his bicycle and rode to the sign-in, got back on his bicycle, and returned to his team car. Sitting inside it with his head down as he fiddled with his shoes, he avoided a small crowd of fans and photographers until it was time to begin the race.

Then he was out of the car, up again on his bicycle and off to the starting line. He had no time for small talk.

The race began under dark, low-lying clouds that threatened rain all day but never fulfilled the promise. Racing south to Tours, the 167 riders fought a strong and chilling headwind much of the way through the Loire Valley. Where sunflowers had stood golden by the thousands a few months before, the few survivors had turned black. Winter is coming, and in the countryside they are prepared: Corncribs brim in the fields, bales of hay are piled in barns, and firewood is stacked next to houses.

The riders remained bunched for hour after hour of the trip. Finally, with 20 kilometers to go, the Belgian rider Hendrick Redant managed to open a small gap ahead of the pack. He was quickly joined by Gino Furlant, an Italian, and Fignon.

Relaying one another, they maintained a respectable lead as the race moved through the suburbs of Tours and then into the city. Clearly Fignon was trying to prove something to the trailing pack.

But, with four kilometers to go, he looked back over his shoulder and saw that the breakaway had failed: The other riders had stormed back and were at the point of overtaking him. Fignon did not sit up and coast, as riders usually do when they are being recaptured, but he seemed to shrug. The fire went out of his pedaling.

On the long straightaway to the finish line, the sprinters maneuvered for position and unleashed their final kick, with Jelle Nijdam, a Dutchman, beating Eric Vanderaerden, a Belgian, across the line.

Fignon came in 86th. "Another race," he said, "just part of the job." He confirmed that he would be riding next in Italy, competing in the Tour of Lombardy, the second "Race of the Dead Leaves." After that, the golden season of his comeback would be finished.

Part Two

THE '90s:
A DECADE OF TURMOIL

A CLASSICAL APPROACH

1990

Somewhere between Mozart's "Haffner" Symphony (Köchel 385) and his "Jupiter" (K. 551), Gianni Bugno learned, allegro vivace, how to become a champion bicycle rider.

Given a month of musical therapy to cure vertigo, Bugno blossomed from a timid rider who seemed able to win only small races into the man who leads the computerized rankings of the world's top 600 professionals.

He is also at the front of the Italian renaissance in the sport: Moreno Argentin is first in World Cup standings, and Marco Giovannetti won the Vuelta a España and finished third in the Giro d'Italia.

In March 1990 the 26-year-old Bugno won the Milan-San Remo classic in Italy and then dominated the three-week Giro from start to finish. Based on his form in the Giro, many riders and observers rate him high among the favorites in the Tour de France once the race reaches the Alps.

"He was very impressive in the mountains in the Giro," said Bernard Hinault. "He's not my main favorite, no, but he's certainly on the list of those who have the best chance."

That is high praise for a rider who finished 62nd in 1988 in his first Tour de France and 11th in 1989. That was before Bugno was remade by psychologists, allergists, racing counselors, and, of course, his musical therapist.

One of the Italian rider's undetected problems was vertigo, or dizziness and fear of falling, when he descended from a mountain peak at high speed. Bugno finally bared the secret after he was first over the top in the 1989 Milan-Turin classic but was easily caught by the pack on the descent.

"A priest in a soutane could have made it down faster than I did," Bugno said. "I felt so dizzy that I slowed down almost to a stop."

The trouble was attributed to a bad crash in the 1988 Giro and to a congenital obstruction in the canals of his inner ear.

As a cure, Bugno tried ultrasound treatments laced with music. "I listened to Mozart at different speeds and degrees of loudness for a month," Bugno said. "After that, the vertigo was gone."

Then he visited an allergist, who discovered that he could not tolerate wheat, milk, or milk products. A combination of pills was prescribed and his diet was changed.

Afterward, he was put into the hands of Claudio Corti, a veteran Italian rider, who taught Bugno how to take charge of his Chateau d'Ax team.

Finally he began seeing a psychologist, who helped resolve Bugno's timidity. This problem was traced to his childhood. Bugno was born in Brugg, Switzerland, where his father was a carpenter, but grew up with his grandparents in Italy while his parents worked in Switzerland.

All these adjustments took place in the winter of 1989 and then Bugno was unleashed.

The rider who had won only the minor Tour of Calabria in 1988, the Tour of the Appenines in 1986, 1987, and 1988, and the semi-classic Tour of Piedmont in 1986 suddenly was storming down the Poggio hill to win Milan-San Remo while other riders took the descent more prudently and slowly.

Bugno's victory in the Giro was just as impressive. He won the prologue and never gave up the lead, finishing first by a huge 6 minutes, 33 seconds.

Many Italians advised Bugno to skip this 77th Tour de France, reasoning that he had nothing further to prove this year and that his chances were slim. No Italian had won the Tour since 1965.

"The Italians just aren't used to such a hard race," said Bernard Thévenet, who won the Tour de France twice in the 1970s.

"And, coming a month after the Giro, the Tour is just too much for most riders who went all-out in Italy."

Bugno knows that. But, as he says, "the Tour de France is the summit of cycling: more fans than any other race, more reporters, more pressure.

"The Tour's climbs are usually longer than the Giro's but the time trials are the key to winning.

"I still have a lot to learn but if I didn't feel I had a role to play, I wouldn't be here."

THE HARD FACTS

1991

Despite abundant anecdotal evidence to the contrary, there are no block-heads out there: At its thickest, the human skull measures no more than a centimeter, or four-tenths of an inch. At its thinnest, the skull measures nine-tenths less than a centimeter.

The average highway, on the other hand, measures 4 to 6 centimeters of tar, concrete, or asphalt laid over a hardened roadbed many times deeper. In any sudden meeting of skull and highway, the highway always prevails.

This truth causes about two hundred bicycling deaths annually in Britain, for example, and about eight hundred in the United States. (Deaths from other cycling injuries raise the total by a third; nonfatal injuries are fifteen times more frequent.)

Even at the professional level, a death or disabling injury occurs nearly every year.

These statistics have led to a ruling that rigid helmets must be worn by all riders in races sanctioned by the International Cycling Union, which governs amateur and professional competition. Until the ruling, few professionals wore helmets other than a thin, aerodynamic shell in time trials.

At the heart of the rule is a 1988 report in the respected *New England Journal of Medicine* concluding that helmets could reduce the risk of injury by 85 percent and the risk of brain injury by 88 percent.

But professional riders have reacted to the imposition of mandatory helmets with a rare vehemence. Never, they say, has a rule been so worthy and so unfair. Complaints range from the extra heat helmets will generate on a summer's climb, to the perceived autocratic manner in which the rule was imposed, to the Darth Vader stormtrooper look produced by helmets combined with riders' omnipresent sunglasses.

The rule is so controversial in the European professional pack that it has inspired talk of a possible mass boycott of helmets. Just before they set off on the Paris-Nice race, groups of riders buzzed with rumors that the boycott would be staged at the first major classic, from Milan to San Remo in Italy.

"At the moment there's a lot of talk," confirmed Sean Kelly, the star Irish rider of the PDM team.

"Everybody's talking, but I haven't seen any organization yet," added Paul Sherwen, a former English rider who now is an official of the Motorola team.

The rumors have been heard also by Hein Verbruggen, the 49-year-old Dutchman who heads the International Federation of Professional Cycling. Known as the FICP for its initials in French, the language of bicycling, the federation governs the professional sport.

"Anybody who doesn't wear the helmet is out of the race," Verbruggen said by phone from his home in Brussels.

"Anybody who doesn't wear the helmet to the start won't depart. Anybody who takes his helmet off during the race will be disqualified.

"Security is more important than how hot the helmet will be or how much it makes everybody look alike."

He got no argument from Ron Kiefel of the Motorola team.

"It's a pretty good idea," the U.S. rider said. "It's like when the National Hockey League made helmets mandatory. There was a lot of fuss at first, but I don't know how many guys would think now about going on the ice without one. I feel much safer with mine on."

Kiefel admitted that he was not bothered by the added heat, which even veteran wearers of the helmet could not quantify.

"It will affect some people and not others," added Jim Ochowicz, the Motorola general manager. "Some people aren't affected by the heat and others are just going to melt away with that on their heads."

"That" is a rigid plastic shell with a liner of expanded polystyrene, also known as Styrofoam, that crushes on impact, absorbing shock that would otherwise pass to the skull. Anchored by a chinstrap, the helmet can be reinforced with a Kevlar or nylon ring. Costing usually between $75 and $100, the helmets worn by professionals are relatively lightweight, about 225 grams (8 ounces). In 1986, when Greg LeMond pioneered the rigid helmet, it weighed nearly twice as much.

"I strongly believe in their use," LeMond said before starting the Paris-Nice race. "There's a lot of risk involved in cycling, it's a very dangerous sport. I would advise anybody riding or training at almost any level to wear a helmet at almost all times."

Then he began to tick off the riders' complaints: "I think we're adults and would have liked to have freedom of choice. The riders' frustration is over the lack of input we have at the FICP level.

"I used a helmet 90 percent of the time last year, but I think it should be left to the rider's intelligence. There are times when they're not desirable, and that's on a six-hour mountain stage in the Tour de France in 100-plus-degree weather.

"Regardless of any studies, you do six hours in 100-degree weather and a helmet's a lot hotter. I know it is. One way of keeping the heat down on your body is dousing cold water over your head. How are you going to douse your head if you're wearing a helmet?

"Then there's recognition. For the television and spectators in the mountains, it's nice to see the suffering and the expressions on the riders' faces. It's probably what attracts many people to the sport."

Other former riders worried more about the extra heat.

Roger de Vlaeminck, the champion classics rider of the '70s who now coaches the Tonton Tapis team in his native Belgium, was one of them.

"I've got a rider, Dirk de Wolf, who can't handle the heat of a helmet already, and it's only March. Sweat pours off his head and into his eyes now. What's he going to do in July?"

One solution proposed by LeMond was not to have to wear the helmets on excessively hot days. He noted that, despite pressure from his helmet sponsor, he chose to ride in his showdown time trial in the most recent Tour de France in the cloth cap that has been standard headgear for decades.

"I thought it was too hot for a helmet at the Lac de Vassivière," he said of the stage that gave him his third victory in the Tour. "I trained in the helmet and took it off, and there was a world of difference."

When LeMond's suggestion was relayed to him, Verbruggen appeared to be unyielding.

"We have carefully studied all elements in this rule," he said. "There are 150 race days a year and only three or four could be a problem. It is very difficult to establish criteria for an exception.

"And what would happen if you allowed an exception because of the heat and that day you had a fatal accident? But the possibility is not excluded. Also, we're convinced that helmet manufacturers can come up with a solution."

Manufacturers themselves seemed less sure.

"Climbing that hill at Alpe d'Huez is never fun and there's no way to make it fun," Jim Gentes, the founder of Giro helmets, said by phone from California. "But we're not talking discomfort here, we're talking protection. Let's face it: Bike racing is a very dangerous sport.

Riders die of head injuries. I'm amazed how many times people land on their heads.

"We all have the attitude that it can't happen and then all of a sudden somebody dies," Gentes said, citing the case of Joaquim Agostinho, a leading Tour de France rider who was killed in his native Portugal after a heavy fall in 1984.

At that time, professionals occasionally wore striped leather helmets known as hairnets.

"Hairnets offered minimum protection because they had no shock absorption," explained Charles Luthi, the managing director of Bell Helmets Europe. "They were better than nothing, but not by much."

IN DARKEST DELAWARE

1991

Is there life after Donald Trump?

The answer began to emerge as the Tour Du Pont started with a short prologue through the streets of Wilmington. Some 1,100 miles later, the sixteen-team international race will end in the same chemical corporation fiefdom.

The Tour Du Pont succeeds the Tour de Trump as the major U.S. bicycle road race. After two years of lending his name to the event, the beleaguered Donald Trump decided that dealing was one thing, wheeling quite another.

"We had two good years with the race but it's too expensive to put on," he said in a phone interview from New York.

"It loses money and I didn't want to lose money. With the economy in the shape it's in, I didn't want to stay involved."

Trump put the race's loss at "a couple of million dollars." Little, if any, of that sum was his, since the real estate developer mainly lent his name and prestige to the organizers, who sought out sponsors eager to share in the razzmatazz.

This year there will be no *Trump Princess* anchored in Baltimore Harbor, no Trump jet winging into Albany, no Trump stretch limo plying the back roads to Richmond, and no Trump, Donald, firing the starting pistol in front of his Plaza Hotel in New York.

Standing in is stolid Du Pont, represented by platoons of power-dressed executives yearning to discuss such chemical products for cycling as Cordura nylon, Delrin acetal resin, and Hytrel polyester elastomer. Where have you gone, Joe DiMaggio?

"Du Pont is a first-class organization," Trump said, "and I'm sure they'll do the race well. It's in good hands."

Yet he was decidedly pessimistic about the future of the sport in the United States.

"It will be a long time before bicycle racing becomes an American sport," he felt. His point of reference was the Evander Holyfield-George Foreman heavyweight title fight in his Trump Plaza Hotel Casino in Atlantic City the month before.

"We put on a fight and drew the biggest TV audience ever but the bicycle race never came close," he said. "The most disappointing thing about the bicycle race is that the TV coverage didn't measure up. They had the wrong hours, the wrong days, they showed the race when people are doing other things."

The "other things" include such current television sports fare as the National Hockey League and National Basketball Association playoffs, not to mention baseball.

The Tour Du Pont hopes to hold its own by showing the race in the afternoon or early evening, well before prime time. Television coverage this year will comprise a total of two hours on the CBS network both Sundays of the race and a total of four hours on ESPN, a cable network, nearly every other day.

A half-hour recap will be televised in eighty-eight countries every day.

The Tour de Trump format has been followed, basically: more than $300,000 in cash and merchandise prizes, making this one of the richer races anywhere; an emphasis on point-to-point road stages with a handful of looped time trials, criteriums, and circuit races; demanding climbs in the Blue Ridge and Pocono Mountains; passage through Delaware, Maryland, Virginia, and Pennsylvania; and a mix of amateur and professional teams.

Among the leading professional teams assembled in Wilmington are Z from France; Helvetia from Switzerland; PDM from the Netherlands; Seur from Spain; Tonton Tapis from Belgium; and Motorola, Coors Light, Subaru-Montgomery, and Spago from the United States.

The better amateur teams include those from the Soviet Union, which nearly ran away with the 1990 race, and the United States. Each team, amateur or pro, will field seven riders.

Leading riders include Greg LeMond, three-time winner of the Tour de France, of Z; Erik Breukink and Sean Kelly of PDM; Gilles Delion and Gérard Rué of Helvetia; Steve Bauer and Phil Anderson of Motorola; Ronan Pensec of Seur; Alexi Grewal and Davis Phinney of Coors Light; and Dmitri Nelubin of the Soviet Union.

Part of the attraction is that the Tour Du Pont will award FICP points, which determine a rider's ranking and, often, salary. The Tour de Trump did not grant points.

"It's a fine race with a fine field," LeMond said in a roadside chat. Troubled by cold sores around his mouth, he has not trained much in a week and is rarely at his best in May. Nevertheless, as the leading American rider, he is the favorite of Wilmington's fans, who got a taste of the race in 1990 and turned out in big numbers.

As Trump put it, "We had good crowds, good enthusiasm wherever we went. I started something that I'm proud of. It's just something that's too expensive for us now."

A RACER WITH A CAUSE

1991

Marion Clignet's calling card identifies her as a bicycle racer and a spokesperson—two understatements. She is more than just another rider since she is the French women's road-race champion. And she is more than just another spokesperson since she is a crusader.

What she crusades for is a better understanding of epilepsy. Clignet knows what some people think and say about an epileptic because she is one herself.

"It's not a problem and it really shouldn't make a difference," she feels. "That's what motivates me to race: to do well because epilepsy was supposed to be an obstacle. I thought, 'You think it's an obstacle, well here we go.'"

She does indeed go. In the 1990 U.S. national championships she repeated her 1989 victory in the team time trial, a race against the clock. In those same championships, she was second in the road race and third in the individual pursuit. She also won the first stage in the 1990 Tour of the European Community and led the race for three days.

Clignet raced then as an American, a distinction she earned when she was born 27 years ago in Illinois. Since December she has raced as a Frenchwoman, a distinction she earned when she was born the child of two French citizens who were living in the United States while her father taught sociology at Northwestern University in Evanston, Illinois.

"I have always felt very French," she said. "My family is French, I grew up speaking French in a French home. But my education is American and I have a lot of ideas that are American."

The only culture shock she reports having had is in understanding temperatures given in centigrade rather than Fahrenheit.

"When they say it's 30 degrees outside, I have to transfer my thought process into the metric system," she said. Still, she quickly gives her height as 1 meter 70 (5 feet 7 inches) and her weight as 60 kilograms (132 pounds). If she has any accent as she speaks English, it is the soft glottals of the state of Maryland. Her parents moved there from Illinois when she was 15 and her father began teaching at the University of Maryland at College Park.

Seven years later, while she was majoring in physical education at the university, she had an epileptic seizure. That sign of neurologic disorder indirectly started her down a road that has led to the 1991 French championship and victories in the Tour of the Drome and the Canadian Tire Cycling Classic.

All this came about because, after her first epileptic attack, she lost her driver's license. She explained that Maryland law then decreed a year's loss of driving privileges after a seizure to determine what caused it.

She still had to get to her job at a health club more than 10 miles from home, so she began traveling by bicycle. Then she started working out at the club and doing fitness programs. "One thing led to another and I got into racing."

As Clignet developed as a bicycle racer, she began campaigning for understanding of epileptics. They are rare among high-level athletes even if, like Clignet, they can control the disease with twice-daily doses of medicine.

"Basically I wanted to educate mostly parents of children who have epilepsy," she said. "I wanted to educate parents to be a little more liberal instead of saying, 'Oh, my God, my kid has epilepsy, he's handicapped.'

"And I wanted to inspire kids not to let it be an obstacle in the way of their doing anything they wanted to do. In the States there was a tendency to put the kids in special ed classes and that would start them on a cycle where the child would think he was stupid and therefore act stupid. I was trying to campaign against that but mostly educate the public."

With the support of the pharmaceutical company Ciba-Geigy, which remains her sponsor, she made a speaking tour of the United States. She continues to speak in France—hence the "spokesperson" on her calling card—but mainly she battles by example: The woman calling for understanding is, after all, wearing the blue, white, and red jersey of a national champion.

Clignet's attitude is straightforward. Do people really discriminate against epileptics, do they really care if she is one?

"I don't care if they do care," she says. "If somebody's going to treat me different because of something they can't tell I have, I don't need people like that."

She has developed a manner of introducing her illness that is based on her philosophy that "If you present it as a problem, then it'll be a problem."

Instead, she continued, "if I have to tell somebody, I make a joke about it. I try to make them comfortable with it by letting them know I'm comfortable with it, that it's not a problem for me and it shouldn't be a problem for them. If they act weird about it, I tell them two or three of my epileptic jokes. If they don't settle down after that, I write them off."

Occasionally there are people who have to be written off.

"People have so many prejudices," she noted. One reason she shifted her base from the United States to France was her perception that U.S. racing officials downgraded her ability because of her epilepsy. Despite her strong performances in 1990, she was not invited to join the American team at the world championships in Japan.

"And the U.S. lost the team time trial," she added pointedly.

Why was she not invited?

"You'll have to ask them. They don't come out and say it but there were a lot of insinuations. It motivated me and still pushes me because I hear some of that in my mind from time to time."

She also has positive reinforcement.

"I get letters from kids who are epileptics or in some institution and I raced for them a lot this year."

Despite plans to spend an October vacation in the United States, she said she did not intend to live there again. Her bitterness toward U.S. bicycling officials, especially the United States Cycling Federation, is obvious, especially when asked if she regarded her victories this year as revenge.

"I wouldn't say I was trying to prove something but. . . . Put it this way: They've already asked me what they could do to make me come back and I said, 'There's nothing.' So."

Clignet's immediate goals in racing are the world championships in Germany and the 1992 Olympic Games in Spain. She feels that her move to her new base near Lorient in Brittany will help her immensely.

"I always wanted to move back to France for at least a year and see how it was," she said. "I was doing well in the States but in terms of learning, I was at a plateau there.

"It's not the same racing there and racing here. I race with the men here. I only race with the women internationally. Locally and region-ally, only with men. I did that in the States too but it's much harder and faster here.

"Everybody's much more experienced here. The guys I train with have been racing ten, twelve years and their fathers raced ten, twelve years. I learn stuff every day from these people. I've worked hard. I've progressed more in a few months here than I did in two years there. Results speak for themselves."

Her first victory of the season, she remembered, came at the expense of the very men she trains with.

"I went on a training ride with the men and I changed their attitude about women's cycling. Now they realize there are women who can race with men and even beat them, make them hurt in training. We've gone on lots of training rides where they've hurt more than I have.

"That in itself is a real victory."

IN THE BIG SHOW

1993

Lance Armstrong has made it to what he calls "the big show, the big deal, the Super Bowl" and what everybody else calls the Tour de France. Armstrong can be excused for his excitement because he is 21 years old and hardly anybody else in the bicycle race, including the kid who distributes soft drinks at the finish line, is even close to being that young.

"This is my style, this is what I like," Armstrong said with a beatific smile. "From what I've seen, this is my type of race." At that point, he was reminded, he had seen nothing more than the perfunctory medical examination that all riders pass through.

"There you are," he replied. "Just the medical exam and all that attention, photographers, reporters, the room full of people, the electricity. It's the Super Bowl."

If Armstrong could generate that much enthusiasm for a test of his blood pressure, how would he react to the race itself? To judge from his first few days in the Tour de France, just fine. The American rider for the Motorola team finished the second stage in 20th place among the 180 riders, finished the third stage to Vannes in 7th place, and was not close to hyperventilating.

Not turning 22 until September 18, Armstrong is one of the youngest men to start the Tour in years, along with Andrea Peron, an Italian with Gatorade who also is 21. Because Armstrong is also a neo-pro, as first-year professionals are called, his entry has caused a bit of controversy.

Miguel Indurain, the current Tour champion, was also a 21-year-old neo-pro in his debut in 1985. There was no similar controversy then because Indurain, who dropped out after four of the twenty-one stages, had not shown the great potential that Armstrong has. In other words, the Spaniard was regarded as cannon fodder—as Gatorade's Peron is—and the American is considered a star of the future if he is not misused.

The possibility of burnout troubles some observers, but not Armstrong or officials of his team.

"I'm here to learn, really," the native of Plano, Texas, said in an interview before the Tour started. "I don't expect anything. I don't expect to win a stage, I don't expect to take a jersey.

"But I'd like to," he added hastily. "I'd really like to win a stage. I definitely think it's possible." He acknowledged, though, that his goal was "rather lofty."

Armstrong is open, extremely likeable, and sincere, but not brash, about his desire to succeed. In his short career, he has won a few big races—including the recent U.S. professional championship and a $1 million bonus—and done well enough in others to be recognized as a major future talent.

The future is not quite now, Armstrong conceded.

For now, his plans are to race only the first two weeks of the three-week Tour. The Alps are on his calendar but not the Pyrenees.

"We'll take it day to day," said Jim Ochowicz, the Motorola team's general manager. "We'll see how he's recuperating each day. He'll be monitored by Max Testa, the team doctor. I'd like to get Lance through the Alps because he needs to know some of those climbs. He's never done them. You need to get through this first time to know the roads, the climbs, all the atmosphere, all the things that come with the Tour de France that you don't find at other races.

"This is a learning experience," Ochowicz said. "I definitely don't think he's too young. If I were worried about that, I wouldn't have had him here."

Armstrong is not worried either, he said as he sat in his hotel room, stripped to the waist, wearing a silver outline of the state of Texas on a chain around his neck, and awaiting a rubdown. Nor, he insisted, is he intimidated.

Two years ago, when he was a teenager riding for the U.S. amateur team in the Tour Du Pont, he admitted that his long-term goal was to win the Tour de France. Now he was putting it into broader perspective.

"When you're a kid you say you want to ride the Tour, but realistically I've been thinking about it just the last couple of months," he said.

In that time he finished second in the Du Pont; third in the Tour of Sweden; and first in the K-Mart Classic, the Thrift Drug Classic, and the CoreStates Championship—the so-called U.S. triple crown that earned him the $1 million bonus. (Rather than accept $50,000 a year for twenty years, the team chose a $600,000 settlement, with $210,000 taken immediately by the Internal Revenue Service. The rest was put into the team pool and Armstrong's share, still under discussion, may amount to no more than $30,000.)

No, Armstrong continued, he is not intimidated. But he is excited.

"I feel like I'm ready," he said. "I'm not necessarily ready to make it into Paris but that may not be in my best interests either. I'm ready to start, I'm ready to race the beginning part. I'm not even scared of the mountains. I'm looking forward to that part."

By constant practice, he has become a good climber. "When I first came into cycling, time trialing was my forte," he said. Now the race against the clock is his weakness, one that cost him possible victory in the Du Pont.

He blamed his emphasis on improving his climbing.

"You work on one, you lose the other," he said. "I didn't used to be able to climb at all. If we saw a hill," and here he snapped his fingers, "I was gone. I worked so much on my climbing—always climbing, climbing, climbing—till it came around. I still have to lose some weight, though, to make it easier going up the hills."

Measuring 5 feet 10 inches, Armstrong weighs 165 pounds.

"I was a big kid when I was growing up," he said, "because I was swimming so much from a young age—12." He competed as a swimmer in Texas before he decided he was too slow to succeed and turned to the triathlon and then to bicycle racing alone.

"At age 13, 14, those years when your body develops and you go through so much growth, I was swimming 10,000 meters a day," he said. "That's all upper-body work, so you can imagine that when I was 14 years old I was this incredibly buffed-out little kid. Not the Hulk but definitely bulky. And I'm still trying to shed it."

A Motorola masseur was knocking on the door and Armstrong prepared to leave for his rubdown. He had a few final words.

"There's been a lot of talk: People say a 21-year-old neo-pro, putting him in the Tour. . . ." He left the sentence unfinished.

"The fact of the matter is I'm physically 100 percent right now, mentally I'm very motivated, and I want to do it. That can't be harmful. I know it's going to be tough but I'm not risking anything.

"Where guys risk burnout and the remainder of their season is in the third week, the last ten days," he continued, "and I'm going to be gone by then. I'll get the benefits of two weeks of racing and get out before I start to kill myself."

There is absolutely, positively no chance he will continue into the grueling Pyrenees?

Armstrong thought about that.

"I'd have to be in a pretty good position to stick around," he finally said. He thought about that, too. He said not another word but the sly smile on his face said it for him.

INDURAIN AGAIN

1993

The Motorola team went to a Tex-Mex restaurant. The Banesto team went to a night club. Most everybody who finished the 1993 Tour de France went somewhere in Paris afterward to celebrate.

It's certain that a little time was spent during the festivities in discussing the 80th Tour and how it will be ranked. A difficult one, certainly. A fast one, surely—the fifth fastest. A great one? Not really.

The problem was that once again Miguel Indurain dominated the race from the first day's prologue until he reached the victory podium on the twenty-third day. Having won his third straight Tour after two successive Giros d'Italia, the Spaniard can look back and see how intimidated his opponents were and how unwilling to attack him.

After the first individual time trial, the ninth of twenty stages, Indurain was in the familiar yellow jersey of the overall leader and he was barely challenged from then to the finish. The Tour de France basically became a battle for second and third places.

"I tell you, it would be a great race if he wasn't in it," said Lance Armstrong, the young Motorola rider, as he watched the final time trial. "It would be much more exciting without him.

"It might even be better for the sport—a serious, serious race. But you can't blame the guy for that. He dominates."

Armstrong, who dropped out after the Alps because, at age 21, he had put enough demands on his body, rejoined his team for the final two stages and then the traditional Tex-Mex celebration party. "A Texas boy like me wouldn't miss a time like that," he said.

Like the rest of the 180 riders who started the Tour, Armstrong was impressed by Indurain. "Very impressed," he said. "He's definitely the best bike racer around. I look at him as the ultimate. If I came close to idolizing anybody, it would be Indurain.

"I'd love to ride with a guy like that. Had we not gotten the renewal, I would have loved being on his team next year," Armstrong added, referring to Motorola's agreement to continue sponsoring the team for another year, after it earlier said it would bow out at the end of the season, its third as financial backer.

Looking fit and relaxed at the time trial's start in Brétigny Sur Orge, south of Paris, Armstrong paid a meaningful personal compliment to Indurain.

"He's got a super attitude," he said. "He's not obnoxious, he's quiet, he respects the other riders, he never fusses. He's so mild-mannered. I really like him."

So much so that the 29-year-old Spaniard seems to have become a role model for the likeable and sensitive Armstrong, who has occasionally been considered brash. "I still have a temper and an attitude sometimes," he confessed.

"I wouldn't mind molding myself into his sort of character," he said. "Really quiet, just goes about his business."

That is the admiring way to put it. Another way began turning up in the French press even before the Tour ended.

"We could have expected the Spanish champion to impose himself with more panache," commented *Le Figaro*. "He had the means and the possibility." But he had not shown panache, the newspaper said. "A question of temperament, certainly."

As the Tour neared its finish, observers frequently charged Indurain with a lack of panache, an absence of flair and attitude. His willingness to allow rivals to win individual stages as long as he won the Tour came under criticism, too. Where was the emotion, the rage to win, that marks a great Tour de France?

"I follow my own road without worrying what people say," Indurain replied when he was asked about panache. "Only I know what this third victory has cost me in energy."

The truth is that much of Indurain's strength is based on his lack of emotion. Is he too kind to his opponents, the newspaper *L'Equipe* asked. "I try to be calm, to give the maximum, to be the best possible, the most professional possible. When I win, it's perfect, but when I lose, I don't make a big thing of it."

He has adopted a formula—the same one Jacques Anquetil used to win five Tours de France between 1957 and 1964—of crushing his rivals in time trials and staying with the best climbers in the mountains. Power is the key, not emotion. For panache, substitute reserve.

Indurain was asked if thought he could win five Tours de France, like Anquetil, Eddy Merckx, and Bernard Hinault. "That's a lot for one lifetime," he replied. "I'll take them one year at a time."

Tony Rominger, the Swiss rider who finished second, is considered computerlike in his training and racing habits. When Rominger's doctor said he would peak in the last week of the race, Rominger followed the programming: two second places in the Pyrenees and a victory in the final time trial.

Indurain, whose results are just as predictable as Rominger's, has somehow not yet been accused of being a computer.

"I can be beaten," he said at a news conference just after Rominger did beat him, by 42 seconds, in the time trial. "I never pretended that I can't be beaten."

Indurain did not look happy at the thought but he did not look unhappy either. He spoke in his usual monotone. His job was to answer questions; he answered them. His job was to win the Tour de France; he won it.

ON THE TRACK

1994

Soaring on wings of suspect wax, Francesco Moser hopes to break the most revered speed record in bicycling. Around and around and around an outdoor track in Mexico City he will go, propelled more than 25 feet with each revolution of the pedals as he aims to travel farther than anybody has ever gone in a one-hour ride.

Can he do it? In the Italian's favor is the fact that he set the record once before on the same high-altitude track. But that was ten years ago and he is now nearly 43 years old and has been retired from competition since 1988.

In his day—the late 1970s through the mid-1980s—Moser was a formidable rider, victorious in Paris-Roubaix three times, a winner of the Giro d'Italia, a world champion on the road and track. Lately, he is a prosperous maker of wine and bicycles and a familiar figure at Italian races as a spectator and official.

Until the summer of 1993 he rode his bicycle solely for exercise. Then his record for the hour's ride was broken and Moser announced that, assisted by the sports doctor Francesco Conconi, he would be back for another shot. Not to try to regain the record, Moser explained, but to see if he could better his own mark. A personal best was all he sought, he said unconvincingly.

Among those most unconvinced is Chris Boardman, the 25-year-old Briton who holds the hour record of 52.270 kilometers, or 32.270 miles.

"I've never considered that Francesco was going for a personal best," Boardman said in a telephone interview. "It's not logical to go to Mexico, have a track resurfaced, assemble some of the best doctors in the world, work with Professor Conconi, have a bike developed—you don't do all that for a personal best.

"For a personal best," he continued, "you hire the track in Stuttgart for the day, you get your old bike and you try to beat your old record."

Agreed, then, that Moser is going for Boardman's record, which was set on the indoor track in Bordeaux. The question remains: Can Moser do it? While the general feeling is no, two men who understand the record better than most think that he can. Neither sounds convinced that he will.

"Nothing's impossible," said Graeme Obree after a humming mantra of thought. Obree mastered the impossible when he rode his homemade and revolutionary bicycle around the track in Hamar, Norway, fast enough to break Moser's record. The 28-year-old Scot covered 51.596 kilometers, or 445 meters farther than Moser's 51.151 kilometers in 1984. A week later in Bordeaux, Boardman outdid them both.

The ebullient Obree said he was pleased that Moser was going for the record.

"He's a true champion—he's come back," he said. Obree is even pleased that Moser has copied his handlebars, his bicycle design, and his aerodynamic riding position.

"That's very nice," Obree said over the phone. "No problem at all."

Even better, the Scot continued, was what nearly everybody else regards as one of Moser's major flaws. "I think the best thing is the age, trying to break it at his age," he said. "If you've got it, why not carry on?"

Boardman was more cautious. "Forty-two is not a huge disadvantage when you can afford to commit yourself to the task for a long period and you have the resources to prepare in any way you see fit," he said.

"He's been out of competition but he hasn't stopped riding a bike," Boardman said. "The body doesn't change overnight; you develop something over many, many years and it doesn't just disappear. He's never stopped riding the bike and he won't be unfit till the day he dies.

"It's feasible that he will break my record," he concluded. "I don't think he can cruise it but I think it's possible he can pip it." In American English, Boardman meant that if his record was broken, it would not be by a wide margin.

The thin air in Mexico City will help Moser since it offers less resistance than Boardman encountered at sea level in Bordeaux. That thin air is notoriously polluted, however. Boardman noted this, saying, "What has deteriorated in the ten years since Moser set his record is the air quality in Mexico—that should be a big consideration."

If Moser does reclaim the record, both Boardman and Obree intend to go after it again.

"Yes, definitely," Boardman said. "But in the longer term, not the shorter one. I've got my plate filled for the next year, trying to establish myself in the pro world." He has signed with the Gan team based in France and will be competing mainly on the road.

"Gan is very supportive of my going for the record again," he said, "but in 1995, not 1994."

There will be no such wait for Obree, who had already planned an attempt this year to beat Boardman's mark. If Moser gets there first, he said, he will shoot for the new record instead.

Obree, who organized his successful record attempt when he was broke and living on welfare payments in Scotland, was impressed by the vast technical and financial support behind Moser.

"If I'd had any of that," he said with a laugh, "I would have done a breakdance."

AN OLD TRICK?

1995

The last time the enigmatic Tony Rominger appeared in the Tour de France he was not so much appearing as disappearing, explaining in the six languages he speaks how he had collapsed physically but certainly not psychologically.

In second place overall and trailing Miguel Indurain by an insurmountable five minutes, Rominger had coasted to the side of the road and quit with nearly a third of the Tour ahead. Stomach problems, the Swiss rider insisted, definitely not a loss of morale.

In French, German, Italian, Danish, Spanish, and English—definitely not a loss of morale.

The news conference was held in the red-brick city of Albi in a hotel meeting room and, on the wall behind Rominger, a Rotary Club plaque proclaimed, "Service Before Self." He posed for one more photograph dozens of times and then he was gone.

Back in his tax-haven home in Monaco, he rested for a few weeks, enjoying a vacation with his wife and their two young children, and then rehabilitated his psyche by winning bicycle races.

First was the Grand Prix des Nations, then two successful attacks on the world record for the hour's ride. This year he began slowly before winning the Tour of Romandie and then the Giro d'Italia. At 34, he remains No. 1 in the computerized standings, comfortably ahead of No. 2 Indurain. It was Indurain's record for the hour ride that he broke in the fall.

Indurain, Indurain—there's that name again.

"I admire him," Rominger says. "If I don't win this Tour, I hope he does." He explained in his six languages how his defeat in the previous Tour had enriched him.

"I learned to lose," he said. "I learned that I have nothing to lose. That is also important. I learned to accept."

If he did not win this Tour, would he accept defeat? "The world would not end," he said. "That is what I learned."

Surrounded once again by cameramen, he spoke after taking the Tour's cursory medical inspection. Despite traces of the flu in the recent Tour of Switzerland, which he did not finish, and minor stomach problems in the Giro, which he won easily, he appears to be in splendid condition.

"In Switzerland, he looked ready," Lance Armstrong said. "I've never seen Rominger look like that. He was lean. Straight away, I thought, 'Whoa!'"

So Rominger is ready physically. Is he ready psychologically? Perhaps his bland, almost casual, attitude toward the Tour de France is part of his new code of acceptance. Or perhaps it's a mind game.

"I was more motivated for the Giro than I am for here," he said. "Now I am here and we will see what I can do.

"Besides, my goal is not to win the Tour de France but to win one big Tour a year, the Giro, the Vuelta, the Tour de France," he continued. "That is enough for a cyclist. I have already done it in the Giro. So I have fulfilled my goal."

He won the Vuelta a España in 1992, '93, and '94. In that period, his best finish in the Tour was second in 1993, and he was a co-favorite with Indurain in 1994 until the Spaniard dominated him and everybody else in the first time trial.

A few days later, Indurain sped away in the first mountains and the Tour neared its finish for Rominger. Sapped by dysentery, he quit after the Pyrenees.

What about his comment that this Tour is really a race for second place behind Indurain? He smiled, not embarrassed by his apparent concession.

"But he has to be the only favorite," he said of the Spaniard, who is seeking his fifth consecutive Tour victory. "For now, there are a lot of guys who want to have a great race and make life difficult for him. I am here, I will do the best I can. More you cannot ask."

Armstrong, among others, asks for more.

"Don't fall for it," warned the American. "He's playing a game: If he gets second, he said all along he'd get second. If he wins, oh God, he's really great.

"If he says he's going to win and gets second, he's disappointed everybody. It's an old trick."

Yes, but is it this time? Only Rominger knows.

BACK FROM A BAD CRASH

1996

Chris Boardman feels so confident about his comeback and prospects that he can afford now to joke about his terrible crash in heavy rain during the evening prologue of the 1995 Tour de France.

The double fracture of his left ankle that he suffered ended his season just as he and everybody else thought it was about to begin, with a victory at the start of the Tour and the leader's yellow jersey.

"I had a good holiday," the 27-year-old Englishman said with a laugh about the months he spent first mending his body and then rebuilding his stamina and power.

As he pointed out in an interview, "I'm about 15 percent smaller in my left leg, but it doesn't seem to be a problem. It will just take time. It's more noticeable than causing me a problem."

How far back he has come is what he is trying to learn in the Paris-Nice race. "This is really the first race of the year for me," he said, dismissing his seventh place in the Tour of the Mediterranean a month before, "and the point is to see what my level is compared to the other riders."

So far, his level seems high: Two days before the finish in Nice, he ranked fourth overall after a 199-kilometer sixth stage from Vitrolles, near Marseille, to St. Tropez. The Riviera beaches were empty in windy and sprinkly weather.

Boardman came in a surprising second in a sprint finish among all the overall leaders and a handful of others.

Boardman, the Olympic pursuit champion and current king of the prologues, will be a favorite in the concluding time trial over 19.5 kilometers.

"I don't know how well I'm time trialing," he continued, since Paris-Nice did not open with the traditional prologue, a short race against the clock. "But if I can arrive at Nice with the time differences where they are now, it's possible to think of second or third place."

The leader of the Gan team and its sole hope in the 1995 Tour, Boardman came in for scattered criticism after his crash for being alone in taking risks on the slippery prologue course. Once the downpour started, all other leading riders played it safe. Only he went all out for victory—and skidded and crashed on one of the last curves.

Boardman dismisses his critics: "If you get round and win the prologue under those conditions, people say, 'What a star, what bike handling, fantastic,' and if you fall off, they say, 'How very rash, very irresponsible.' I don't think it was rash. I just think I made a mistake.

"That's my first major crash in about one thousand race days I've had, so I'm not really complaining."

If he had it to do all over again, would he? "I'd ride in a similar vein," he answered, "and hope not to fall off." That was good for another laugh by Boardman.

FIRST YEAR IN EUROPE

1997

Chris Horner will not be at the start of the Tour de France in Rouen, of course. As a first-year professional, he hardly expected to make the team. No loss, he said with a shrug, no loss this year at least. Instead he will spend the time back home in the United States, getting well.

Horner can describe all the symptoms but has not yet diagnosed his classic ailment. "Honestly, they were the hardest four months of my life," he said. "Incredibly hard. Every aspect you can think of, it was incredibly hard for me to be over there."

"Over there" is Europe, specifically France, where Horner, a 25-year-old Californian, arrived in February to join his new team, La Française des Jeux.

He arrived full of hopes and ambition after a splendid career as an amateur in America—"Everything went my way last year in the States," where he won thirteen races and "finished top 10 in more than sixty"—

and then discovered what so many other American riders have learned before him.

The language, the weather, the isolation, the loneliness all overwhelmed him. "It's been a hard year in Europe," he admitted in Pennsylvania, where he rode strongly in a series of races in the Tour of America. He enjoyed being back home, Horner said. It was all so familiar.

"I'm glad to be back with my friends and family, getting back to normal, getting back to my normal training, communicating again.

"Without any other Americans on the team, that makes it difficult," he said, echoing a dozen American riders before him. Almost all of them lasted briefly with their European teams, an outcome that Horner, who holds a two-year contract, insists he rejects.

"Being an American going to Europe—there's nothing you can really do to make it easy. You just have to adapt. It just takes time. You've got to adapt, got to."

His team has been understanding, he continued. "I think they expected this. I haven't got any real results, just been working for the leaders, so I don't think they're happy but I think it was expected.

"They've done everything they can to make it easy for me. It's a great squad and the management has done a good job of trying to make me feel at home."

And yet, and yet. "No one to talk with, and calling home is quite expensive, and I don't have my girlfriend in Europe and so not doing too much talking for a four-month period makes it quite difficult.

"The racing's hard there, but it's not so much the racing that makes it hard. It's the style outside the racing that makes it hard, and unfortunately that carries over into the racing."

Horner, who lives near Paris, next door to a team official, Alain Gallopin, speaks little French. "A little bit, a little bit only," he said. "I'd like to be able to study it, but you really can't as a cyclist because you never have a set schedule where you can say, 'OK, I can go to school Mondays, Wednesdays, and Fridays.'

"If I hadn't got so homesick and left, I think I would have got much further with the language because I was just starting to pick it up."

Although his program called for him to return to San Diego at the start of June, he left France two weeks early.

Don't misunderstand, he added, he looks forward to returning to

Europe at the end of July and picking up his career. Until then, he's recuperating. There's a lot to recuperate from.

"It's good to get the break," he said. "It was necessary. I was gaining weight because I was bored, and the only thing for me to do was eat. And you can't race heavy over there. From 145, 147 pounds, I went to 155, 156. I would go back down to 150 as soon as I started racing—a couple of days of racing and you get pretty hammered and drop a couple of pounds, but you never get down to race weight."Looking trim in Pennsylvania, he credited the four to six hours of training he does daily in San Diego and his return to health after assorted ailments in Europe.

His problems started when he came down with a heavy cold shortly after the season began in February. Despite that, he finished a creditable 26th overall in the Etoile de Besseges, including a top 10 finish in the last daily stage. "Then in the Tour of Navarre I pulled a hamstring muscle and missed a couple of days of riding. Then in the Tour of Murcia I got food poisoning the night before the race started. So I missed the whole race plus three days more.

"I missed a lot of training and a lot of racing and when I got back to France it was 0 degrees Celsius, so it was difficult to train. You train two hours maximum. I'm used to the heat.

"So you go back into the house and I don't have my girlfriend there, I don't have friends to call and go out with, it's too cold to be outside, so you just sit inside the house and eat. Right from there, it started coming downhill." Working for the team by setting a pace for its leaders and letting them ride in his slipstream, he rode hard in some of the spring classics and failed to finish any. "It's more of a job in Europe," he said, comparing racing there to the American version. "Everyone's there to do their job. And in the U.S. the riders aren't making that kind of money. Everyone's doing it in the U.S. for fun, so they're your buddies, even riders on other teams.

"In Europe, it's much more cutthroat, everyone's trying to hurt everyone else to win the race, whatever it takes to win the race. In the U.S., it's kind of whatever it takes but they're not willing to kill each other over it. Everyone's there to have a good time.

"No one's going to retire rich from racing in the U.S. That's the difference."

AS STRONG AS LANCE

1997

On the far side of 30, Darren Baker is preparing to end his career as a professional bicycle racer, to leave Europe and return to the United States and become a businessman, somebody in financial services. Baker, who has a degree in finance from the University of Maryland, and his wife are already looking for an apartment in San Francisco, not far from their home in Santa Rosa, California.

"I have more aspirations than being a bicycle racer until I can't physically do it any more," he says.

But first he knows just the farewell present he would like: "A victory," he said during the just-completed Tour of Holland. "That would be a nice way to go, wouldn't it?" A consistently high placer and occasional winner in American races, he has yet to win in Europe, where he has competed as an amateur and professional since 1991.

After riding for the U.S. Postal Service team in the Tour of Holland, Baker is getting ready for the start of the Vuelta a España.

"One last chance," he said. "I'll look for my opportunity, do my best, and hope."

If not, he continued, it's been fun.

Yes, it has, and fun is important to him. The bright and lively Baker is rarely seen without a smile, never less so than during races in the United States, where his mother, father, and wife often show up with one and sometimes two small dogs dressed in a miniature version of Baker's team jersey. The dog barks, Baker's parents hold up signs saying, "Go, Darren," and he rides by, beaming.

Once he leaves Europe, the native of Chambersburg, Pennsylvania, will not be tempted to continue riding solely in America. "It's time to get going with the rest of my life," he said. "We want to start a family. The big goal is to retire before I'm 50 with enough money to buy a sailboat and sail around the world.

"Races in America are familiar and comfortable and not quite as difficult as they are in Europe," he said, laughing at his understatement. He was speaking the day before the Paris-Roubaix race, about as tough as it gets in a one-day classic.

"I don't mind difficult races," he continued, "but I like to be at least a little bit competitive. I don't feel I'm very competitive here." He blamed an intense spring schedule of races and then a long layoff.

"As a professional athlete, you want to excel. I speak for myself: I want to excel at every race. If you can't do that, it takes away a lot of the fun.

"I love racing my bike. It's the most fun thing in the world—you can get out there and viciously attack guys and not get in trouble. And you can win doing it."

When he turned professional in 1993 with the Subaru-Montgomery team, a lot was expected of Baker because he had been so promising the previous two years with the U.S. national amateur team. "I was strong," he said. "Most of the time I was just as strong as Lance Armstrong," his teammate, "maybe even stronger on the climbs.

"But he was always more hungry for the win than I was. I envied him. Strong as anything. But I was, too. I could put the hurt on guys, ride away from them."

Then, early in 1993, after a few races in the south of France, Baker got sick and wound up in a hospital in Dortmund, Germany, with pneumonia and a chest infection.

"I had a high fever for about a week, above 105," he recalled. "I don't know, I never really made it back after that. Some people say I was pretty close to dying."

After that week of fever and hallucinations, his chest filled with so much liquid that his left lung collapsed and his heart was pushed to the right side of his chest cavity.

"I'm basically dying, wasting away," he said, talking about that time.

Showing a scar, he told how he finally went into surgery. "They cut my chest open, put seven tubes in to drain the liquid but it had coagulated, so they cut my side open and scooped two and a half liters of junk out.

"Ever since then, I haven't felt the same. I've had spurts where I felt good but I've never seriously felt that I could stomp the way I did in '92. Every year I get better but it's never going to get back to where it was.

"So I have some regrets. My career wasn't what it could have been. But what can you do? I've seen a lot of the world, I've met some incredible people. It's been a great journey."

He was hoping to ride the Tour de France and end on what he described as a bang, but he was not selected for the U.S. Postal Service team.

"That's all right," he said. "The Tour of Spain, that's not a bad hand of cards to be dealt either."

STONY SOIL

1998

England, this royal throne of kings, this sceptered isle, would be even more so, in many people's opinion, if it accommodated professional bicycle racing at the level of such major local sports as cricket, darts, and snooker.

But it doesn't. In a bizarre reversal of sentiment in the rest of Europe, bicycle racing is a marginal sport here. Not only marginal but jinxed: The multiday Milk Race, which began in 1958, ended in 1993 when its sponsor, the Milk Marketing Board of England and Wales, was curdled by European Union bureaucrats. A year later, the Kellogg's Tour of Britain, which began in 1986, also ended.

All the rest is silence, as the Bard also said, or was silence until the nine-day Prutour began an 825-mile (1,320-kilometer) journey from Stirling, Scotland, to London. According to Alan Rushton, head of The Events Group, the organizer of the race, it is the biggest race Britain has had in terms of promotion and prizes, with £100,000 ($165,000) for the riders.

Road racing has a long if inglorious history in Britain, Rushton pointed out. "It really didn't kick in until after World War II," he said. "Not until the '60s did the sport begin to take hold. So, for decades, it just didn't get under the skin of the people the way cricket did."

Other students of the sport offer supplementary explanations. They include traffic, school curricula, and, this being Britain, class.

"I think traditionally bike riding was seen as something you did if you couldn't afford a car," said Clare Salmon, consumer marketing director of Prudential, the race's sponsor.

Rushton agreed: "It was a class thing. The working man had a bike and the bosses had cars. That was true until the '60s, when the working man bought a Ford Anglia and left his bike behind. In the '50s there were huge cycling clubs around this country and then the car took over."

But today, Salmon said, the sport is seen differently in Cool Britain. "What's happened now is it's taken on a more glamorous image: lycra, carbon fiber, and incredibly rapid speed. It's become upmarket, a fashion thing."

In another explanation, Phil Liggett, the cycling journalist and television commentator, points an accusatory finger at school sports.

"You go with what you've got," he said, "and here in England what you've got in the school curriculums are cricket and rugby, the Oxford and Cambridge games, the old public school business."

As an organizer should, Rushton also bemoaned the lack of major races in Britain to attract youngsters, "to let people see the bicycle racer as a hero."

"The beauty of having a domestic calendar," he said, "is that Chris Boardman can be seen here and it will affect that little kid who saw Boardman ride into his city in the red jersey of the Prutour's leader. That little kid—we don't know which one, but surely one of those watching—will want to race bicycles, too. But if Boardman's perpetually racing abroad, nobody British can see him and get behind him."

Besides Boardman, who leads the France-based Gan team, there are no more than two or three other Britons racing professionally in Europe. One of the pioneers, for a decade starting in the late 1970s, was Graham Jones, who is working on the Prutour.

"We have so many sports here, but cycling is not high on the list," Jones said. "When I was a boy I was discouraged from racing. I was chased by a lot of people from soccer and athletics but not to do cycling.

"I realized at 16 or 17 that if I wanted to be a professional rider, I had to go live in another country. So I did: I had £200 in my pocket, a bike, a spare pair of wheels, and a suitcase."

Jones spent a year in the Netherlands and another in Belgium as an independent amateur rider, and in 1978 joined the ACBB team in France, a pipeline to the professional Peugeot team, with whom he made his debut.

"You had to go abroad," Jones said firmly. "It's still the case."

HOLD THE MEAT

1998

As a bicycle racer, Dudley Hayton never won anything major outside Britain, but he rode honorably and did represent his country in ten world championships and the 1976 Olympic Games. Now he coaches a team in his image: hardworking and direct, nothing fancy. A meat and potatoes kind of team, one could say—but shouldn't.

Make it a wheat germ and potatoes kind of team, or a soya and potatoes kind of team, or a veggieburger and potatoes kind of team. Hold the meat. For Hayton is directeur sportif of the Linda McCartney Pro Racing Team, the first in memory to be sponsored in the cause of a vegetarian diet.

Why not? Insurance companies and supermarkets sponsor teams, as do lotteries and the manufacturers of industrial adhesives and rattan furniture.

If the sport has room at the table for McDonald's fast food (a secondary sponsor of the Polti team in Italy) and Hot Dog Willy (a sponsor in Belgium), it has room for nutburgers.

"Linda was into Green issues, very much so," said Hayton, referring to McCartney, who died earlier in the year. "She thought cycling was a good trailer for what she believed in. She was for people going out and getting more exercise."

A photographer, a keyboardist with two of her husband Paul's post-Beatles bands, and a champion of animal rights, she also published two cookbooks and started a line of frozen vegetarian dinners.

The team was put together in March 1998 with the idea of not only winning races but also promoting a meatless, fishless, and eggless diet. Unlike his riders in the Prutour in Britain, the 45-year-old Hayton is not a vegetarian but says he has gone on the diet and "You can't tell the difference in taste."

A typical breakfast, he explained, would include baked beans, lasagna, cannelloni, coffee, and toast. "And cereals, of course. We love muesli."

For dinner, "veggies, vegetable pies, veggieburgers—which are really nice—and pasta."

Bicycle riders pack away the groceries on a race day, consuming seven thousand to eight thousand calories each. It's fuel, of course, and the machine—their bodies—stops without it. But instead of the red-meat meals of yore, the trend is to lighter cuisine.

"The old-fashioned way was red meat in the morning and evening," said Johnny Weltz, the directeur sportif of the U.S. Postal Service team and a former rider. "Always steak at night. For breakfast you would have veal or chicken. Now you have muesli, rice, pasta in the morning and soya milk, pasta, and rice in the evening. Lots more fish than before. If you have meat, it's mostly chicken.

"Look how long it takes to digest red meat. It takes so much of your energy. You're supposed to race and you're using your energy instead to digest a steak," he said.

"Think of a racehorse: He runs fast on a diet of grass."

Still, there are dissenters. Mark Gorski, the manager of Weltz's team and a gold-medal winner on the track in the 1984 Olympic Games in Los Angeles, has recalled differences in eating habits.

"I've used special diets, like a vegetarian diet with lots of vitamins," he told the writer Peter Nye. "Then I'd see the East Germans at the next table, gorging themselves on greasy French fries and wiener schnitzel. The East Germans would go out on the track and set world records. It does make you wonder sometimes about diet."

There are no similar doubts for Robert Millar, a Scot who was a formidable climber in the Tour de France and once finished second overall in the Vuelta a España. He was a pioneer vegetarian a decade ago. "Not for ethical reasons," he explained, "it's that a vegetarian diet suits me better. I recovered better, I didn't have the intestinal problems that so many riders develop in long races."

Millar, the directeur sportif of the Scottish team in the Prutour, recalled the negative attitudes of officials and riders on his French teams when he declined meat, fish, and eggs.

"At first they thought I was doing it to annoy them," he said. "It was a bit of a hassle the first couple of years, but when you're one of the best riders in the team and you win, the French think of it as some kind of whim."

Watching his six riders prepare for the start, Hayton said that his role involved no proselytizing when he met with officials and riders of rival teams. "We just talk cycling," he said. "If we do talk about a vegetarian diet, we don't go into it deeply. But you'll find there are more vegetarian riders than you think. The ones that aren't, they won't eat as much red meat as you think."

Just behind him as he spoke was a fast-food outlet with its heavy air of hot grease. No chance, was there, that Hayton might sneak in and grab a Double Whopper?

He looked astounded. "No, no, no," he protested. "I've never. . . ." Then he realized he was being teased and broke up laughing. It was a small joke and he had no beef with it.

THE FESTINA AFFAIR

1998

The Tour de France and the Festina team riders finally parted company in the back room of a café near the finish of the seventh of twenty-one stages.

Jean-Marie Leblanc, the Tour's director, met with six of the team's nine riders there to confirm that they had been thrown out of the race.

"They are out of the race, period," he said over his shoulder as he hurried away.

A quarter-hour after he left the steamy café, Chez Gillou, the Festina riders began to emerge in the blue uniforms of their team. Their spokesman was the team leader, Richard Virenque, 28, a Frenchman who finished second overall in the 1997 Tour and who has won the king-of-the-mountains jersey four years running.

"We've been ordered out," he said. "OK, let the Tour continue without us. It has to continue because it's such a great, popular event.

"We asked to continue because there are no charges, no witnesses against us. They said no. This is very difficult personally and professionally for the riders. We'll continue as a team and ride the Vuelta in September," he added.

"We'll be at the start of the Tour de France next year and we'll come to win. Vive le Tour de France 1998," Virenque concluded as his voice cracked and he began weeping.

Leblanc announced that the entire team was being expelled after its coach said that he had supplied the riders with illegal, performance-enhancing drugs.

"The object was to optimize performance under strict medical control," said a statement issued by Bruno Roussel, 41, the team's directeur sportif.

Roussel has been formally charged with violating French laws against buying, transporting, and distributing drugs and was in police custody in the northern city of Lille as the investigation continued.

"Those words constitute an oath," Leblanc said, citing Roussel's statement. "An oath that doping was conducted in the Festina team and that it was even organized doping."

The drugs reportedly included amphetamines, steroids, masking drugs, and EPO, an artificial hormone that thickens the blood to carry more oxygen to muscles.

Other riders supported the Festina team after the news was made public. "Guilt by association and innuendo isn't the way to go," said Bobby Julich, an American with the Cofidis team, after he finished third in a 58-kilometer (36-mile) individual time trial. "These guys haven't been proven guilty. It's bad for them and worse for the sport."

"The Mapei team is stunned," said Freddy Viaene, a Belgian masseur with the predominantly Italian team, which shared a hotel with Festina prior to the announcement. "It's like a hammer is coming down on everybody and the riders say, 'Who's next to be accused?'"

That was a good question. Although the use of illegal drugs has long been suspected in the professional ranks, the thousands of drug checks carried out every season implicate fewer than a dozen riders. A major question has been whether the rumors are unfounded or whether the doctors that most teams employ are far ahead of the drug inspectors.

As a Festina official, who refused to be identified, said: "We're the scapegoats. They're using us as an example for a practice that is widespread in the sport."

The drug scandal began unfolding more than a week earlier, when a team worker was arrested in an official Tour team car that was full of illegal substances.

"The scandal's a shame; it's terrible for the sport of cycling," Tyler Hamilton, an American with the U.S. Postal Service team, said. "But maybe this is going to open some eyes and change things."

ROAD CAPTAIN

1998

His eyes locked ahead of him, Bjarne Riis rode solemnly to the sign-in for the twelfth stage of the Tour de France. He barely acknowledged his introduction as winner of the 1996 Tour, scrawled his signature on the list of entries, and hurried off alone. The bicycle race still had ten days to go but for Riis, the former champion, it was over.

Overnight he reverted to a road captain, the rider who dictates tactics in the heat of action when the directeur sportif is unavailable. Road captains do not win the Tour de France, Riis's stated goal for the race, but help others win it.

"I'm here to win," he said in Dublin before the start of the race. "My goal is to win the race, to be in yellow in Paris."

The 34-year-old Dane was speaking at a Telekom team presentation at Dublin Castle in a hall lined with portraits of dukes, earls, and other grandees. The next speaker was Jan Ullrich, a decade younger than Riis and the defending champion in the Tour.

"My goal is to win the race, to be in yellow in Paris," Ullrich said, echoing his teammate.

Something had to give, and it was Riis.

He lost 3 minutes, 44 seconds to Ullrich in the first long time trial and 3:09 in the second climb in the Pyrenees. Seven minutes behind the German when the twelfth stage set off, the Dane was told on the race's rest day that he could no longer ride for himself but had to dedicate himself to his leader.

Riis did that during the 222-kilometer (138-mile) journey from Tarascon Sur Ariege in the mountains to the unhandsome Mediterranean resort of Le Cap d'Agde. When Telekom was at the head of the pack chasing three breakaways in sticky heat, the Dane took his turns at the front, setting a fast pace while Ullrich rested in his slipstream.

Neither rider participated in the inevitable final mass rush in the flat stage. That is a job neither for team leaders nor for road captains but for sprinters.

Ullrich continued to wear the yellow jersey. Riis remained in 15th place, moderately high for a road captain.

He knows his new role well since it was for so long his old role. Before his victory in 1996 he had worked himself up from domestique (literally, "servant") to road captain of teams in France and Italy. After he finished third in the 1995 Tour, he moved as the leader to Telekom, where a certain Jan Ullrich was a first-year professional.

The Dane won the 1996 Tour with a splendid display of power, while the unheralded Ullrich finished second. A year later, the German was an easy winner while the Dane finished seventh, twenty-six minutes behind.

"I'm in better form than I was last year," Riis insisted in Dublin. "I feel more relaxed. Last year I was sick. This year I'm healthy."

He has not ridden like an overall winner, however.

As he promised, the Telekom directeur sportif, Walter Godefroot, waited until the halfway point in the Tour to decide which of his two big riders would lead. Making the decision public, he pointed to the seven-minute difference between them.

"I wanted to win the Tour," Riis said. "But with those seven minutes separating us, I have no choice.

"I have total confidence in Jan," he added. "He's very strong now."

That was spoken like a road captain, not a rival.

THE END OF THE ROAD?

1998

The Tour de France, plagued by drug scandals, was stopped twice in one day by rider protests and faced a premature end for the first time in its ninety-five-year history.

The riders agreed to resume racing only if the French police modify their tactics in a spreading investigation of some of the twenty-one teams in the world's greatest bicycle race. Not until Jean-Marie Leblanc, the director of the race, consulted with government officials and promised a change in police methods—including questioning in team hotels rather than police stations—did the riders call off their second sit-down.

But they ripped off their numbers, making the stage unofficial, and then rode at a moderate speed without competition, reaching the finish line nearly three hours late. Three teams quit en route in protest, as did a handful of individual riders. A fourth team quit later.

The turmoil was unprecedented. Six teams are under suspicion; the riders are divided in their response to the investigation, and Tour officials spent the day trying to keep the race going to its scheduled end in Paris. They had been successful earlier, when the riders refused to start as a protest against media treatment of the drug scandal, which began before the race started in Dublin.

The focus of the second protest was a police hotel raid in which four riders from the TVM team were taken to a hospital and tested for drugs in their urine, blood, and hair. A TVM car had been seized by French police in March and found to contain what was described as a huge quantity of illegal, performance-enhancing drugs.

"They treated us like criminals, like animals," said one of the Dutch team's members, Jeroen Blijlevens. "They took Bart out of the shower, made us sign some papers, and took us away," he continued, referring to his roommate, Bart Voskamp. The riders were held more than four hours for the tests and released half an hour after midnight.

Word of their treatment did not reach the full 140-man pack until it was rolling in the seventeenth of twenty-one daily stages, 149-kilometer (92-mile) from Albertville in the Alps to Aix-les-Bains. The riders also learned then that the police would visit the hotels of three more teams: Casino, which is based in France; Polti, based in Italy; and ONCE, based in Spain.

Three officials of the Festina team, based in France, had previously been arrested, and two officials of the TVM team are being held in a French jail. Another French team, Big Mat-Auber, came under suspicion Tuesday when one of its vans was stopped by the police and found to contain medication that was sent to a laboratory for analysis.

As the news of the TVM treatment and the police investigation at the three hotels filtered among the riders, they stopped for twenty-five minutes after 32 kilometers.

"I'm fed up," said their spokesman, Laurent Jalabert, the French national champion and the world's top-ranked racer. "I can't continue under these conditions, being treated like a criminal." He entered a team car, quitting the race, and was followed shortly by the other ONCE riders.

His directeur sportif, Manolo Saiz, a Spaniard, said: "We may never come to race in France again. This may be the end of cycling. It's the biggest crisis we've ever had and we're a family heading for divorce."

Leblanc, the Tour director, pleaded with the riders and their coaches. "I ask you, directeurs sportifs, my friends, I ask you, the riders, my friends, to continue the race," he said on the radio that links the race.

"We were as astonished as the riders about the way TVM was treated," he said on television later. "We are discussing with the authorities how further investigation of the Tour de France riders can be handled with the utmost dignity."

With that promise, the race resumed, but only for a dozen more kilometers. Since Jalabert was gone, Leblanc met with the riders' new spokesman, Bjarne Riis, a Dane with Telekom and the winner of the 1996 Tour.

"If the riders can be assured that the investigation will be held with a certain dignity, they will continue with the Tour de France tomorrow," Riis said.

The riders then resumed the journey at a speed about half their usual 40 kilometers an hour. At the feeding zone, the Banesto team, like ONCE from Spain, and the Riso Scotti team from Italy dropped out. So did individual riders, including two TVM riders.

After the stage, the Vitalicio team, also from Spain, withdrew.

By the end of the day, the field was down to 111 riders.

Although representatives of teams with riders among the leaders were not threatening further disruption, team officials and riders condemned police tactics. The police, who are under the orders of an investigating magistrate in Lille, far to the north, had no official spokesman and could not present their side.

"I understand the riders' unhappiness," said Alain Bondue, a former racer and now manager of the Cofidis team from France. "You have to let them do their job. The TVM riders left the hospital at 12:30 without eating and without being massaged. That's not right.

"That the police want to investigate is logical, but why not wait till Monday, a day after the race ends?" Asked if Cofidis expected a visit from the police, Bondue said, "Who knows? They don't telephone ahead."

The police were waiting at the hotels of ONCE, Polti, and Casino when the race pulled into Aix-les-Bains. The four TVM riders remaining, including some of those taken to the hospital Tuesday night, led the pack across the line and were applauded by a large crowd of fans who had remained for that moment.

"If the French police want to ruin their national race, they're doing it," said Bobby Julich, an American with Cofidis who is in second place behind Marco Pantani, an Italian with Mercatone Uno.

"We haven't been treated like human beings," he added. "Which TVM wasn't last night. That's what we're protesting against. That's why the stage was ruined today."

IL PIRATA

1998

Marco Pantani returned home to Italy to more than a hero's welcome after his victory in the Tour de France. He will surely be acclaimed campionissimo—champion of champions, a title that is not easily earned.

The last authentic one was the fabled Fausto Coppi, the winner of the Tour de France in 1949 and 1952; the winner of the Giro d'Italia, the world's second-most-important bicycle race to everybody except Italians, in 1940, 1947, 1950, 1952, and 1953; the world road-race champion in 1953; the Italian national champion in 1942, 1947, 1952, and 1955; the record holder for the hour's race against the clock in 1942; and the winner of every major Italian one-day classic and then some.

That's pretty swift company, but Pantani has won his right to be included. The 28-year-old leader of the Mercatone Uno team is the first Italian in thirty-three years to win the Tour de France. He is also the first bicycle racer since Miguel Indurain in 1993 to win both the Giro and the Tour in the same year.

The only other riders to have done it are the big stars: Coppi, Jacques Anquetil, Eddy Merckx, Bernard Hinault, and Stephen Roche.

"He's a throwback, the old-fashioned kind of rider," said Italian prime minister Romano Prodi in a telephone interview. The prime minister, a big fan of professional racing and the riding companion of such Italian stars as Gianni Bugno, meant that Pantani did not base his season on one major race.

"A real star," Prodi said. "It's unbelievable what he's gone through, the sacrifices and pain he's known."

The charismatic Pantani was hit by a car during the minor Milan-Turin race late in 1995, fracturing his left leg. He spent the rest of that season and most of 1996 on crutches, learning to walk again.

A year later he had recovered well enough to finish third in the Tour, the same placing that he had in 1994. But bad luck struck him again in the Giro in June 1997, when a black cat—yes, really—crossed the road and caused a mass crash of riders trying to swerve around it. Pantani went down and was out for a month, returning for the Tour.

In 1998, though, all went right. He won the Giro by dominating his opponents in the mountains, just as he did in the Tour, and then riding a superlative time trial to finish third.

Acknowledged to be the sport's swiftest climber, the 1.7-meter (5-foot-7-inch), 60-kilogram (132-pound) Italian came into the Tour with many complaints: The mountains were not difficult enough, he said, and only two of the five daily stages in the Pyrenees and Alps ended on a peak. In the three other stages, his rivals would have the chance to catch him on long descents. Nevertheless, he finished second and first in the Pyrenees and first and second in the Alps. The final Alpine stage was annulled by the riders' protest against anti-doping investigations.

With a lead nearing six minutes before the final time trial, he again finished a surprising third, guaranteeing himself victory when the Tour finished in Paris. The margin was enough to subdue panic when he had a flat during the ten laps on the Champs-Elysées and had to be rushed back by his teammates to the main pack.

But Pantani rarely gives in to panic. "His biggest virtue is his intelligence," says Felice Gimondi, the last Italian until now to win the Tour de France. "He has an acute sense of the race."

Pantani, who used to be known as Il Elefantino, the Elephant, because of his Dumbo-like ears, has reshaped his image in recent years. Now he prefers to be known as Il Pirata, the Pirate, with his ears hidden under a bandana, his head shaved, an earring in his left ear, and a suave mustache and goatee.

Possibly to match his yellow jersey, he had his black facial hair dyed blonde for his appearance atop the final victory podium. His teammates were all yellow-haired too.

As he says, his beard will have to turn gray before he also attempts to compete in the sport's third major stage race, the Vuelta a España. Not even "throwbacks" still ride the three big races in one year.

Nor does he plan to appear in the post-Tour criteriums, basically exhibition races, though they enrich many riders. But he has an offer to move from Mercatone Uno to the Mapei team in Italy at a salary reported to be above $2 million a year.

Pantani admits to only one unsettling moment in the Tour.

"That was when I fell in the descent from the Aubisque," the first of four major climbs on the first day in the Pyrenees. "My hands were frozen, and I had almost no feeling in the tips of my fingers. But the fear of losing wasn't in vain, because it caused me to react, to take nothing for granted."

He arose from that fall, remounted his bicycle, and finished second. The next day, in the mountains again, he won. He had started to construct his overall victory.

RUMORS AND DOUBTS

1999

Lance Armstrong has heard the rumors and doubts.

"Innuendo," he bitterly calls speculation that he is dominating the Tour de France because he is using illegal drugs. How else, some of the European press is asking, can somebody who was undergoing chemotherapy for testicular cancer two and a half years ago be so dominating now in the world's toughest bike race?

He strongly rejects all suspicion. Asked flatly whether he is or has been doping, Armstrong said, "Emphatically and absolutely not.

"I'm not stupid," he continued in an interview as he had dinner at his team's hotel in the mountain resort of Alpe d'Huez. "I've been on my deathbed.

"My story is a success story in the world of cancer," he said, asking why he would jeopardize that. "A lot of people relate to my story. In America, in France, in Europe, they relate to this story."

His comeback from three months of chemotherapy and more than a year away from the sport began the previous fall, with fourth places in the Vuelta a España and in the world championship road race and time trial. Now he is the overall leader of the Tour de France and the center of attention, most of it adulatory, but some not.

Armstrong, a 27-year-old Texan, leads the race by nearly eight minutes. He has won three of the eleven daily stages so far: the short prologue, a long time trial, and then the first of two climbing stages in the Alps. He finished fifth in the demanding ascent to Alpe d'Huez.

Speculation about the reasons for his performance mounted after the climbing victory in Sestriere, Italy, with veiled references in newspapers and television to the power of a man who has never been known as a dominating climber and who did not return full-time to racing until May 1998, more than a year and a half after his cancer was diagnosed and treated in the United States.

"I've heard the questions and speculation," he said. "The bottom line for me is the same as for Miguel Indurain: Sweat is the secret of my success."

He referred to the Spaniard who won the Tour de France five consecutive times and then retired late in 1996, a man he described as "a good friend and one of my heroes."

"There's no answer other than hard work," Armstrong said. "This team has done more work than anybody else.

"Look, I'm not going to get mad about the questions because I understand them after the events of last year. I expected this."

He was talking about the drug scandal in the 1998 Tour that resulted in the expulsion of the nine-man Festina team on charges of systematic use of illegal performance-enhancing drugs—mainly an artificial hormone, EPO.

That case led to police searches of riders' hotels and to protests and slowdowns by the teams, almost scuttling the race. Although investigations have continued in France and Italy since the summer and riders and officials are still being questioned, this 86th Tour de France has not been hampered since it started.

The innuendo does bother him, Armstrong said. "It's bad for the sport, so I can get worked up. It's disturbing for the sport. I think it's unfair."

Armstrong was willing, even eager, to discuss the rumors. Asked if he was taking any medication, he said: "Vitamin C, multivitamins. This is the Tour de France. You need certain recovery products, but certainly nothing illegal."

His defense was considered. He did not repeat his denials, knowing that other riders have made them too and then confessed to drug use under police questioning. Instead he built his case on his record and reputation as a clean rider.

"Who was the world road race champion in 1993, when nobody had heard of EPO?" he asked rhetorically. "Who? The second-youngest world champion of all time?" The answer? Armstrong, not quite 22, in the race in Oslo.

"Everybody in cycling knows that France is a dangerous place to be," he said, "especially considering that they have extremely aggressive police and the scandal du jour. There are a lot of riders that never, ever come to France.

"But I live in France, I race the whole year in France, my Tour de France preparation was done in France. If I want to dope, that would be ridiculous.

"I'm not a new rider," he said. "I showed my class from the very beginning. I've never focused on the Tour de France and when I decided to, I was in France the whole time."

He explained his climbing strength by saying that his focus in the first years of his career had always been on the spring and fall one-day classics.

"At my highest level, though—'93, '94, '95, '96—when was I tested in the big mountains? I wasn't. It's true," he said. It was "only last year" in the Vuelta, Armstrong said, "'when that was an objective. Because of my success in the Vuelta, naturally the team, because the Tour is the biggest race for them, they wanted me to focus on the Tour."

He also credited his climbing skills to a loss of weight, 6 or 7 kilograms (13–15 pounds) to his present 158 pounds.

As well-wishers came to his table to congratulate the Texan on his performance, he said that he would possibly be moving from Nice to another country. "I like Nice. I like France a lot," he said. "But we have people looking through our trash, just bad stuff. The possibility of somebody sabotaging me or pulling some funny business, it's not worth it.

"As Miguel said before the Tour started," he said, referring to Indurain, "you spend ten years building a career and a reputation and they can tear it down in fifteen seconds. It's scary."

CLOSING ON A HIGH NOTE

1999

That was some victory party for Lance Armstrong and his U.S. Postal Service teammates.

Two hundred of their closest friends and sponsors filled two rooms of the chic Musée d'Orsay a few hours after Armstrong became the second American to win the Tour de France and take a victory lap with his teammates on the Champs-Elysées as the American flag fluttered behind the man in the yellow jersey.

"My baby," his mother greeted him as he arrived at the museum.

Linda Armstrong, who is what the French would call a pistol if they spoke English, is still mistaken, at age 45, for his wife. Like many others at the celebration, she had a few T-shirts she wanted him to autograph.

Everybody found a T-shirt, in fact, on the chairs at the sit-down dinner that followed the champagne reception. It said "1999 Tour de France champions" and had an American flag. There were also yellow caps, similarly inscribed, for each guest.

"We planned to have a party for seventy, but it grew," said Thom Weisel, the president of the team's management staff. The former head of Montgomery Securities, Weisel had earlier sponsored the Subaru-Montgomery team that had as its goal a place in the Tour de France. When it was offered half a berth, with the other half to be shared with a German team, Weisel rejected the offer and vowed to be back soon with a team that would get a full share.

He looked triumphant. So did Mark Gorski, the 1984 Olympic gold medalist on the bicycle track, who put together the present team with Dan Osipow. They hired Armstrong in 1998, when there were no other takers because of his treatment for testicular cancer in 1996 and subsequent season off his bicycle.

Now one of his new trophies—a big golden key with the names of peaks in the Alps and Pyrenees that the Tour climbed—was posed in front of a Musée d'Orsay bust of Jeanne Balze, identified as the daughter of the painter Raymond Balze, a student of Ingres a century and a half ago. Painted nymphs cavorted on the ceiling, and an ice sculpture of a bicycle rider slowly melted in the summer heat, dripping into a ring of pans that protected the parquet floor.

The 27-year-old Armstrong was customarily gracious. He signed autographs, chatting with representatives of the team's two dozen secondary sponsors and posing for photographs with his wife, Kristin, who is expecting their first child in October.

He looked comfortable, surrounded by friends and well-wishers. For all his ease, however, he acknowledged that he had just spent three weeks as demanding on his mind as on his legs. The man in the yellow jersey is supposed to have time during the race to relax, and Armstrong spent most of his days fending off suspicions, doubts, and innuendos about drugs.

This was the Tour of Renewal that wasn't.

"We didn't quite make it," said Jean-Marie Leblanc, the Tour de France's director, shortly before the finish in Paris. "We closed a lot of back doors, but we accomplished only part of what we hoped to do." Other officials and observers agreed.

One early way to measure whether the Tour had recovered luster with its millions of fans after a drug scandal the previous year was to check the size of the crowds that turned out to watch the three-week race. By that standard, the results were mixed.

Although immense numbers stood as usual at the sides of most roads, they were people through whose villages and cities the riders were passing. In other words, they merely had to step out of their homes to watch the riders pass swiftly on the flat.

Where the crowds thinned out was where they are customarily thickest: atop the mountain passes where diehard fans often camp for days beforehand to watch the action unfold for an hour far down from the peak.

For the just-completed Tour, the turnout on the fabled Galibier climb in the Alps, where fans usually pick out favorite riders' names with stones in the yearlong snowfields, was about a third that of the year before. On the ascent to Alpe d'Huez, which is usually two long lines of camping vans on either side of the twenty-one hairpin curves, there was plenty of room. In the Pyrenees, the crowds were even sparser, with the Tourmalet climb, often on the verge of a riot, strangely quiet. The Piau-Engaly stage was a study in bucolic calm.

So, if the spectators were there, perhaps the real fans were sitting home or at the beach, disenchanted.

They would have had much to be further disenchanted with. An atmosphere of mistrust and, as some saw it, paranoia was prevalent.

"Everybody was waiting for a bomb to explode," a French television official said, accurately.

The Tour de France was stung by the drug scandal and subsequent rider revolt against police investigatory methods the previous year. In 1999 it attempted to avoid trouble by having the International Cycling Union, which governs the sport, increase blood tests that hint at the use of such illegal performance-enhancing drugs as the artificial hormone EPO. The Tour also conducted its customary urinalyses of the daily stage's winner and runner-up, the overall leader, and two riders selected at random.

To general lack of surprise, the Tour's tests detected nobody using drugs—only one rider has been caught in this way in the 1990s. By contrast, blood tests for three riders, including Marco Pantani, the winner of the previous Tour, came back positive in the Giro d'Italia in May. Did this mean the Tour riders were clean? Not according to a segment of the press, which reckoned, probably correctly, that the riders were being more careful to beat the tests. Whatever the reason, some newspapers, especially in France, were full of daily doubts.

Laughing at the spectacle was Manolo Saiz, the directeur sportif of the ONCE team from Spain and a man whom Tour authorities tried unsuccessfully to ban because of his derisory attitude toward the race and the country the year before.

"The Tour has found a new boss to dominate the race," Saiz said midway through. "And look how he isn't allowed to enjoy his victory. The press dirties him with its suspicions.

"You're dirtying not only a rider," he warned, "but also an illusion that nourishes millions of fans."

Part Three

THE NEW CENTURY

2000

An American who began living in France more than two decades ago as a Francophile (don't they all?), and over the years believed he had become a Francophobe (don't they all?), was having dinner in Rouen and, as he ate his way through the cheese course, was thinking about what those years had taught him.

For one thing, he had learned how to eat cheese. Since this was Normandy, he selected Pont l'Évêque, Livarot, and Camembert, three regional cheeses made within a few miles of each other, all soft and covered with a crust. With Pont l'Évêque and Livarot, those many years had taught him, the crust is cut away; with Camembert, the crust is eaten. Get that wrong, the French snicker at you.

They snicker at you anyway, he told himself.

The fellow was not feeling favorably about his host country this evening. Like all relationships, theirs had its on- and off-days, and which this one was could easily be guessed. His hotel in Rouen was as charmless as the view from his window: During World War II, the city had been plastered by Allied bombers trying to cut the bridges over the Seine and to destroy a major German rail-marshaling yard. Now, instead of half-timbered houses in the Norman style, the streets along the river were lined with blockhouse apartment and office buildings.

Anything else wrong? It was raining. The cathedral front that Monet so famously painted in all changes of light was now blotchy and hidden in scaffolding. And the restaurant was suddenly being filled with a noisy crowd, probably one of those two-week guided tours of Europe for elderly swingers.

There were about twenty people in the group and, swingers or not, they were definitely elderly. Intent on his brooding, the fellow paid no attention as they took seats at tables that had been pushed together at the other end of the restaurant. He devoted himself to his Camembert.

Then he heard a familiar voice, the foghorn timbre of a former official of the Tour de France. For years, that voice had ordered people in cars—the press (this very fellow, for one)—to clear the road for the riders. The voice had never cajoled or pleaded; it had bellowed and threatened whenever a car seemed to get too close to the front of the race, as reporters tried to do their job. It was not a voice of sweet reason.

This time, though, in this restaurant, the voice was loudly affectionate. It was welcoming the group to the start of the Tour the next morning and promising one and all a warm reception as honored guests. And now, the voice boomed, a splendid dinner awaited. The voice finished with a jolly laugh.

Outside, a bus announced the group: the surviving members of the French national team that helped the late Jacques Anquetil win his first of five Tours de France forty years before. And this was the year the race was honoring Anquetil, a native of Rouen, where the Tour was starting.

A painting of him in the leader's yellow jersey decorated the bus, which also carried the names of his teammates: Gilbert Bauvin, Louis Bergaud, Albert Bouvet, André Darrigade, Jean Forestier, François Mahé, René Privat, Jean Stablinski, and Roger Walkowiak. Privat had died a few years ago, Anquetil in 1987; maybe some others since the start of that 1997 Tour.

What a team that was! The fellows in the restaurant helped the 23-year-old Anquetil win by nearly fifteen minutes in his Tour debut. He and his teammates won twelve of the twenty-three stages, with Anquetil winning four stages, Darrigade and Privat three times each, and Bauvin and Stablinski one stage each.

The grouchy American lifted his glass and saluted the old men, who were too busy talking about the old days to notice. For them, the 1957 Tour was still rolling around the country in that summer's heavy heat and Anquetil was preparing to don the first of his many yellow jerseys in Charleroi. They were rolling now through the Alps, the old men, and then the Pyrenees, where their leader faltered on the final 1,500 meters of the Aubisque and had to be helped up and over. And then, do you remember, two days later, Anquetil, looking fresh as a daisy, won the final time trial.

Listening to their stories, the fellow so down on things French only an hour before felt the old affection stir. It was hard, he decided, to dislike a country where the Tour de France in all its glory and color could sweep right through a restaurant.

There are other ways to follow the Tour, of course, and some are more immediate than a dinner table in Rouen. They include by car, by bicycle, by television, and by foot.

By car: Jean-Marie Leblanc, who oversees the Tour, often has a guest in the car that precedes the riders by about 100 yards and tucks in behind any significant breakaway. The sightlines are superb and the company is first rate, but the A list is generally composed of French politicians, captains of industry (a priority to race sponsors), and such visiting nabobs as European crown princes.

Leblanc's B list is often seated in another official car with Bernard Hinault, who won the Tour as many times as Anquetil and now is the race's head of public relations. Nowhere near as companionable as Leblanc, Hinault was, on the other hand, a somewhat better rider than the Tour's director, and he can offer unique insights.

Other privileged cars in the caravan include a few dozen reserved for the French television network that shows the race—not for its journalists, naturally, but for such guests as advertisers and the dim stars of obscure quiz shows. Press cars have to fight off this armada to get a view of a breakaway, one reason that fewer and fewer press cars join the caravan. (Another is that most reporters prefer to speed directly to the finish, plunder whatever buffet table is available and then watch the Tour all afternoon on television. Their accounts do not burst with local color, but they do get fed.)

Then there are the team cars, two for each outfit in the race. The first holds the directeur sportif, a mechanic, and spare gear, in addition to the bicycles clipped to the car's roof rack. The seat in the front next to the directeur sportif is sometimes available for a guest, especially if the team is not French. If it is, the sponsor will surely have somebody booked for each day of the three-week race. (Kelme, which makes shoes in Spain, seems not to have a friend or salesman outside the motherland and always has an open seat; ditto Liquigas—an Italian heating specialist, not a gastric affliction.) Depending on the rank of the team in the Tour, a seat in its first car is close to the action; the second team cars are usually so far back that they may carry a small television set to watch proceedings.

By bicycle: Cycling tours, some of them luxurious, have proliferated. But although cyclotourists get a chance to ride the routes and climb the hills that the Tour uses, they can't do that and watch the race at the same time, except when the race comes by the point they have cycled to.

By television: French television coverage, the basic international feed, is good, especially when voiced over by any commentator not French. The locals are notorious for their chauvinism: Viewers will learn everything, down to his shoe size, about a French rider in a breakaway, while his companions will often be identified only as "the Belgian" or "the Spaniard." Television, however, remains television, a long step removed from being there.

By foot: This can be sketchy. On one occasion, two women drove from their homes in Paris to Pau, the doorsteps of the Pyrenees, to see a mountain stage. After finding a hotel, they arose early the morning of the climb through "the Circle of Death," drove as close to the Aubisque as they could before the police stopped all vehicular traffic, and then set off on foot.

The Aubisque is high—1,709 meters, or 5,606 feet, at the top—but these are two spunky women. For hours, they trudged higher, higher, higher, neither complaining. Finally, they made it to the perfect vantage point, a small rise on the shoulder of the road a little way before the peak, where they could see down the valley and watch the Tour de France rise to them.

Rise it did. And as it rose, a heavy fog descended. Fogs—or low-slung clouds—can be common near the Pyrenees' passes. It was a whiteout, and the women saw nothing of the stage.

They said that they perhaps made out the glare of headlights, while never spotting a bicycle rider. And they knew the entire race had passed when everybody standing around them began walking back down the Aubisque. By that time the fog had turned to rain. Foot-sore and drenched, the two women finally reached their car and drove straight back to Paris, a twelve-hour trip. The next time they went out to watch the Tour, they had seats in a grandstand on the Champs-Elysées for the final stage in Paris.

By foot, improved version: Pick a day with a few puffy clouds in a pale blue sky, a blazing sun, a cooling breeze—a grand day for a picnic or a bicycle race. Do what Constant Pointet, a worker in a charcoal factory, and his apprentice fiancée, Denise Grundet, a cleaning woman, did some years back, when they drove in the Alps toward the Col des Saisies, 1,633 meters high and the first of three first-category climbs in the stage.

Parking their car below a cow pasture full of mauve wildflowers, walking for a while to a spot with a view of the climbing riders through willow and fir trees, and unpacking a picnic table, two chairs, and a hamper of food and wine, the couple settled down for a good time.

They were doing exactly what hundreds of thousands of others did that day in the Alps, and what millions did around the country during the three weeks of the Tour.

The couple saw only a small part of the stage, of course. But whether in the mountains, where the race can take an hour to pass a given point, or on the flat, where it can whiz past in a handful of nanoseconds, the important thing is to have seen the race go by. That's why parents hold up their infants for an uncomprehending glance: It's the Tour de France, the parents explain. And once, long ago, those parents were held aloft by their own parents and given the same explanation.

As they passed the pâté, the slices of ham, the crusty bread, the pickles, and the red wine between them, the couple in the Alps saw the pack pursuing the first breakaways, and then the many splintered groups as the race exploded. They saw the stragglers, too, and they continued with their picnic long after nothing was left to see.

So take a holiday. Set up a picnic by the side of the road and follow the Tour de France. It's free. And remember: If cheese is part of the picnic, with Pont l'Évêque and Livarot, the crust is cut away; with Camembert, it's eaten.

THE PERFECT LIFE

2000

Best-selling author, inspirational speaker, endorser of products ranging from cereal to sunglasses, foundation official, family man, and wearer of the Tour de France's yellow jersey as its leader and defending champion, the conglomerate Lance Armstrong confirmed that life is good.

"Perfect," he said. "I don't know what perfect is," he quickly admitted, "but this is perfect enough for me."

Just plain living is good, he said, referring to his recovery from cancer and the effects of chemotherapy in 1996. Beyond that, he continued in an interview, his way of life is good. His wife, his son, his job—he's happy.

How does it feel to be the proverbial man who has everything?

"I think a big part of my success is the lifestyle, the comfort that I have now, the happiness that I have now," he answered. "Not that I was unhappy before, but this is certainly the happiest I've ever been in life, period. I don't know if I have everything, but I have everything I need. I don't know what everything is, but I have enough.

"The money thing is relative. I have enough to not have to do this, but I love this, this makes me happy. The bike, the training, the sport, the atmosphere. Even the travel, the training camps, everything that goes with it."

He paused in his litany of euphoria. "Not this hotel." Lounging on his bed after a forty-five-minute massage, Armstrong gestured around the tacky room with water stains showing through the plush on the walls.

Especially when he is feeling feisty, the 28-year-old leader of the U.S. Postal Service team is famous for complaining about the sometimes dreadful hotels that race organizers assign. There was no doubting his feistiness now.

"We still have a lot of racing to go," he said cautiously before the start of three stages in the Alps.

"I'm surprised at my fitness. I focused totally on this event and wanted this result, but I didn't expect to be entering the Alps with a five-minute lead. That really surprises me. Five minutes is a lot."

He brushed aside his three previous second-place finishes in Tour stages. "It's not important to win stages," he said. "What's important is to win in Paris."

Armstrong was equally uninterested in judging whether he is the best climber in the race. His power in the mountains he ascribes to his loss of weight—from 82 kilograms (180 pounds) in 1996, when he dropped out of the Tour a few months before his testicular cancer was diagnosed, to 72.5 kilo in 2000 (159 pounds)—and his use of a smaller gear and increased pedal strokes as he moves uphill.

"I don't care to be called a climber," he said. "I don't care to be called a time trialist," a discipline in which he also excels. "It's important to be a complete rider.

"If I'm the second-best climber and the second-best time trialist and that wins the Tour de France, perfect. Perfect."

He turned to a saying from golf, a hobby at which he likes to think he shows skill: "Short game—drive for show, putt for dough."

The talk turned to his motivation to repeat as Tour champion. First, he said, was his continuing inspiration to other cancer survivors.

"That is not as big a story as it was last year, but it's still my main purpose. It's still a big part of my motivation. This race is about surviving and survival. To do it, at least to participate, to try to win again, hopefully win again, is survival.

"Cancer people survive now. People live the rest of their lives normally."

There is another side to his motivation, and that is Armstrong's quiet rage against the people he thinks showed him no respect after his victory last year. These include the reporters who suggested that he used illegal drugs and the rivals who he feels implied he would not have won if they had been in the race.

"It gives me drive. Absolutely. Absolutely. You've got to get motivated by something."

What about the positive influences?

"It's a package. There's the good energy, family stuff, my place in the cancer world, all the right reasons. Then there are the other things that just make me mad. Like somebody having no respect for me in the race. That I use as well. You need both."

Time for the team dinner was nearing and the Texan rose from his bed and edged around his open suitcase on a table. "Not much room to move in this room," he grumbled. He straightened the clothing, including his latest yellow jersey, in the suitcase.

Final question: A Danish reporter, possibly just returned from years on the moon, had asked some probing questions about Armstrong. Did he have brothers or sisters (no), where did he live in America (Austin, Texas), did he and his wife (Kristin) have children (Luke, ten months old, twenty-one pounds), was Armstrong a good person?

What does Armstrong himself think?

"We have an obligation to be good people," he replied. "I can be mean, I can yell and scream and cuss and be seemingly a bad person. But at the end of the day, I'm going to do whatever it takes—if I was checking out that night—to prove that I was a good guy.

"Whether it was giving back to the world of cancer, giving back to the world in general, giving back to my family, giving back to the sport—whether it's financially or your time, whether it's that yellow jersey in the suitcase, if it's just giving it away, that's what you've got to do."

THE MORNING AFTER

2002

After the usual lavish victory party the night before, Lance Armstrong woke up and prepared to spend the day as just another American tourist in Paris.

Or not quite, since the four-time victor of the Tour de France had several television commitments ahead of him, then a return to his in-season home in Spain before he flew to Manhattan to compete in a race there.

Even without this heavy schedule and the need to relax after the three-week Tour, it was doubtful that Armstrong, his wife, and their son and infant twin daughters could spend much time strolling in the Latin Quarter or window-shopping along the Rue de Rivoli.

With his face prominent on television every day during the race and his photograph on the front of many French newspapers and magazines, the leader of the U.S. Postal Service team is a major celebrity in Paris. Add his photogenic family and there is no mistaking the Armstrongs for folks from Milwaukee on a package tour.

This rock-star status is well earned. Unlike any other recent Tour de France champion, Armstrong is bright, charming, and vividly articulate in English, while getting there in French. His battle against cancer in known and respected by the French. His wife is beautifully blonde and his children adorable.

But his standing with the French is not entirely a love feast. A former resident of Nice, he is being pursued by the authorities to pay taxes on the money he has won in the Tour and then donated to his teammates. A judicial inquiry into suspicions of doping by his team in 2000 has not yet been closed, even though the main investigator said months ago that no acceptable evidence had turned up.

And then there are the hecklers, the spectators who have jeered Armstrong occasionally during the race, insinuating that illegal drugs have assisted his four consecutive victories.

Between Armstrong and the French, the relationship can be complicated.

Flash back three nights to the French town of Chatillon sur Chalaronne, which seems to be a lively place even when its annual late-night market is not being held, as it was when the U.S. Postal Service team was trying to rest in the appropriately named Hotel de la Tour (referring in this case to a tower, not the bicycle race).

Near midnight in the Place de la République in front of the hotel in the eastern heartland, throngs were picking through movie and music cassettes, checking the prices on pieces of country furniture and inspecting clothing. On the Rue Pasteur alongside the hotel, cotton candy was being spun and music was blaring. On the Rue Président Carnot nearby, a merry-go-round was whirling and Spanish pottery was drastically marked down for the occasion, as a salesman kept shouting.

"I didn't have to go to the fair," Armstrong said glumly the next morning. "It was right there in my room with me."

Yes, it was noisy, but also jolly. Although several members of the team wandered out after dinner to check the scene, Armstrong remained in the hotel. He was not bothered there since the public heeded a sign asking them "to respect the intimacy and relaxation of the riders" by not entering the premises except to eat in the restaurant.

Why had he not gone outside to join in the fun, the Tour de France champion was asked.

"I can't do that," he explained. "It would be a mob scene with all the people wanting autographs."

Yet two days later, he was noting again that he had sometimes been booed during the race, unusual treatment for a Tour de France winner.

Usually the focus of the jeers is doping. As the French sports newspaper *L'Equipe* pointed out, the people who have been most vociferous against Armstrong, who denies any suggestion of doping, also applaud Richard Virenque, a Frenchman who has admitted taking illegal performance-enhancing drugs and was the leader of the Festina team that gave its name to a doping scandal in the 1998 Tour.

"The day on Mont Ventoux was the worst," Armstrong said, referring to the Tour climb in Provence that Virenque won.

"It was a minority, but anytime you have those people, you really hear them.

"Instead of people encouraging you, you have them jumping in the road, making hand signals, drunk out of their minds, fat bellies. So it's louder, more obvious than somebody who's encouraging you."

The evening after that stage, he complained, "If I had a dollar for every time somebody hollers 'Dopé, dopé,' I'd be a rich man.

"Don't come to the bike race if you want to yell at the riders," he continued. "It's an issue of class—do you have class or don't you?"

At a news conference, he returned to the subject of some fans' and journalists' suspicions about the use of illegal drugs.

"The mentality is, 'He came back from cancer, he never did this before'—meaning win the Tour de France—'how can he do it now?' It's a sick mentality.

"When you're clean, clean, and clean, I don't see how a guy can stand out in the road and say, 'Dopé, dopé.'

"My biggest fear is that somebody might try to do something violent—jump out at me to hit me or stop me or a team. That would be not good."

Eddy Merckx, the great Belgian rider and five-time winner of the Tour three decades ago, understands the fears of Armstrong, his friend and protégé. Merckx was punched in the stomach by a French fan on a climb in 1975 and blamed the injury to his liver for his final second place in the race.

Armstrong also understands the peculiar attitude of the French to winners—or, rather, to losers. Napoleon was never so popular as during "The Hundred Days" when he returned from Elba for his final drubbing at Waterloo. There exists, even now, a somewhat revered Pretender to the Throne, a seat abolished in 1848.

The national bicycle-racing hero remains Raymond Poulidor, three times second in the Tour, five times third, and never a winner. Poulidor still travels with the race, representing different sponsors, signing autographs more than a quarter century after he retired and smiling at the shouts of "Poo-poo," a nickname he detests.

"The French are against winners," Merckx explained recently. "They were against me until I was beaten in the 1975 Tour, and then I became popular."

In other words, if Armstrong really wants to stop the heckling, he better lose the race. There appears to be no chance of that anytime soon, so he might as well get used to the disrespect.

A DUBIOUS CONSULTANT

2001

"It's 'rip Lance' time," Lance Armstrong had said pleasantly and cryptically in a conversation just before the start of the 88th Tour de France. With the race underway, his meaning is clear and the ripping has begun.

The question is how long it will continue. To judge from a random poll of European reporters traveling with the bicycle race, the latest storm over drugs will not end soon. The many reporters who were not present when Armstrong defended his relationship with a controversial Italian doctor were mostly planning to write follow-up articles based on reports in some morning French newspapers.

The name of the doctor, Michele Ferrari, rang many alarms. Ferrari is facing trial in Italy on charges of procuring and supplying to riders a variety of illegal performance-enhancing drugs, including EPO, human growth hormone, steroids, and testosterone.

Ferrari was also the physician for the Gewiss team, whose riders finished first, second, and third in the Fleche Wallone race in 1994 and then fired him when he defended the use of EPO.

In short, his reputation is "sulphurous," as the newspaper *L'Equipe* twice described him. As Armstrong said in the statement issued in his name, Ferrari "has had a questionable public reputation due to the irresponsible comments he made in 1994 regarding EPO." He is not generally regarded as the sort of doctor a rider would see for ordinary advice about his training.

Yet Bill Stapleton, Armstrong's agent, insisted in an interview that "Dr. Ferrari is not a witch doctor. He knows physiology and when he discusses gearing, Lance listens."

Armstrong sounded the same note, saying that he had consulted Ferrari "on dieting, altitude preparation," and other "natural methods of improvement," including "my testing and my form on the bike."

"He has never discussed EPO with me and I have never used it," the leader of the U.S. Postal Service team and defending Tour champion added.

He was replying to an article by the award-winning reporter David Walsh in the *Sunday Times* of London, heavy with circumstantial evidence. Walsh has long argued that Armstrong has to use drugs since so many others in the sport do and Armstrong has easily crushed them all in the last two Tours.

In his article, Walsh quoted a former professional "who rode with Armstrong for four years at Motorola," the Texan's team before he joined U.S. Postal Service in 1998. He was out of the sport from the fall of 1996 until 1998 as he recuperated from testicular cancer.

Motorola, "Armstrong believes, was 'white as snow,'" the article said. "That is not what his one-time teammate says. This rider tells of a decision by certain members of the Motorola squad to use the blood-boosting drug erythropoietin (EPO) during the 1995 season: 'The contract with our main sponsor was up for renewal and we needed results. It was as simple as that.'"

Walsh said that his source is retired and "agreed to speak on the basis that his name would not be used. Should it become necessary, though, he will come forward and stand up for his account of the Motorola team."

According to the former rider, before the 1995 Tour de France, "the picture was becoming clear: We were going to have to give in and join the EPO race. Lance was a key spokesperson when EPO was the topic."

Discussing Armstrong's ties to Ferrari, Walsh cites records held by "the carabinieri of the Florence-based NAS team who enforce Italy's food and drug laws."

"Sources close to the investigation of Ferrari," Walsh continued, "tell of a series of visits by the rider to Ferrari's practice in Ferrara in northern Italy: two days in March 1999, three days in May 2000, two days in August 2000, one day in September 2000, and three days in late April/early May of this year."

Their relationship was not generally known. "In the past, I have never denied my relationship with Michele Ferrari," Armstrong said in a statement. "On the other hand, I have never gone out of my way to publicize it."

In what Stapleton admitted was a preemptive move before the publication of Walsh's article—which the Postal Service camp had been tipped off was coming—Armstrong granted an interview to the Italian newspaper *Gazzetta dello Sport,* in which he said he was working with Ferrari in an attempt to better the world record for the hour's ride against the clock.

When the interview was reprinted in the French press Sunday, it raised eyebrows. A few hours later, Walsh's article began circulating with its account of the visits and the Armstrong-Ferrari relationship since 1995. The ripping began.

His team remains solidly behind Armstrong in the latest controversy, which follows unproven allegations of drug use by Postal Service in the last Tour.

"I have known Lance for a long time and I have a hell of a lot of confidence and belief in his values, him as a person, and his decision-making abilities," said Mark Gorski, the team's general manager. "In managing this team, I have given Lance a lot of room to make his own decisions and I don't believe there's any reason to question his decisions about the people around him. I believe in him 110 percent."

NOVICE RIDER

2002

"I was warned," Floyd Landis said of his first Tour de France. "People told me what it was like, so I had a pretty good idea. It's a tremendous amount of stress."

Landis, a 26-year-old American with the U.S. Postal Service team, was speaking while the race was on the plains. After a strong time trial, he ranked 15th among the 182 riders still competing. While he spoke, he seemed to be under minimal stress.

That changed a few days later when the race entered the Pyrenees.

Floyd Landis, meet stress. As the pack started climbing the Aubisque mountain, rated beyond category in difficulty, Landis was left behind. A rider who made the Tour team to help Lance Armstrong, the defending champion, in the mountains, Landis lost more than twenty-one minutes and finished in 117th place. He started the next stage nearly twenty-five minutes behind Armstrong, in 70th place.

"I was disappointed, but everybody's had their rough days," Landis said. "There were teammates in the back earlier and I guess it's my turn now."

He explained his problem simply: "Just bad legs. Very bad legs." Riders call the condition a jour sans, a "day without" in French, the language of cycling.

"When a team's leading a race, it's great for morale and everybody's happy. A bad day is not nearly as bad. Nobody's depressed. It's been a great experience," he continued in an interview.

"If Lance hadn't won the stage, I would have been more disappointed, but he was OK without me. He just said, 'Don't worry about it; tomorrow's another day.'"

Armstrong, and Scarlett O'Hara before him, got that right. Landis rode for a long while at the front for his team the next day in the Pyrenees, sheltering Armstrong and keeping the pace high enough to leave opponents behind.

He finished in 43rd place, 9 minutes, 15 seconds behind Armstrong, moving up to 53rd place overall. The day after that, he continued to do his share of the team's work, finishing in the main pack with Armstrong in his slipstream.

Now in his fifth year as a professional and first year with Postal Service, Landis is highly regarded by team officials.

"I think he could be a leader of the future, and the future is coming up real quick," said Dan Osipow, the director of operations, alluding to Armstrong's approaching 32nd birthday and his hints that he will not continue beyond another year or two.

"It's good for us to have a rider who can climb, time-trial, and is gaining experience," Osipow said of Landis. "He's becoming more comfortable, especially in the European mode. We'd love to keep him on the team and become a team leader of the future."

Things have happened quickly for Landis, an Ephrata, Pennsylvania, native who now lives outside San Diego. He started in the sport as a mountain biker, leaving home at 20 for California. "I decided I don't want to train in the snow any more. The wintertime, the cold weather," he added with a shudder.

A former junior national mountain bike champion who won the Pro Rookie of the Year award in that discipline in 1995, he was basically a walk-on with the Mercury team late in 1998.

"I was in California near their training camp and I did their races," he remembered. "There were twenty of them and one of me, but I finished second in one race and third in another. John Wordin, their directeur sportif, gave me a call and asked if I wanted to race with them.

"I wanted to do road racing for a long time, but I didn't know how to get on a team, so I was happy he called."

When he finished third in the Tour de l'Avenir, a French showcase for young talent, in 1999 and fourth the next year, he began attracting major attention. After Mercury failed to get an expected—and deserved—

Sean Kelly, at Paris-Roubaix in the
photo above, excelled in the spring
classics, and was a contender in the
major tours as well. Not for nothing did
the French call him "King Kelly."

Alexi Grewal, opposite page, rocketed to fame with a gold medal in the 1984 Olympics but suffered mightily on the Continent. "My legs need to start talking," he said, but instead they stayed mum.

Grand Old Man Joop Zoetemelk, left, finished a record sixteen Tours de France, and finally retired at age 41.

Greg LeMond and Bernard Hinault, below on L'Alpe d'Huez in 1986, shared a team, ambition, and glory, but little else.

Irishman Stephen Roche, in the Giro d'Italia's pink jersey at left, angered the natives by having the temerity to win their national tour.

Andy Hampsten, riding for 7-Eleven in 1989, was outspoken about drug cheats. "If they fail, they're out of the race," he said.

Greg LeMond embraced technology, and the aerodynamic handlebars he adopted from triathlon helped him close a 50-second gap on the last day of the 1989 Tour de France.

Miguel Indurain, above, the silent
Spaniard, won five consecutive Tours
de France without uttering a single
significant sound bite.

American Chris Horner, opposite
top, stormed through the U.S. ranks
and arrived in Europe with high
expectations but low results. He did
better his second time around, in 2005.

Richard Virenque, lower right,
the nabob of sob. He protested his
innocence for two years after the
Festina team was busted for drugs in
1989, only to finally admit, weeping,
that indeed he was a user too.

Marco Pantani, above, was ousted for doping on the penultimate day of the 1999 Giro d'Italia, a sad end for a once-great star.

Bjarne Riis, at left leading teammate Jan Ullrich, won the Tour in '96 but became a somewhat unwilling support rider thereafter.

The irrepressible Mario Cipollini, above, brought a touch of glamour, with his Armani suits, and a touch of theater, with his many racing costumes, to a sport that badly needed diversion. For his sartorial excesses, he was often fined by racing's grand viziers, but his popularity with the *tifosi* never waned. It did not hurt that he was also one of Italy's greatest sprinters.

Jeannie Longo, much admired if not much liked, was one of France's longest-running hits, compiling a huge medal count over the years and competing in the 2004 world championships at the age of 46.

Paolo Bettini, above, with Mapei in happier days. The powerhouse Italian team outspent all comers and won more races, too, until 2002, when a doping scandal at the Giro put an end to it all.

Andrea Tafi, above, and Laurent Jalabert,
below, were steady riders throughout one of
cycling's most turbulent eras.

Belgium's problem child, Frank Vandenbroucke, was a celebrated classics winner early on but never recovered from a drug bust in the winter of 2002. The drugs, he said, were for his dog, a defense that earned him immediate suspension.

David Millar was world time-trial
champion in 2003 and busted for EPO
in 2004, the evidence plain to see on
his bookshelf.

Jesus Manzano, above, broke the
silence about the goings-on at team
Kelme and was dropped by the squad
shortly thereafter.

Johan Museeuw, below right, the Lion
of Flanders, compiled 101 victories and
finally retired at age 39. "Above all,"
he said, "I want to avoid the image of a
Johan Museeuw in decline."

Jan Ullrich, left, won the Tour in 1997 and great things were predicted for his future. But a series of personal stumbles and the arrival of Lance Armstrong ended those hopes.

Tom Boonen, below, emerged as a great classics rider and was proclaimed the new king of cycling-mad Belgium after winning Paris-Roubaix in 2005. But his hero, he insisted, was not Museeuw, as you'd expect, but Indurain.

Tom Danielson, below, established himself as the American star to watch with victory in the Tour de Georgia and a strong ride at the Vuelta a España in 2005.

invitation to the last Tour de France and then dropped its European campaign because of financial difficulties, Landis signed with Postal Service.

He has become a protégé of Armstrong's as well as his neighbor in Girona, Spain, during the racing season.

"I trained the last two months almost every day with him and learned a lot," he said.

Landis is forthright about his admiration for his team leader. "The most important thing he does for himself is stay focused," he said. "Even when he doesn't have the yellow jersey, everybody looks at him as if he should be in control of the race."

He's teaching you how to win the Tour de France, somebody suggested.

"I hope so," Landis said with a laugh. "But I have a long way to go."

ONE WORLD TO ANOTHER

2003

When the Tour de France rolls out, it will pass through a microcosm of the country: from the soured streets of Saint-Denis, a town of immigrants and unemployment just north of Paris, through the capital itself and its mythic squares, and into the country, through quiet villages like, say, Coulommiers in a gentle valley to the east.

Carlos Da Cruz, a Frenchman who will be wearing the mainly white jersey of the FDJ.com team in the 198-man field, knows the way better than most.

He was born in Saint-Denis, where his mother and father were janitors, as Portuguese commonly are in Paris. Now he lives in Coulommiers, which he describes as being farther from Saint-Denis than just 100 kilometers, or 60 miles.

"Another world," he said. "Nicer than Saint-Denis," he added with a laugh. "It's in the country, lots of horse farms, sheep, all that. It's really different from Saint-Denis, nothing like it."

Da Cruz, 28, a professional since 1997, has lived in Coulommiers with his wife and young daughter since 2000. "It's much easier to train there than in Saint-Denis," he said. "Open roads, not too much traffic. It's hard to train in the city."

Training is important to him because he was hampered the last two years after operations on the iliac veins in his legs. "Two lost years," he said.

This year he returned in a new role—an attacker. Before he was a domestique, one of the personally unambitious riders who carry water bottles to teammates and shelter their leader from the wind.

Now he has turned to the long-distance attack, bolting from the pack and chancing his luck at staying away. He tried it first in the Milan-San Remo classic in March and was caught. Off he went again a month later and won the Circuit de la Sarthe. Although unsuccessful, later attempts gained him the reputation of an aggressive rider and a place on the nine-man FDJ.com Tour team. This will be his second Tour after the one in 2000, when he was with Festina.

"My principal role will be as a lead-out man for our best sprinter, Baden Cooke, and maybe for Jimmy Casper, too, if he's in form," he said.

He also has his own goals. "To win a stage," he said. "Especially in the first week since I won't be far from home."

He left it vague which home he meant, Coulommiers and its few thousand inhabitants or Saint-Denis and its eighty-five thousand. He noted that the Tour's first stage will begin at the Stade de France, a stadium 500 meters from where he grew up.

His father is retired. His mother plans to retire at the end of July. Both worked forty years in Saint-Denis after they left Portugal. "There was no work there," Da Cruz said.

There is no work in Saint-Denis now for its mainly North African immigrants. "People hang out, they look for jobs but can't find them. If I wasn't a racer, I'd be in the same place, hanging out in the same cafés. Nothing much has changed there.

"People work a month, three months, and their contracts run out. They go on welfare, come off welfare, and maybe find another job that lasts three months. It's not easy for them."

It was not easy for him either, Da Cruz admitted. He was inspired by the elder of his two brothers, an amateur rider.

"When I was 13, 14, I saw him bringing home bouquets and trophies, and I decided I wanted to do that, too."

Now Da Cruz hopes he is a role model for the youth of Saint-Denis.

"The young people in my old neighborhood, whenever I visit my parents, they come out to encourage me. They know what I've accomplished—

they read the newspapers, they see me on television. They see what I've done, they see that I'm in the Tour de France. And I hope I encourage them.

"Maybe some of them are thinking, 'I can do that, too.' They can, you know. It's possible. I'm the proof."

WHERE IT ALL BEGAN

2003

The steak at the Reveil Matin in the Paris suburb of Montgeron is tender, the house wine thin but acceptable, the service no worse than the usual inattentive, the bill a bit less than it would be in a more chic and higher-rent restaurant in the capital.

A town of twenty-one thousand, Montgeron is hard to find in the southeastern suburban sprawl, and the Reveil Matin (Alarm Clock) lies at the northern end of town, a thirty-five-minute slog, much of it uphill, from the train station.

Worth the trip, as the Michelin guide would put it? Not at all for the food, absolutely for the occasion. The Reveil Matin is a shrine.

At 3:16 p.m. on July 1, 1903, a crowd in the dozens outside the inn watched sixty bicycle riders set off on the first Tour de France. It began in Montgeron and finished on July 19 in another suburb, Ville d'Avray, because the police ruled that a bicycle race in Paris would interfere with daily life.

A century later, French officials have changed their minds: For a few days the Tour de France will rule Paris.

The prologue to the three-week race will start at the Eiffel Tower, with all nearby streets blocked to traffic and the usual throngs of tourists. When the Tour ends, it will monopolize, as it has since 1975, the broad Champs-Elysées in the heart of Paris.

For the Centennial Tour—actually the ninetieth edition of the race, which was halted by both world wars—the organizers have scheduled a series of celebratory events in and around Paris, including parades, concerts, fireworks, exhibitions, and mass bicycle rides open to the public. The aim, in the words of Jean-Marie Leblanc, the Tour's chief director, is to affirm the race's role as a "sporting, social, historic, and festive" event.

That it is. What started as a gimmick to boost circulation for the newspaper *L'Auto* has grown into the world's third-largest sporting event, after the Olympic Games and soccer's World Cup, as measured by spectator interest.

Since neither of those is scheduled for the summer, more than the usual 15 million Frenchmen and women should flock to the sides of the Tour's roads and more than the usual 160 million viewers should be watching globally on television. The number at the finale along the Champs-Elysées, however, should remain constant; because nobody counts, it is always estimated at 250,000 fans.

The crowd in Montgeron alone should reach into the tens of thousands, including spectators; the 198 riders, divided into twenty-two teams of nine men each; their automobile armada of officials, coaches, mechanics, and masseurs; and several hundred journalists—a permanent supporting cast of more than 3,500 people.

What a change those twenty-two teams will be from a century before, when just a few riders signed up early. Almost nobody, it seemed, was ready for a 2,428-kilometer, or 1,509-mile, race in six daily and sometimes nightly stages, with one to four rest days between each stage. The distance was twice that of the record holder, Paris-Brest-Paris, and the prize list of 20,000 francs, then nearly $4,000, was quite high.

L'Auto and its editor, Henri Desgrange, fighting a circulation war with the newspaper *Le Velo*, proclaimed it "the greatest bicycling test in the world. A month-long race—Paris-Lyon-Marseille-Toulouse-Bordeaux-Nantes."

After the race's length was reduced to three weeks, the entry fee cut from twenty francs to ten and the overall eligibility rules relaxed, seventy-eight men signed up and sixty set off.

Watching over the crowd at the Reveil Matin were a few policemen on horseback. Their successors will be back for the first stage in a parade by mounted members of the Garde Républicaine.

Otherwise, and not unexpectedly, much has changed.

The original first stage, from Montgeron to Lyon, lasted an overwhelming 467 kilometers. Lyon is on the schedule again, as are the five other original cities, but it will not be reached until the seventh daily stage, 226.5 kilometers from Nevers.

Instead of six stages, there will be twenty. Instead of 2,428 kilometers, there will be 3,427. Instead of the 6,075 francs carried home by the first winner, Maurice Garin, there will be €335,000, or $385,000.

The Tour will also pass through the mountains, not added until 1905 (the Vosges) and now including the Pyrenees (1910) and the Alps (1911). The leader will wear the distinctive yellow jersey, introduced in 1919 and the same color as the newspaper *L'Auto,* now the daily sports newspaper *L'Equipe.*

Even the Reveil Matin has changed.

New owners took over in 2002 and, after coats of white and yellow paint were slapped on its ancient stucco walls, the place reopened under the name Hacienda Reveil Matin. The owners will soon begin renting rooms, which are now being redone.

One thing that has been left untouched is the plaque on an outside wall, placed there in 1953 to mark the fiftieth anniversary of the Tour. A centennial plaque will be unveiled July 1.

Inside, the restaurant menu is divided between Tex-Mex and traditional food, although the new decor leans to a western theme: posters of the death of Jesse James, plus a six-shooter on a wall among vaguely Mexican artifacts. The menu offers burritos, fajitas, and tacos along with tortilla chips and a bland salsa. "Traditional" dishes include veal chops, broiled kidney, steak tartare, several kinds of fish, and that steak. It's tasty medium rare.

PROMOTED FROM LIEUTENANT

2003

Modest, polite, a brute for endurance and now a champion, Tyler Hamilton was a charter member of the U.S. Postal Service bicycle team, joining it in 1997 and serving as lieutenant to its drab first leader, Jean-Cyril Robin, and its spectacularly successful second one, Lance Armstrong.

On climbs, Hamilton was the last man with Armstrong, pacing and sheltering him. In time trials, he was the pilot fish, setting off ahead of his leader to gauge the course, with his times and observations radioed back.

Late in 2001, after, as he says, "helping Lance win three Tours de France," Hamilton decided that with his 31st birthday approaching, he wanted to try to ride for himself.

"I wanted to see what I could accomplish, how far I could go, as a team leader myself," he recalled in an interview. "If I hadn't tried this, I never would have known."

He was speaking as the leader of the CSC team from Denmark, although, courteous as always, he insisted that he shared the main role with Carlos Sastre, a Spaniard with CSC. "Whichever of us is going better, the other will help him," Hamilton said.

There really was no question who would be going better. Hamilton had just finished second in the Giro d'Italia, the three-week race rated second only to the Tour de France.

He might have even won the Giro if he hadn't crashed twice and hurt his left shoulder. "I fractured the arm bone that goes into the shoulder and hurt the tendon," he said.

How had he been able to ride for two weeks after that?

"Look at my teeth," he replied. "They're all worn out." In fact, this winter his dentist had to cap eleven teeth that he ground down while trying to ignore his pain.

"I suffered a lot," Hamilton said. "I suffered more than people thought. It was pretty much two weeks of hell."

He had suffered before, too, he added. For example, there was the Tour de France where he was so weakened by salmonella that Postal Service gave up on his chances and left him behind, alone, on a torrid stage.

Just beating the time limit, Hamilton managed to finish not only that daily stage but also the Tour itself.

The fine showing in the Giro was the first thing he learned he could accomplish as a leader.

He learned another: The native of Marblehead, Massachusetts, became the first American to win a so-called monument of cycling. These are one-day classics: Milan-San Remo, the Tour of Flanders, Paris-Roubaix, and Liège-Bastogne-Liège.

Finding himself at the front with two other riders near the finish of the 258.5-kilometer Liège-Bastogne-Liège race, Hamilton "gave it a whirl, put my head down, went as hard as I could."

Under a cold rain, he crossed the line twelve seconds ahead of Iban Mayo, a Spaniard with Euskaltel, and fourteen ahead of Michael Boogerd, a Dutchman with Rabobank. Only 88 men finished what 196 started.

Suddenly Hamilton went from being "another American" in the European sporting press to "the other American." Armstrong, of course, is "the American."

Hamilton regards his former leader that way, too.

"Lance was the strongest guy in the race," he said, although events proved otherwise. Despite his usually forceful ride in Liège-Bastogne-Liège, where he has twice finished second, the Texan was unable to pull away while in the lead with 15 kilometers to go.

"Lance got away with three or four other guys," Hamilton related. "Lance is a friend of mine and it was OK with me if he got away. I would have been happy if he won the race."

Teammates arrived to help Hamilton—Armstrong was isolated through much of the long haul over ten hills and through the Ardennes—and he overtook the Texan and then attacked.

"This was one of my objectives for the spring," Hamilton said of his victory. "I have other goals in July." By that, he meant the Tour de France.

He was soft-spoken about his goals in the Tour, where he was 15th last year.

"Lance has been the strongest by far in the Tour de France the last four years," Hamilton said. "Until somebody shows they're on the same page with him, he's going to be a tough man to beat."

NOTHING IS NORMAL

2005

Normally, this would be a peak time in the bicycle-racing season for Tyler Hamilton. Recent races include the one-day Liège-Bastogne-Liège classic, which he won two years ago, and the six-day Tour of Romandie, which he won in 2003 and 2004. Now the Giro d'Italia, in which he finished second in 2002, has just begun.

Normally, Hamilton would have been a favorite in the three races as he prepared for the Tour de France, in which he finished fourth in 2003.

"Normally," he said, slowly repeating the word. "Normally," he said, swirling the word in his mouth like a sip of wine. "Not much is normal these days."

Hamilton was speaking on the phone from his home in Boulder, Colorado, before a six-hour training ride. "This is great country for training, and I have a lot of good riders to go out with," he said.

Training is all the 34-year-old American does these days. He has not raced since September 2004, shortly after he won the gold medal in the time trial at the Olympic Games in Athens and then was told that he had twice failed a new test to detect doping.

He was accused of using another person's blood to increase his supply of the red corpuscles that carry oxygen to tired muscles. Officials said that he failed the first test of his blood—the A sample—but that the confirmation test—the B sample—had been ruined because of a laboratory error in Greece.

Therefore, despite continuing litigation, he has kept the gold medal. But he also failed a test in September in the Vuelta a España, and this time the B sample confirmed the finding.

Hamilton has vigorously denied the charge of blood doping. "Number one, I'd be risking my life," he said last autumn. "It could kill me. Number two, I could get a disease, AIDS, hepatitis, the list goes on. Number three, I could endanger Haven," he said, referring to his wife, "and everyone knows how much I love her."

He appealed the finding but was rebuffed in April when a three-man arbitration panel ruled two-to-one that he had not proved that the new test was flawed. That decision meant Hamilton was banned from the sport for two years.

Under the laws of the new ProTour, he cannot ride for any of the top 20 teams for four years.

Hamilton called that decision by the independent American Arbitration Association-North American Court of Arbitration for Sport "a tragedy" and pledged to fight it.

"There's a reason that hundreds and hundreds of people in the medical profession have come to me in support," he said on the telephone. "Many of them have no knowledge about bicycle racing, no interest, but they see the flaws in the testing."

His defense, which he has outlined in more than two thousand words on his Web site, does not rely on his reputation as a soft-spoken and polite straight arrow in the sport, nor does it mention his courage in finishing second in the Giro despite a broken right shoulder after a crash, or a fourth-place finish in the Tour despite a double fracture of his right collarbone.

Instead, the defense is highly technical, nearly incomprehensible to a layman. It cites false positives, the possibility of a lost twin when Hamilton was in utero (a phenomenon known as a chimera), homologous transfusions, and the differences in testing for red corpuscle count between his team's equipment and that of the International Cycling Union and the World Anti-Doping Agency.

He summed it up: "I'm guilty until proven innocent."

Other elements verge on melodrama. They include an extortionist who warned Hamilton's Phonak team, based in Switzerland, that he and a teammate, Santiago Pérez, would be found guilty of blood doping unless money was paid. It wasn't and, weeks later, both men failed the tests in the Vuelta. Pérez, a Spaniard, has also been banned for two years.

"It's like a trashy novel," Hamilton said. "I'm trying to cover every angle."

Carrying his appeal to the next and presumably final level, Hamilton will be heard by the Court of Arbitration for Sport, which usually sits in Lausanne, Switzerland.

"They're coming to the United States, probably to Denver, in late June," he said. "There are so many witnesses here, it will be easier and cheaper for them to come here.

"So much waiting, that's the hard part," he continued. "But I'm not fighting for myself alone. I want better tests for all athletes. I'm in this for the athletes who don't have the resources to challenge the tests—a gymnast, for example, whose family had to take out a second mortgage just to afford a coach. This fight, it's a lot of money, a lot of time, a lot of stress. It's been hard."

Nevertheless he sounded cheerful after what he described as "a small break from all this trouble." His wife said they had just returned home after a few days in Florida where "we swam, ran on the beach, just got away from the stress here."

But what if the next appeal fails and there is no further court to reinstate him? What does he plan to do with the rest of his life?

"I'm not even thinking about that," he answered.

Hamilton addressed a suspicion that has been raised on bicycling Web sites: that he did not intentionally use another person's blood but that he and Pérez were transfusing their own blood and that the samples became confused.

"Certainly not," Hamilton said. "I've never transfused blood in my life."

He is convinced, he continued, that he will win his appeal and resume his career.

"Otherwise I wouldn't be busting my butt every day in training," he said. "On November 1 last year, I began training for this season and thought I would be racing again by now. I'm still riding in Phonak gear and hope when this is all over that I'll be back with the team. Now I'm shooting for a return in August—that's the plan. I haven't done my last bike race, that's for sure. You'll see me again."

NOT ONE FOR TALKING

2003

Jaan Kirsipuu never likes the limelight, especially the one bathing him now. While that was quite a milestone he passed in February—his 100th victory as a professional bicycle racer, joining only thirteen other men—he doesn't want to talk about it.

During a weekend of races in Belgium, as some riders drifted up to him beforehand and said a few congratulatory words, he looked distracted. At the sign-in for the Kuurne-Brussels-Kuurne race, he hurried past a clutch of expectant photographers. Reporters? Not often do they get a quote.

"He doesn't say much," agrees Kirsipuu's longtime directeur sportif, Vincent Lavenu. They have been together, under four sponsors, since 1992, when Kirsipuu, not that long arrived in France from his native Estonia, made his debut as a professional at age 23.

"You have to understand the road they've taken and their history," Lavenu says, referring to riders from the former Soviet bloc "They say only what's essential. For him, what's meaningful is victory."

It would be interesting to question Kirsipuu about that meaning, since his victories have predominantly been in minor races: four stages of the Tour of the Mediterranean, eight in the Etoile de Besseges, eight more in the Four Days of Dunkirk, three victories in the Classic Haribo. He has won the Tour of the Vendée twice, Chôlet-Pays de Loire three times, the Route Adélie twice, the Grand Prix de Denain twice. Small races all.

The higher points have been three stages in the Tour de France, where he wore the overall leader's yellow jersey for six days in 1999, and one stage in the Vuelta a España. Otherwise, there are two stage victories in Paris-Nice, a first place in Kuurne-Brussels-Kuurne, the time-trial championship in Estonia three times, and the road race championship in that country twice.

Add them up, though, and they come to 100. Only Mario Cipollini (158) and Erik Zabel (130) have more among those still competing. Eddy Merckx leads the list of retired racers, followed by such grand names as Rik van Looy, Roger de Vlaeminck, Freddy Maertens, and Sean Kelly. Francesco Moser, Bernard Hinault, and Laurent Jalabert are also in the mix.

That's strange company for Kirsipuu, a workhorse among thoroughbreds.

Does he begrudge the fact that Lavenu's teams have always had small budgets and thus few stars and rarely enough points to qualify for major races?

When Zabel and Cipollini are winning the Milan-San Remo classic, Lavenu's AG2R team—like its predecessors Chazal, Petit Casino, and Casino—habitually rides the same weekend in the unsung Chôlet-Pays de Loire in France.

Even the Tour de France, which packs its rolls with French teams, usually admits Lavenu's teams at the last moment and after much politicking. For the centennial Tour this year, AG2R is hoping for a wildcard invitation, and there are just four left.

Wherever he finds himself, Kirsipuu keeps grinding out victories. The 100th, in the small Classic Haribo, was his third of the 2003 season, which began in February.

"He's a special rider, always does well in the early season, he's always strong then," said Erik Breukink, a former top Dutch rider in the crowd at Kuurne.

That strength at the start of the year is a testimony to arduous training during the winter, when many others are lazing through their off-season.

"He's a good sprinter, and a good sprinter wins a lot," Breukink said. "He's a smart rider, too. He knows what his strength is, and he takes advantage of it.

"Kirsipuu knows he can't beat the top sprinters now, so he picks his spots—he'll go solo and avoid a big sprint. That's smart."

In remarks to the French sports newspaper *L'Equipe* after he won his 100th race, Kirsipuu agreed with that judgment.

"Instead of a sprint, you can win a race thanks to tactics," he said. "And that's just as pleasurable.

"When I turned professional, I never thought of how many races I could win, only about winning them, even the small ones. One hundred, that's a significant number, but 100 victories doesn't put me among the greats.

"It's not the number that makes a difference," he concluded. "I'm not a star."

Does that sometimes trouble him? Would he trade all his victories in the Etoile de Besseges and the Four Days of Dunkirk for one Tour of Flanders? Will he be satisfied once again to be riding in Chôlet-Pays de Loire while the big teams and the big names are riding in Milan-San Remo?

There are so many questions to ask him, but Kirsipuu prefers not to answer.

R.I.P. MAPEI

2002

While nobody was paying attention, the Mapei team—usually referred to as the powerhouse Mapei team—went out of business.

It was not a surprise; the decision was announced months beforehand. The major factor was humiliation and anger over a drugging case, one more of those scandals that continue to undermine bicycle racing.

While sponsors have pulled out before over doping, they have been discreet and usually blamed economic conditions.

Sometimes a sponsor—Festina comes to mind—has even capitalized on a scandal and boasted that the publicity surrounding its team's ouster from the 1998 Tour de France helped sell its watches. Mapei left not with a smirk or alibi but with a rage.

It closed up shop after one of the final races of the season, the insignificant Japan Cup. Most European teams skip the race, since it is so far from home and scheduled when most riders have quit for the winter. But Mapei almost never missed a start. Europe, Asia, Australia, the United States—plan a race, and Mapei riders would be there.

One reason was that the sponsor sells his adhesive bonding all over the world, so an appearance at Le Tour de Langkawi might help win a contract to paste tiles on Malaysian floors.

Another reason was that Mapei had an enormous squad: twenty-eight men on the main team and thirteen on the development team of those under the age of 23. In all, that was twice the number of most other teams, and Mapei kept its workers busy by entering races big and small wherever they were run.

The big number called for a big budget, of course, officially put at €7.63 million, or $7.63 million, and probably closer to €10 million—twice what most other teams spend.

Dr. Giorgio Squinzi, the Mapei owner, did not seem to begrudge a cent of it. An admitted bicycle racing nut, Squinzi hired and developed stars, stayed loyal as they aged, and surrounded them with lavish support and facilities.

Taking a leaf from the Oakland Raiders' playbook, he asked one thing in return: Just win, baby. And win they did. When the season finished, Mapei led the World Cup team rankings comfortably, and its riders had finished first in scores of races, including two big classics. The Tour of Flanders? Winner: Andrea Tafi of Mapei. Liège-Bastogne-Liège? Winner: Paolo Bettini of Mapei. Wearer of the world champion's rainbow-striped jersey most of the season? Oscar Freire of Mapei. Overall World Cup champion? Bettini.

In a decade in the sport, Mapei won more than six-hundred races, dominating the one-day classics. In 1996, for example, it pulled off a rare one-two-three finish in the grueling Paris-Roubaix race. In Johan Museeuw, it had a World Cup champion twice and a world road-race champion once. In Gianluca Bortolami, it had another World Cup champion.

But the team did not often present a challenge in multiday races, especially the Giro d'Italia in its home country or the Tour de France. Its last winner in the Giro was Tony Rominger in 1995. Since then, Mapei, a team built around tough one-day riders, has lacked the combination climber and time trialist who could excel in a three-week race.

Until this year, that is, after it lured Stefano Garzelli, the winner of the 2000 Giro, away from a rival. At age 28, Garzelli was primed for the race this season and flanked by some of Mapei's best support riders. He started as a favorite, won the second stage, and seemed well launched toward overall victory.

Then, disaster. Squinzi, who shocked the sport by declaring a few years ago that nobody could win a three-week race without benefit of illegal performance-enhancing drugs, proved in this case at least to be accurate. Garzelli failed a doping test in the first week and was ousted from the Giro. The outraged sponsor then announced the team's end. Call it pique or call it betrayal, Squinzi is not talking.

So it's all over. Freire has signed with Rabobank in the Netherlands, Tafi with CSC in Denmark. Cadel Evans, a bright young Australian, has joined Telekom in Germany, as has the veteran Daniele Nardello. Miguel Martinez will ride for Phonak in Switzerland and Tom Steels for Landbouwkrediet in Belgium. Bettini will find a new home, as will most of the promising members of the under-23 team.

Luca Scinto has retired, along with Andrea Noe. They will probably be joined by Elio Aggiano and Stefano Zanini. From A to Z, they were part of the Mapei team, the powerhouse Mapei team, now history.

GOOD WHILE IT LASTED

2002

This is an obituary that would have been unimaginable a few years ago: The Grand Prix Midi Libre, 53, one of France's most enjoyable bicycle races, has died after a short and complex ailment.

Never more than the fourth-ranked multiday race in the country, it was known nevertheless for attracting top riders in a tune-up to the Tour de France, for the warm hospitality of its organizers, and for the enchanting countryside it crossed.

The race leaves many friends.

But send no flowers yet, advises Jean-Pierre du Guglliermotte, promotion director for the race's organizer, the Midi Libre newspaper, which is based in Montpellier and circulates in much of southwestern France. He insists that the race is not dead, just sleeping.

"Suspended," he said by telephone. "There will be no race next year, but we hope to resume in 2004."

Of course, he admitted, that was merely a hope. "We are seeking new partners," he said, "but obviously that will not be easy under these difficult conditions."

Those include not just the stumbling French economy and the reluctance of corporations to ante up the €460,000, or $451,000, it costs to organize a five-day race, including prize money and the bills for team hotels and meals, plus police protection on the road.

Staff expenses seemed low since many workers were volunteers, happy to spend a few days in May traveling in congenial company in a low-pressure race.

The Midi Libre—known generally on its turf as the Grand Prix—was the kind of event that was small enough for most teams, journalists, and officials to stay in the same town and spend time together before or over dinner. (They were good dinners, too—usually cassoulet, the white-bean-and-things classic; in Carcassone, add lamb; in Castelnaudary, hold the lamb, add preserved goose and pork.)

There was always somebody connected to the race to recommend the best cassoulet in whichever town the Midi Libre ended its day, and usually somebody to offer a ride to and from the restaurant. In other words, the race verged on a mom-and-pop organization in a globalized world—a recipe not for cassoulet, but for extinction.

The race also had other challenges.

One was that the sport's calendar was changed a year ago to accommodate a rival race in Belgium, not to mention the concurrent Giro d'Italia, and the Midi Libre lost one of its habitual six days of competition.

Another challenge was that since 2000, the owner of the Midi Libre newspaper has been *Le Monde,* no friend to bicycle racing. *Le Monde,* while exemplary in its investigation of drugs in the sport, rarely bothers to report an actual race. Nor does it believe that a newspaper should organize a race.

The possibility of conflict of interest is, in fact, real.

Although newspapers have traditionally sponsored bicycle races, some newspapers have occasionally been suspected of covering up doping cases that would have reflected badly on their race.

Doping—there's that word again.

"Yes," Guglliermotte said with what seemed to be a sigh. "Doping."

The Midi Libre race this year had a prominent doping scandal. "We lost three major sponsors," Guglliermotte said.

Fare thee well, Grand Prix Midi Libre. It has been won by champions and by lesser riders, too. Whoever won, it was always a good time and a good race, which can serve as its epitaph.

SUPER FAN

2003

While Lance Armstrong has many fans from the United States cheering for him on the sides of the roads the Tour de France is traveling, Sammarye Lewis is hands-down the most fervent.

Forget the guy draped in the American flag who sometimes runs alongside Armstrong as he labors uphill.

Another noncontender is the fellow who wears what appear to be steer horns to celebrate Armstrong's Texas heritage. Pay no attention to the man who is wearing and selling "Lance Is God" T-shirts.

From tip to toe, nobody equals Sammarye Lewis.

Tip, first: She always wears a yellow cap, to match Armstrong's usual leader's jersey, with the words "Go Lance" written on it.

Toe, next: Her right big one is painted yellow with a "5" for Armstrong's goal of five successive Tour victories, and it has the Lone Star of Texas on it. (The other toes on that foot are colored a relatively lackluster red and blue.)

"It's wearing a little thin right now," she said, but the big toe on her left foot bears a painting of the U.S. flag "with little sequins for the stars."

"The gal who does my nails painted those before I left for France," Lewis explained. "She said 'I'm going to do a treat for you.'"

That was back home in San Jose, California, where Lewis works at her paid job as an independent contractor, helping to coordinate volunteers for organizers of major American bicycling races.

That is also where she had her left index finger painted yellow. And where she had the tattoo "Go Lance" put on her left calf.

And where she made the big yellow sign that says, you guessed it, "Go Lance" that she has raised over her head in France for the last three Tours.

Lewis, a joyful woman of what the French call "a certain age," one she does not disclose, says she has lots of fun with these demonstrations.

But her devotion to Armstrong also has a serious side. She runs one Web site dedicated to him and another dedicated to his team, U.S. Postal Service.

"The one for Lance is called the lancearmstrongfanclub.com for lack of a better name," she said in an interview. "I do searches, and everything about Lance I will put a link to it and say, 'Hey, catch this.' I have a lot of photos up that I've taken, and I have a spot where fans can send in their photos."

The site gets about ten thousand visits a week, she said. "I think Lance realizes I do a lot of work for him," she said. "Maintaining a Web site is a big job, a couple or three hours a day, at least.

"I just started in September www.postiefans.com, and that focuses on the team. It's basically an information and referral site, and it kind of goes out of business during the Tour because I'm over here."

While in France, she is writing a daily report for Armstrong's own site, lancearmstrong.com, on an unpaid basis.

"There are eight of us who are writing, and it's very, very popular with the fans," she said. "We're getting an incredible amount of appreciative e-mail.

"I kind of give a fan's perspective of what happens at the Tour, find some human-interest stories, just odds and ends. If I'm near the team bus, I'll say Lance looks really good or the guys are relaxed, whatever.

"It's not a spy-and-tell about the team. It's what it's like to be a fan, the people you meet, the obstacles you run into."

Those obstacles include often having to drive alone from start to finish for all twenty stages over three weeks.

"I spend most of my time lost," she admitted, "especially finding my hotels. They're pretty far from the finishes, and I put in a lot of miles.

"But, c'est le Tour," she said, nearly exhausting her French. "I'm having a ball."

She added that her son and daughter, both adults and "great kids," support her work.

"They just love that I'm doing this, that I'm traveling, that I've created a niche for myself."

Why Armstrong as her labor of love?

"I've been a fan of his since his cancer struggle," which began in 1996 and included chemotherapy because his testicular cancer had spread to his brain, abdomen, and lungs.

"I knew of him before that, but I can't say I was a rabid fan. I was intrigued by his courage, his tenacity."

Bright and bubbly, Lewis is proud that in her relation with Armstrong she is all give, no take, which she ascribes to being "respectful and not pushy and never asking Lance for anything."

He does answer her infrequent e-mails instantly, she said, and has invited her to a sponsors' dinner during a training camp in Arizona.

"He's a very thoughtful man," she said, "very lovely."

Lewis added that an article once reported that "Lance looked out the team bus window and saw me standing there with my yellow banner and said to Tyler Hamilton: 'See that fan out there? She's the only fan who doesn't want a piece of me.'

"So they invited me into the bus, and I met the team."

That's where it began. Will it end when Armstrong retires?

"No, I'll probably continue to follow the Postal team as long as it exists," she said.

PROBLEM CHILD

2003

Belgian fans of bicycle racing rank among the most intense in Europe, as supercharged as the Italians and the Basques. Those in Flanders are the most fervid in Belgium.

It was no surprise, then, to see the hordes at the race Het Volk waving the flag of Flanders, yellow with a black lion rampant. Or the dozens wearing red caps that proclaimed them "Supporter Peter Van Petegem," the Lotto rider who has won Het Volk three times, or the roving squads that kept disrupting television interviews by raising huge posters behind riders, squarely in the cameras' view, that said "Nico Mattan Fan Club," honoring the solid Cofidis rider.

But how to account for the platoon with banners that read "Frank Vandenbroucke, Allez VDB"? How to deconstruct the scrawl on the roads that said "VDB is Back, God is Back'"?

The divinity in question ranks 571st in the world. "God?" said the Belgian journalist who furnished the translation from Flemish. "He's not God."

No, not now, but once, most fans felt, he was nearly so. Four years ago, he ranked third in the world.

Vandenbroucke, who is 28, has already recorded forty-two victories, including the esteemed Liège-Bastogne-Liège classic and the Paris-Nice race. He also won Het Volk in 2000.

Since then, disaster. Too old to be referred to any longer as the problem child of Belgian racing, Vandenbroucke has been dogged by accidents, illnesses, doping allegations, lawsuits, suspicion, surliness, and suspensions. He has changed teams five times, an abnormally high number, even abandoning one led by his uncle, since he turned professional at 20.

At Cofidis, which signed him to a big contract five years ago, he was known as "the headache."

For the past three years, just when he should have been approaching his peak, he has done nothing but make terrible headlines. The man known in all of them as VDB is a textbook case in disaster control.

"The last three years he was not so good," admitted his latest directeur sportif, the kindly and patient Patrick Léfevère of the new Quick Step team in Belgium, who rescued Vandenbroucke from sulky exile with the Lampre team in Italy for the 2002 season. In return, VDB was busted last winter by the Belgian police, who found illegal performance-enhancing drugs in his home. They were for his dog, he said.

That defense earned him a suspension by the bicycling federation in Flanders, where Vandenbroucke lives, near the French border.

Despite his name, Vandenbroucke is not Flemish. His family speaks French. Wallonia, the French part of Belgium, did not honor the suspension imposed by the Flemish-speaking federation, and Vandenbroucke was free to ride in the Walloon part of Belgium. (It is not true, although widely reported, that in a daily stage of the Tour of Wallonia that passed through a village half-Flemish and half-Walloon, the pack rode on one side of the street—Flemish—and he rode on the other—Walloon. "Folklore," another Belgian journalist said.)

What is true is that the International Cycling Union also suspended him, that he appealed and more or less won but sat out most of the season. Last autumn he returned and finished second in the minor Tour of Poland and then crashed and broke an elbow in the Paris-Tours race, ending his season on the accustomed downbeat. That made three years without a major victory for the rider once considered the next great talent.

"He did it to himself," Léfevère said in an interview. He is kindly and patient only up to a point. "It's his own fault," he said of Vandenbroucke. "Shame on him.

"There's a lot of doubt about him," Léfevère said, "but he's on a good path now. I've paid him already for a lot of months to get to this point. We're hopeful."

The suspension in Flanders has just expired and Vandenbroucke is free to ride there with his team. While he has competed this new season in France, he was not able even to train with his Quick Step colleagues in Flanders but had to ride alone when they scouted the routes for spring classics.

Het Volk is not one of these. At 200 kilometers, it is not long enough to be a major one-day race, and with ten short but steep climbs, it is not difficult enough, either. But the weather is always bad—cold and usually rainy—and those ten cobblestoned hills make it a race for tough men.

Vandenbroucke showed his toughness in the race. Despite a tender left knee from a race in France, he finished fourth and came across the line with his arms up in a victory signal when his Quick Step teammates took two of the three places ahead of him, including the top one.

The winner was Johan Museeuw, at 38 still the king of the classics and semi-classics. Afterward, he said the results had proved that he could still win races. And, he added, they proved that Vandenbroucke was back.

"We hope to see the same Vandenbroucke in the classics," Lefevère said later. "He did a very good race." For now at least, Léfevère looked carefree.

IMPORTED TALENT

2002

Anybody seeking symbols of the fragility of professional bicycle racing in France had to look no further than the official presentation of the fdjeux. com team, which, after twenty-five victories this season, proclaims itself as the country's best among the six teams in the sport's First Division.

To pounding music, a video of the season's triumphs kept returning to the major ones: the French national championship, two gold medals in the world track championships, a gold medal in the Commonwealth Games, and a stage victory in the Tour de France. Heady stuff, no?

On the stage of an auditorium in a Paris suburb, the riders looked proud. So did their team officials and representatives of the major sponsor, La Française des Jeux, the French lottery. Even dignitaries of the team's twenty secondary sponsors, from Lapierre bicycles and sportswear down to Cristaline water, looked proud.

That's the purpose of the annual and hallowed ceremony of an official presentation: to show off the riders and introduce the new ones; to boast about what a great season it was and how the next one will be even better; to thank anybody who poured goods, services, and money into the €3.5 million, or $3.59 million, budget, set to rise by a million euros in 2003.

A seat down front, please, for the people who make the tape that gets wrapped around team handlebars! Everybody connected with the team traditionally shows up. But this time they didn't. Four riders among the twenty-one were missing.

One of them was Jacky Durand, king of the kamikaze attack. The rider who never saw a road he didn't like to speed down solo arrived late, earned a glare from his directeur sportif, Marc Madiot, and blithely explained that he had been stuck in traffic.

The three others had a better excuse. From a velodrome in Australia, Brad McGee appeared on closed-circuit television to wish the crowd a good time and talk about how he, Baden Cooke, and Matthew Wilson, all three of them Australians, were spending what is the summer Down Under and absolutely not neglecting their training.

On the stage, Jimmy Casper, fdjeux.com's top French sprinter and sixth in the world championship road race, and Nicolas Vogondy, the French champion, listened intently. So did Sandy Casar, second in Paris-Nice.

Their accomplishments are not negligible, but came nowhere near matching those of the team leader speaking on the big screen. Gold medal on the track in the world championships and in the Commonwealth Games, and a Tour de France stage victory all belong to the 26-year-old McGee. Cooke, 24, had a good year as well, winning nine races, finishing second in the Tour's final and showcase stage on the Champs-Elyseés in Paris, and vaulting from 373rd place in international rankings to 21st. Wilson, 25, won a stage in the Tour de l'Avenir and wore the leader's jersey there for two days.

In short, the three are major parts of the engine of the French team and none of them is French.

The situation is the same on most other French teams. A Scot, David Millar, 26, is the leader of Cofidis; Jaan Kirsipuu, 33, a Lithuanian, leads AG2R; and Jens Voigt, 31, a German, Stuart O'Grady, 29, an Australian, and Thor Hushovd, 25, a Norwegian, lead Crédit Agricole. Only Jean Delatour and the former Bonjour, now Brioches la Boulangère, are headed by Frenchmen, and both teams are feeble.

Where are the French stars? With Laurent Jalabert newly retired and Richard Virenque in decline, who succeeds them? The answer is that nobody does, at least not in the foreseeable future.

These are barren times for bicycle racing in France, a cradle of the sport and home to many of its former champions. Now they come from all over the map: eastern Europe in particular but also Australia, Scandinavia, the United States, Germany, and Colombia, in addition to such traditional spawning grounds as Italy, Spain, Belgium, Switzerland, and the Netherlands.

Everywhere, that is, but France. Why not?

The reasons are complex and, at the same time, perhaps simplistic. Bicycle racing appears to no longer fit the French psyche, which now rejects suffering and sacrifice, the sport's hallmarks. If a young French athlete is looking for social mobility, he takes up tennis. If the lure is simply money, try soccer.

Why spend seven or eight hours a day in the rain on a bicycle when a young athlete can spend a couple of hours in the sun, swatting a ball, or ninety minutes twice a week running up and down a field, booting one? Who needs the cobblestones of Paris-Roubaix, the snows of the Tour of Flanders, the everlasting climbs in the Alps and Pyrenees, the dinky salaries, the temptation to use illegal drugs, the shoddy hotels, the monotonous food, the pain?

So the numbers decrease. The 130 French professionals in 2002 will drop to 115 in 2003, with only eleven of them neo-professionals in their first year in the sport.

Sponsors are increasingly difficult to find—BigMat will withdraw after 2003 and Jean Delatour is yearning to cede its place on the jersey to anybody with a heftier wallet—and races, like the Midi Libre, are disappearing.

The lights are going out, no doubt about it. What if they gave a Tour de France and no French rider showed up?

HAIL AND FAREWELL

2002

The twenty-five teams in the Paris-Tours race mounted the podium before the start and their riders were introduced by name and major laurel, with nearly everybody getting his fifteen seconds of fame.

"X, a winner of a stage in the Tour of Poland," said the announcer as a rider waved. "Y, the revelation of Paris-Bourges last year"—another wave. "Z, a valuable teammate, always a battler"—ditto.

Then it was Laurent Jalabert's turn as his CSC team faced the small crowd in the hamlet of St. Arnoult en Yvelines near Paris.

"World champion in the time trial, 1997; French road-race champion, 1998; winner of Milan-San Remo, 1995; Tour of Lombardy, 1997; Flèche Wallonne, 1995 and 1997."

The announcer paused.

"Winner of the Clásica San Sebastián, 2002; Paris-Nice, 1995, 1996, 1997; Midi Libre, 1996; Route du Sud, 1996; Tour de Romandie, 1999; Milan-Turin, 1997; Classique des Alpes, 1996 and 1998."

Out of sight behind the grandstand, Johan Museeuw, the grand Belgian rider and ordinarily the most phlegmatic of men, smilingly whirled his arm in a cheerleader's "let 'er rip" gesture.

"Winner of the Vuelta a España, 1995; winner of three stages in the Giro d'Italia and four stages in the Tour de France. Tour points champion in 1992 and 1995; top climber, 2001 and 2002. No. 1 in the world for four years."

He paused again. "And now, today, in his last race on French roads. Next Sunday he ends his glorious career in the world championships in Belgium."

Jalabert smiled, whispered something to the teammate next to him—probably "You've been hearing this a lot"—and then thanked the crowd for coming to see him one last time.

Six hours later, at the end of the race, Jalabert was summoned to the podium in Tours, given a celebratory plaque, and heard his record enumerated again.

He would still be standing on the platform in the Loire Valley city if the list had included such minor races as the Tour of the Haut Var, 1998 and 2002; the Catalan Week, 1999 and 2000; the Tour of the Basque Country,

1999; the Criterium International, 1995; and the Tour of Catalonia, 1995; plus the innumerable criteriums, or exhibition races, he has won in the two months of his farewell tour of the European cycling map.

It's true: Jalabert, who will turn 34 on November 30, has only one race left. He said during the Tour that he would retire after the world championship road race even if he won it.

If that 256-kilometer race, to be held over a flat course, is determined by a mass sprint, as expected, he has almost no chance. His best sprinting days are a decade behind him.

But the twelve-man French team is hoping he can mount a strong attack over the final two hours, the sort of breakaway that almost carried him to two Tour de France stage victories this year.

It's a long shot, especially if the sprinters' national teams work together to prevent individual offensives and set up a mass final charge to the line.

But don't underestimate Jalabert's determination. As he said recently after he went on a long breakaway in a minor French race: "I tried to put on a good show. That's my style of riding. Until the end, I want to set an example."

He admits that the final race in Belgium will be difficult.

"The season is beginning to feel awfully long for me," he said last month. "I'm worried that I'm no longer at the level where I can be at the front in the toughest races.

"But I have to stay focused. There's only one race that still counts: the last one."

He has been looking forward to that race since his announcement early in the Tour of his pending retirement.

"It's over," he said then simply. He meant his fourteen-year career as a professional, from 1989 to 1991 with a French team, from 1992 to 2000 with a Spanish team, and for two years with a Danish team.

Even though he was by far the greatest French rider of his generation, his popularity at home fluctuated. Partly that was because he rode so many years in Spain for the ONCE team and competed mainly in Spanish races, not French ones, missing out on a lot of publicity.

Partly, too, it was because he never came closer to winning the Tour de France than his fourth place in 1995. Despite the two king-of-the-mountains jerseys he won, he always vaporized in the Tour's highest mountains; those jerseys were acquired on secondary climbs.

Finally, the rider known to all Frenchmen as Jaja was reserved, private, almost deliberately bland.

He never went public with his reasons for leaving the ONCE team, reportedly a growing distaste with authoritarian rule. Nor did he often discuss his home life with his wife and four children in Switzerland, a refuge from French taxes.

Of his flameouts in the Tour de France mountains, he said nothing, simply soldiered on. He never sought public sympathy even after his spectacular fall in the 1994 Tour, when a policeman taking a photograph caused a mass crash near the finish line.

Jalabert, who lost a couple of teeth and broke his jaw and cheekbone, needed three hours of surgery and six weeks to recover. Then it was back to the races, back to his job, like any victim of an industrial accident.

"That crash changed me," he says now. "Racing became more important. I might have lost everything, and without the bicycle, what would I have done?"

Until the crash, he was a moderately successful rider. The next year he won an amazing twenty-two races, became No. 1 in the sport, and stayed there for years.

Anybody seeking a detailed record of that time had only to show up at Jalabert's final races before the world championship and listen to his introduction.

CIPO'S FIRST RETIREMENT

2002

Who could have guessed that underneath the designer stubble, the Armani suits, and the Via Veneto good looks; apart from the cheetah he kept as a house pet, his disco prowling, and frequent service as a judge at beauty contests; away from such celebrated friends as Ronaldo and Michael Schumacher, all Mario Cipollini sought, like you and me, was love and respect?

He wasn't getting any, he said, despite more than 170 victories in bicycle races during his fourteen-year professional career. Or maybe he wasn't getting enough—Cipo was a tad unclear when he announced his retirement.

Chalk that up to emotional stress. He made the retirement official at a news conference in Florence a week later, just after the Tour de France sprinters' festival that Cipollini dominated for half a dozen years. He has won twelve stages, far from the forty he has won in the Giro d'Italia back home, but still as many as anybody else still competing.

And how did the Tour organizers reward him? He choked on the words: No invitation to his Saeco team the previous year, no invitation to his new Acqua & Sappone team in 2002. He tossed his head and, with it, the flowing mane that has won him the nickname of the Lion King. (He prefers Super Mario, after the video game, or Il Magnifico.)

Cipollini took the high road, not mentioning that his personal style was far too flamboyant for the sober Tour organizers. They did not appreciate it in 1997 when he wheeled out a yellow bicycle to match the overall leader's jersey he wore for four days. Still less did they approve of the toga he wore to a stage start in 1999 to signify that, for the moment, he was the race's emperor. As for the skeleton skinsuit—mimicking every last bone in his body—that he dons for time trials, brrrrr.

Nor did Tour officials comment on his fashion sense. Last year the excuse was that he had never finished a Tour, always bowing out before or early in the mountains, where sprinters bring up the rear, rather than lead the charge across the finish line. He was also, the organizers said, too old at 34; it was time to turn the page for a younger crew.

Finally, and most unkindly, they noted that he was not winning as often as he had just a few years ago.

So this year, Cipo pointed out, he won the Milan-San Remo classic, finished top 10 in the Tour of Flanders, and won Ghent-Wevelgem. He held the jersey of the overall leader of the World Cup, racked up six victories in the Giro, and was the clear favorite for the world championship road race in Belgium—and still he and his team were not invited.

Basta, he said. Finito. The Tour de France had dishonored him. His team had let him down as well: It had no power, perhaps even no will, to set things right with the Tour. How could he continue in a sport full of so many deficienti? He couldn't, of course.

How could he continue to make so many sacrifices by training and racing instead of spending his time at the beach or at the many parties his friends invited him to? He couldn't, of course.

Ciao, he explained. "I'll be back only if the sport misses me."

His snit lasted a little more than a month. Moved, endlessly moved by what he described as an outpouring of love, respect, and admiration from fans and fellow riders, Cipo announced in August that he had found the spark to continue racing his bicycle. By September he was fanning the spark into a bonfire at the Vuelta a España.

He won the third stage of that race, looking less strained than the dozen other riders in the sprint but, abnormally, hunched over his handlebars. The next day he made victory look simple, crossing the line in his familiar pose of upraised arms and fanned fingers, like a pastor blessing his flock. Three days later, he did it again—same pose, same ease of triumph.

"It wasn't difficult," he said, "because for the first time in my career, I have a team entirely at my service."

Cipollini always says that about his latest team and each time it's true. If the conditions are right, who wouldn't build a team around such a dominant sprinter?

That's what Italy is thinking. For the world championship road race in Belgium, the first one in years without a serious climb, the Italians have designated Cipollini as their leader and main hope. Since everybody is predicting that the race will end in a massive sprint, who better to finish it than Cipollini and bring Italy its first victory since 1992?

This will be the first time in his career he has been selected to represent Italy in the world championship road race. Always run on a circuit—

a course that is lapped many times—the road race has heretofore included at least one hill that must be climbed more than a dozen times.

Hills are not Cipo's terrain. In tabletop northern Belgium, there are no hills.

"The world championship is the objective of my life," he said. "The course suits me. Since I was a kid, I've dreamed of the rainbow jersey of the world champion. Something deep inside me says it finally can happen.

"Whatever I said during the Tour de France, you can forget that."

CIPO'S SECOND RETIREMENT

2005

Once again, Mario Cipollini has announced his definite, absolute, unswerving, and irrevocable decision to retire, and this time he means it. Probably.

Unlike previous decisions to hang his bicycle in his garage forever, which were always made in pique, this one sounded sincere. "Announcing my withdrawal one week before the Giro d'Italia is a painful but honest decision," he said. "The public will understand.

"I would have liked to be at the start of the Giro, looking for victory again, fighting for the pink jersey," he said. "Maybe an 'old man' like me, who has given a lot to cycling and has also received a lot, has to recognize when is the right moment to stop."

Everything he said is accurate.

Cipollini would indeed have liked to race in the Giro, where he holds the record of forty-two stage victories, all of them sprints, and where he has worn the leader's pink jersey for six days. The Giro is his favorite showcase.

Further, he is an old man for a racer—he turned 38 in March—and, in a career that began in 1989, he has been a flamboyant figure in the sport, as renowned for his 180 victories as for his flashy dress and lifestyle. Who else would have dared show up for the start of a stage in the Tour de France, where he had twelve daily victories over the years and six days in the leader's yellow jersey, in a toga, as emperor Cipollini did after winning four consecutive days in 1999? Who else traveled with, and rode on, a yellow bicycle when he led the Tour and a green one when he was in the jersey of the same color as points leader?

He liked going to nightclubs in the off-season, when he also judged beauty contests and, to hear him tell it, tended his pet cheetah at home with his wife and children. He boasted that his closets contained a pair of shoes for each day of the year and possibly that many suits, too.

He backed up all the theater: the Giro and Tour triumphs, a victory in the esteemed Milan-San Remo classic in 2002 and in the world championship road race that same year.

Recent years have been nearly barren. In 2003 he registered only four victories, although two of them were in the Giro, and broke his tie of forty-one stage victories with Alfredo Binda, a star in the 1940s. Cipollini scored only twice in 2004, in the Tour of the Mediterranean and the Tour of Georgia, neither the ample stage that he prefers. He has seen victory in 2005 only in a stage of the Tour of Qatar and in a small Italian race.

But why is he quitting now? Part of the answer is that he is no longer in the class of such a top sprinter as Alessandro Petacchi, the Italian who won nine stages in the Giro in 2004 and has nearly a dozen victories in 2005. Cipollini does not like to finish second, at best, in a sprint.

Another part is that he is riding for the strong Liquigas team after three years with weak teams. They had no hope for any victory but one by Cipollini and therefore dedicated themselves to his needs; Liquigas, having potential stage winners in Danilo Di Luca and Magnus Backstedt, will not stake everything on the first week of sprints.

So it's over for Cipo. Assuredly. Certainly. And yet.

What if those Italian fans, who worship him, rebel? "The public will understand," he said, but what if it doesn't? What if the fans, known in Italy as the *tifosi,* put up such a clamor before the Giro starts in Reggio Calabria that Super Mario has no choice but to appear at the starting line?

Let's hear it, *tifosi.*

THE CRICKET

2003

It was a tough week but at the end of it the Cricket was still chirping.

The Cricket is Paolo Bettini, who gained his nickname possibly because of his size (small), his looks (his eyes do bug out a little), or his animation (he talks volubly, he smiles a lot). He is also ranked the No. 1 bicycle racer in the world, he is the Italian national champion, and he has just secured his second consecutive title as winner of the World Cup series of classics.

The 29-year-old Bettini, the leader of the Quick Step team in Belgium, has gone where no man has gone before: He won three one-day World Cup classics in 2003, starting with Milan-San Remo in March, followed by the Hew Classic in Hamburg and the Clásica San Sebastián in Spain, both in August, with a third place in the Championship of Zurich later that same month.

He might have won Liège-Bastogne-Liège in April, as he did twice in four years, if he had not crashed in the Ghent-Wevelgem race beforehand and ripped ligaments in his left shoulder, necessitating an operation and a long recuperation period. Recuperation was on his mind following the final World Cup race, the Tour of Lombardy in northern Italy.

"I haven't had much time to rest," Bettini said after he finished in the mid-20s. "I'm still jetlagged from the world championships in Canada and I haven't had any sleep because my daughter cries every three hours."

His daughter Veronica, his first child, was then three weeks old.

Those world championships made for a tough week before the Tour of Lombardy.

First, Bettini, the overwhelming favorite, finished fourth when he was slow to respond to an attack in the last 4 kilometers by the eventual winner, Igor Astarloa, a Spaniard with the Saeco team in Italy.

What upset the *tifosi,* the normally hyperventilating Italian fans, was that Astarloa launched a Bettini kind of attack, waiting till near the end on a final climb to show his power and zip away.

Just the Sunday before the world championships, Bettini had demonstrated the move in the Paris-Tours race, where he was caught by a pack with the wind at their backs.

It was supposed to be different at the world championships in Canada, where the Italian team was built around Bettini. But he hesitated and all was lost.

"After the finish, the bad thing was that I still had good legs," Bettini said in an interview before the Tour of Lombardy. "That was a sign for me that I had done something wrong.

"Before the world's, you could have complimented me on my tactical abilities, but not so much afterward. Everybody says I ride intelligently, that I use good tactics, but in the world's I wonder if I did right.

"Everything was going great until 4 kilometers from the finish when Astarloa attacked," Bettini said. "When he went, I hesitated for a second—I didn't think it was right to respond immediately, I thought it would be better to wait and then go.

"I thought some of the others would take the initiative," he continued. "So I made the split-second decision not to go."

That translated into a five-second deficit at the finish.

Worse was to come.

Flushed with victory, Astarloa, 27, confided to the Spanish press that Bettini had offered him a monetary bribe, amount unspecified, for the two of them to work together and burn off the opposition before the finish.

"Coming into the final climb, Bettini offered me money to collaborate with him," Astarloa was quoted as having said. "He suggested we break away together and fight out the gold medal between us. I couldn't accept that."

Tipping the scales, the Spaniard added, was not only his moral abhorrence of any such illegality but also the knowledge that Bettini would easily beat him in a two-man sprint.

Call it situational ethics.

Speaking at his team's hotel in Cantu before the Tour of Lombardy, his eyes flashing as he rose from his seat and began to dance around, Bettini called it a lie.

"It's true that we spoke at the foot of the last climb," he said. "I asked him how he was doing because he had crashed and he said he was hurting a bit all over, but was OK.

"We also talked about collaborating. That's normal in a race like the world's," where the riders represent not their usual trade teams but their countries. "There's some collaboration.

"But we didn't talk about money," Bettini insisted. "Absolutely not.

Astarloa has called me and said this is all a mistake. There was never any talk of money."

Astarloa now agrees.

Standing before a huge poster showing him crossing the finish in the world's with his arms outstretched and the words "World Champion 2003" in English, Italian, and Spanish, Astarloa said at a news conference at the Como Yacht Club before Lombardy that it was indeed a mistake.

"I want to close the polemics and say I'm sorry," he said in his squeaky voice. "It was a linguistic misunderstanding. He never offered me money."

In the rainbow-striped jersey of the world champion, the Spaniard then posed for the photographers with a big smile and a thumbs-up gesture. He held the pose for shot after shot.

He also brushed off his role in yet another incipient scandal. According to French and Italian newspapers, Astarloa was one of four riders at the world championships who were asked to give urine samples as well as blood samples to prove that they were not using prohibited drugs.

"It's irrelevant," he said. "I've never had any problems and I'm facing this with tranquillity."

The results of the urine test should be known shortly. A positive finding could cost Astarloa his gold medal and rainbow jersey.

Insisting that he has been cleared of any bribery, Bettini has gone home with his wife and baby to take a couple of months off and sleep by the feeding schedule.

He's fine with the world, he says. No worries. Astarloa, meanwhile, is waiting for the phone to ring.

RETURN OF THE DOMINATOR

2003

Shaking off a crash that left him lying on the road, Lance Armstrong the dominator reappeared in the Tour de France, winning the major stage in the Pyrenees, significantly widening his overall lead and taking a big step toward his fifth consecutive victory.

After he hit a spectator and went down early on the last of six climbs, he said later, he told himself, "Lance, if you want to win the Tour, attack."

Attack, he did. Armstrong remounted, sped to the main group, and then survived another mishap when his bicycle malfunctioned and his right foot came out of its pedal. Once he corrected his wobble, he made it back to the small group of his main opponents.

Led by Jan Ullrich, the German in second place overall, they had slowed at the urging of Tyler Hamilton, Armstrong's former lieutenant and now the leader of the CSC team, who waved his hands and yelled at the group. The sport's unwritten code of chivalry dictates that nobody takes advantage of the leader when he has crashed.

After Armstrong returned to the front and order was restored, he raced away and nobody could catch him. There were about 9 kilometers left in the 13.4-kilometer climb to the resort of Luz-Ardiden. His face set in a grimace of determination, Armstrong rode as he did in the mountains in his four Tour victories and as he had not done previously in this year's race—with facility, power, and suppleness.

"I wasn't angry when I attacked," he said. "I was desperate to gain time on Ullrich before the time trial."

At the finish, he was 40 seconds ahead of Ullrich. Combined with a 20-second time bonus for his victory, minus the 8 seconds Ullrich gained for third place, Armstrong jumped from a 15-second lead at the start of the day to a lead of 1:07 at the end of it.

With huge crowds watching at the finish, Armstrong crossed the line shrouded in fog. On the way up, he overtook the lone survivor of an early two-man breakaway, Sylvain Chavanel, a Frenchman with Brioches la Boulangère. As he passed him, Armstrong patted Chavenel on the back for his long exploit, only a small part of an epic stage.

Discussing his crash, Armstrong said at a news conference, "It was my fault for riding too close on the right side of the road." The strap on the bag of a spectator leaning into the road caught in the Texan's handlebars and down Armstrong went. Crashing atop him was Iban Mayo, a Spaniard with Euskaltel, who was also impeded later when Armstrong's foot came out of the pedal.

Mayo showed the same spunk Armstrong did, finishing second in the stage, 40 seconds behind, and remaining in fifth place overall.

Despite the triumph and show of restored force after a week of subpar performances, Armstrong was wary of talking about a fifth victory before the final of four stages in the Pyrenees and a long time trial. "The Tour finishes on the Champs-Elysées," he said, repeating his mantra. "Ullrich is a great rider. Anything is still possible."

He was asked if he knew that Ullrich, the leader of the Bianchi team, and other riders high in the standings had waited for him after the crash and whether he would have done the same.

"I did know that," he replied. "Would I have done the same? I did do the same when Ullrich crashed on the Peyresourde two years ago. I waited. What he did today was the correct thing. What I did then was the correct thing.

"I appreciate what he did. As we say, 'What goes around, comes around.'"

As he spoke, his body language was totally changed from the last few days, when he looked weary and disappointed. Now he was the old Armstrong, in command and confident.

But, he continued, "This has been a crisis-filled Tour. There have been a lot of strange things happening, things I haven't talked about.

"This is a Tour of too many problems—close calls, near misses. I wish it would stop. I wish I could have some uneventful days."

All in all, he concluded, even if this was not an uneventful day, there were compensations, like the solid hold he now had on the leader's yellow jersey and his sixteenth stage victory in the Tour de France. "It was a good day," he decided.

HOLD THE PUNS

2004

If sarcasm is the lowest form of humor, making puns with somebody's name ranks closely behind. Ask Iban Mayo.

On second thought, don't ask Mayo. Since he's Spanish and the word for mayonnaise in his language—"mahonesa" (sometimes "mayonesa")—is never shortened to "mayo" and since, in any case, his name is pronounced MY-oh, he wouldn't get the joke.

Not that there is a joke, despite what headline writers for the English-language press and Internet sites think. All spring, as he chalked up one victory after another, it was "Hold the Mayo," "Can't Hold the Mayo," "Mayo on a Roll," and "Mayo Spreads It Around."

Enough already. These puns don't cut the mustard.

Despite his 89th place overall in the Tour de France and deficit of 15 minutes, 2 seconds behind the yellow jersey after a crash, Iban Mayo, the 26-year-old leader of the Euskaltel team from Spain, is no laughing matter but a rider to relish. On one of his strong days, his rivals can do no better than play catch-up.

Not that this was one of them. The Tour enjoyed the first of two days off before it ended in Paris and the riders spent their time sleeping, holding news conferences, seeing friends and family, and going on short training rides.

Those rides were on flat roads, which is not Mayo's favored terrain. His is uphill, as in the long stage coming over nine climbs in the Massif Central.

Mayo first rose to prominence in 2001, when he won the Midi Libre and Classique des Alpes races in France. The next year he was fifth in the Vuelta a España, and in 2003 he was sixth in the Tour de France and won the climbing stage to Alpe d'Huez.

He has blossomed in 2004. In May, he won two of three stages and the overall title in the Alcobendas Classic, finishing second by three seconds in a short time trial; then the one-day Subida al Naranco and then the five-day Tour of Asturias. Those races, all in Spain, were staged over eight days.

People began wondering if he was peaking too early for the Tour, but he thought not.

"I've been asked a hundred times, and I keep saying the same thing: No," he said. "My preparation has gone wonderfully, but I still have room to improve.

"Last year at the Dauphiné," he said, referring to the weeklong mountainous race in France, "I was better than I am now, so I still have room to improve."

He finished that Dauphiné in second place, behind Lance Armstrong.

Improve he did. In June, Mayo finished second in the Classique des Alpes and won the Dauphiné Libéré, including the prologue for the second successive year and the individual time trial up the dreaded Mont Ventoux. Those victories made him a center of attention in Spain, especially in the bicycle-crazy Basque region, where he hails from and still lives.

"He's been overwhelmed," Mayo's agent, Sabino Angoitia, told the Spanish sports daily *As*. "Everybody is talking about him, asking for his autograph. He went to the supermarket and had to leave without buying anything because he was so surrounded by fans."

Despite his dark, curly hair and the two golden rings he wears in his left ear, a combination that often leads to comparisons with a rock star, Mayo seems to be a down-home type who is finding it difficult to believe that so many Spaniards feel he may eventually be the successor to the country's last champion, Miguel Indurain.

Helping him keep his balance is his Euskaltel team, a Basque formation so closed to foreigners that riders must have spent three years with a Basque amateur team to be admitted. Euskaltel's riders live in the area around Bilbao and San Sebastián and, among themselves, speak Euskera, the Basque language.

Since the crash just before the Tour reached the cobblestones in the north of France left him so far down in the overall standings, Mayo's accomplishments will seemingly have to be limited to stage victories in the Massif Central, the Pyrenees, or the Alps.

"His Tour is not over," Armstrong said last week. "He'll be a factor, especially in the Pyrenees."

In other words, "Mayo Can Still Lay It on Thick."

THE PEOPLE'S CHOICE

2003

People from Bernard Thévenet's native hamlet of Le Guidon in Burgundy, those from the surrounding village of St. Julien de Civry, and everybody in the small world of bicycle racing who likes Thévenet, which is everybody who knows him, turned out to honor him.

That the occasion was a free lunch of prime Charolais beef from the region was possibly incidental. Nevertheless, the slabs of pan-fried steak accompanied by potato pancakes and washed down with Beaujolais recalled the lost days when the Tour de France was often punctuated with buffets for the press as the race transited the home town of a legendary, or even semi-legendary, rider.

It was fitting that the party was a throwback. Thévenet is a throwback himself, a reminder of the times, now decades past, when the main hope for young French athletes to escape from the farm or factory was to become a bicycle racer. Now they play tennis or soccer and, unlike the racers who often earn no more than the legal minimum wage, make enough money in a season to buy that farm or factory.

Thévenet says that when he was 13 years old in 1961, he watched the Tour de France storm by his family farm in Le Guidon and was so dazzled by the flash of colors, the performance of the riders, and the enthusiasm of the fans that he decided on the spot to become a rider himself.

He did become one, and a fine one too: He won the Tour de France in 1975 and 1977 and was the French champion in 1973. Thévenet was a tough, determined climber who lived down a scandal when he admitted that he had used cortisone to soften his suffering in the mountains, and then became a team director. For more than a decade he has been a race commentator on French television.

Because of that job, he had to leave the party early by helicopter to make it to the finish in Lyon, 107 kilometers away. Before he left, and before some overzealous Burgundians broke into native dance rather than eating, he talked a bit about himself and the Tour.

In its 100 years, he said, the race has passed the family farm three times, but never while he was riding in it. He did not mention, as many others did, that in 1970 he was weeping on his mother's shoulder at the farm because he had not made his Peugeot team's roster for the Tour when a call came through that a rider was sick and that Thévenet was his replacement. Nor did he say that he won a stage in that Tour.

What he wanted to discuss was the farm, a two-story stone building flanked by two barns, all of them with red tile roofs. Out back is a big field holding, of course, cows.

"We raised Charolais sheep, too," he said. "But not here. For them, we had to use fields a little far from home."

Although he left the farm at the age of 22, more than thirty years ago, for a home in the city of Grenoble, he is not forgotten in the hamlet of Le Guidon—the word for bicycle handlebars—or in the village of St. Julien de Civry. The bread at his party came from the Alloin Bakery in St. Julien's main square, the Place Bernard Thévenet.

A TOUR ROOKIE

2003

Thomas Nee is riding in his first Tour de France, working hard, enjoying himself, and learning, learning, learning.

"It's wonderful," he said as the race moved westward across France. "It's a great time, a great experience, a great race. The Tour is a model for the rest of the world. It's why so many people come here to learn."

Although Nee is doing well, do not look for his name in the results of any daily stage. This rookie is not a racer, but the first American to be a member of the four-man international jury charged with overseeing the conduct of the racers. Nee rides not on a bicycle but in a car, looking for infractions.

"Our duties are to make sure everything is done correctly," he said in an interview.

Some of the things that are occasionally not done correctly include a rider's being towed up a mountain as he hangs on to the door handle or the mirror on a team car.

That offense is punishable by expulsion.

Less heinous is the supply of food or water from a team car to a rider in a zone where that is forbidden, or the use of a team car to shelter a rider from the wind or to pace him back to the pack for too long if he has crashed or had a flat. These crimes result in fines and time tacked on to a rider's overall accumulation.

"I think the biggest offense is what you might see in the finals, in the sprints," Nee said, referring to extravagant bumping. Even worse, a rider can leave his line—his straight path to the finish—and swerve to slow his opponents.

"I watch the sprint on television, and there's a technician who can replay it for us," Nee said. "If we see something wrong, we work closely with the organization here, which is probably the best in the world."

Joining the 43-year-old Nee in policing the race, in addition to his three fellow jury members, are six commissaires, as the officials are called, on motorcycles; two judges at the finish line to establish the order of passing; two timers; and a final commissaire in the broom wagon, at the tail of the race, who collects riders who have dropped out.

Nee was appointed by the International Cycling Union, which governs the sport. The honor comes with some drawbacks. While he does receive pay, he described it as nominal. Then there is the matter of arranging to work for the Tour on his vacation.

"It's not too easy to get a four-week vacation in the United States," he said. "My company is very understanding."

He works in Manhattan for Forest Laboratories, which, he said, markets and distributes pharmaceutical products. In his day job, Nee is an assistant vice president in the marketing department.

His wife and two daughters are as understanding as his company when he goes off to a bicycle race, he said.

He entered the sport, he said, because he grew up in Palo Alto, California, and "there's a lot of cycling there, a lot of great cyclists have come from that area, and it was natural."

He added: "I went to Stanford and helped the cycling team there. While I was there I was on the board of directors of the U.S. Cycling Federation and I helped create the National Collegiate Conference."

He also became the youngest international commissaire. Before this race, he said, his biggest assignment was the Tour Du Pont in the United States a decade ago.

"In Europe, what aided my formation was coming in 1987 to the Tour of the European Community," Nee said. "That was a big break for me because I was able to learn how Continental races are run and got to know Tour de France people.

"When I was president of the Tour de Trump in 1989, I was able to bring a lot of their thinking and techniques to the United States."

MISSING HIS BIG DAY

2004

This was to be the day.

"Olympics, Olympics, Olympics," David Millar chanted, heaping his plate with vegetable risotto and smoked salmon, waiting for a glass of champagne not half so bubbly as he was. The date was January 11, 2004, and Millar, then the world time-trial champion, had changed from his rainbow-striped jersey into the dark suit, white shirt, and dark tie of the formal dress of his Cofidis team.

Thirty minutes before, he had stood on a stage in Paris and been introduced as one of the French team's three world champions. Now, affable and articulate as always, he was digging in at the buffet while talking about his goals for the season ahead.

First was the Tour de France. How immense was the pressure on him to win the prologue, as he did in 2000, and perhaps in an early stage carry the team's name on the yellow jersey to Cofidis's headquarters in Wasquehal, in the north of France?

"See, I like that, I like that," he said about the pressure. The world champion's jersey made such a difference, he explained. "Before, everybody expected me to win and, if I finished second, I'd lost. Now I've got the rainbow jersey and I'm really proud, I'm really looking forward to doing the prologue in the rainbow jersey."

Forget that.

His major goal was the Olympic time trial in Athens. He also planned to ride in the road race and, on the track, in the pursuit competition. He was thinking of at least one gold medal.

"Cycling is an anonymous sport in the U.K.," said Millar, born on

Malta to Scottish parents and reared in Hong Kong, where his father is a pilot for Cathay Pacific.

"We're getting very little kudos. What we do is getting no respect. Win at the Olympics and they'll look at us all differently," he said.

"Olympics, Olympics, Olympics—that's my big thing this year."

Forget that, too.

On June 22, 2004, while he was starting to have dinner with two friends at a restaurant in Biarritz, the southwestern French city where Millar lives, three narcotics policemen from Paris came to the table, showed their badges, and asked the 27-year-old rider to accompany them to his apartment.

"They took me out into the car park, took my watch off, my shoelaces, any jewelry I had, my keys and phone," Millar remembers in the September issue of the British magazine *procycling*.

"They took me back to the apartment. They went in with a gun first, as if somebody was going to hit them with a back wheel or something. They sat me down, and I wasn't allowed to move while they searched the house. They search while you're there. It took them four hours."

The policemen were investigating the Cofidis Affair, a teamwide case of supplying and using illegal performance-enhancing drugs, which became public knowledge two weeks after the team presentation and has so far cost more than half a dozen riders and officials their jobs.

Most of them are small fry: a Polish rider who had already signed with another team, a French rider best known for clumsiness that has caused mass crashes, another French rider who was suspended for drug use twice before, an Italian rider at the end of his career, a doctor and team manager who seemed to never know what was going on, a Polish masseur, a French hopeful on the track.

The big name was David Millar, team leader, winner of one Tour de France prologue, second in another, winner of stages in the Vuelta a España and Dauphiné Libéré, world time-trial champion in 2003.

Until that night, he had denied any involvement in the scandal despite the testimony of a teammate, Philippe Gaumont, that Millar had ordered the team doctor to inject him with the banned drug erythropoietin, or EPO, the day before the 2003 Tour ended. Gaumont, Millar said, was a liar and "a nutter."

He stuck to that defense all spring as he sat out the team's suspension from all racing activity for a month to let the dust settle. As he practiced on the track in England, Millar was still denying any involvement until that night in June when the police went into his bedroom.

There they found two empty syringes.

"They were sitting on my books on the shelf in the bedroom," Millar told Jeremy Whittle of *procycling*. "It said Eprex on them," a brand of EPO. Two days later, while in a jail cell, he admitted that he had used the EPO in the syringes before he won the world time-trial championship in Canada last October as well as two other times, in 2001 and 2003.

In the only other interview he has given since that night, Millar talked to *The Guardian* newspaper about the syringes.

"I used them, I forgot about them, left them in my bag, went to Las Vegas, came back, was unpacking and found them. I thought, 'What the . . . has my life come to?' and put them on the bookshelf. It's my most private place, a place no one touches.

"It had scarred me: I had won the world championship by a huge margin and didn't need to have used drugs. I had got to a point where I had wanted to win so much that to guarantee my victory I did something I didn't need to do. I didn't want to forget about it."

The Guardian report, by William Fotheringham, continued: "Asked how he made the journey from an idealistic youth who was adamant that he would never use drugs to a cynical professional who needed 'guarantees,' Millar holds up finger and thumb. The gap between them is half an inch.

"'It's that. I was 100 percent sure I'd never dope. All of a sudden it escalated out of control.'

"It was, he believes, a form of adolescent rebellion against the demands of his sport," Fotheringham wrote. He quoted Millar: "It was the only thing in life that defined me. I resented that. I didn't think about it, there was no twiddling thumbs and wondering if I should or I shouldn't. I just walked into a room one day and did it."

In July, Millar was banned from the Tour. Days later, after he repeated his confession to an investigating French magistrate, he was fired by the Cofidis team.

On August 4, the British cycling federation banned him from the sport for two years and stripped him of his world championship gold medal. His victories in the 2001 Vuelta and 2003 Dauphiné were also voided.

As doping scandals go, 2004 has been a devastating year in bicycle racing.

While the Cofidis Affair was unfolding in March, a Spanish rider, Jesus Manzano, charged that his Kelme team had engaged in systematic doping. In Belgium, three riders are under investigation for drug use.

In Italy, two major drug investigations are entering their second and fourth years. In Italy also, Marco Pantani, the great climber of a few years ago, was found dead in March of a cocaine overdose after years of doping charges.

In August, a Swiss former world road-race champion, Oscar Camenzind, was fired by his Phonak team and retired after he failed a drug test. Again in Belgium, Dave Bruylandts, the leader of the Chocolade Jacques team, was suspended for eighteen months after testing positive for the second time in a suspected use of EPO.

Two mountain bikers, one the Belgian world champion, Filip Meirhaeghe, the other Janet Puiggros Miranda of Spain, have been barred from the Games.

"Do you think that dope-free sport is possible?" *procycling's* Whittle asked Millar.

"That's idealistic," he replied. "As long as human beings compete against each other, there will be guys that cheat. It's unavoidable. But I'm in a position now where I can help younger riders, British riders, to avoid the pitfalls. All you need is a support program."

PRINCE OF THE MOUNTAINS

2004

Say what you will about Richard Virenque (it better not be anything overly admiring), nobody can accuse him of low self-esteem.

Exhibit A: What other rider would call a news conference in a Paris theater to announce that he was retiring?

Usually these are quiet occasions. Laurent Jalabert, who won scores more races than Virenque and far bigger ones, chose a small hall in his team's hotel during a rest day in the 2002 Tour de France to announce that he would retire at the end of that season. Although Bernard Hinault did go out in 1986 with a mammoth 32nd birthday party after he had won the Tour five times, the party was given by his friends and neighbors, not the rider.

When Virenque threw his bash in the Olympia music hall, it's true that he was in a meeting room, not on stage, where he has so often been metaphorically, proclaiming "I live for my public."

That public—mainly young girls who delighted in screaming, "Richaaaard! Richaaaard!" and timeworn couples who saw in Virenque the rage against authority that filled their dreams—was missing for the upscale occasion, limited to the press and bicycling figures.

It's also true that, for a man who spent a major part of his career cheating and lying, he sounded sincere.

"I'm afraid of riding a year too many," he said, referring to the collapse many riders have when they stay too long in the sport.

"I want to be remembered going off the front, not the other way," he continued, noting that he will turn 35 in November. Speaking of the last Tour de France, he said, "After winning my seventh king-of-the-mountains title and winning a stage on Bastille Day, I asked myself, 'What more can I do in cycling?' I want to go out at the top."

Which top is that, exactly?

In fourteen years as a professional, he won one major classic—Paris-Tours in 2001—a handful of minor races and daily stages in secondary races; no big stage race; and no world, Olympic, or national championship.

His reputation rests on the Tour de France. Where he won seven stages in nearly a dozen participations, finishing a distant second in 1997, third in 1994, and fifth in 1994, all years in which he was team leader both in races and in systematic use of illegal performance-enhancing drugs.

He also won the climbers' jersey a record seven times, as he pointedly noted.

Busted in 1998 in the infamous Festina Affair, Virenque spent the next two years denying any involvement in the doping to which other members of his team confessed. They served their suspensions and returned to the races while Virenque insisted that he—mocked nightly on a French television puppet show that portrayed him with hypodermic needles jabbed into his body—was clean.

In 1999, when the Tour tried to ban him, he prevailed and raced with the support of the sport's overlords, the International Cycling Union.

Finally, late in 2000, he confessed and was suspended for nine months.

When he returned to the Tour, he was a different rider. No longer surrounded by the juiced teammates dedicated to him in the Festina days, he now rode for a Belgian team, sponsored first by Domo and then Quick Step, that was constructed for classics, not three-week stage races. Other than Virenque, it had no real climbers.

So, for the last two years, he had to change his methods to win the mountain-climbing jersey, white with red polka dots. Instead of constant attacks in the Alps and Pyrenees with the help of his teammates, he had to content himself with the occasional solitary exploit there while scrabbling for points on hills and minor mountains.

Those points add up. While Lance Armstrong figured in every mountaintop finish in the last Tour, winning four of them, and Virenque was no closer than 17th once, Armstrong trailed the Frenchman in the climbing competition.

Virenque was king of the mountains in 1994, 1995, 1996, 1997, 1999, 2003, and 2004. He recorded a stage victory in 1994, 1995, 1997, 2003, and 2004.

For the record, his favorite animal is the scorpion.

"He's dangerous, he's beautiful, and he loves the heat, like me," Virenque explains. "That's why I had a scorpion tattooed on my leg in 1999 after my fifth jersey."

They still love him in France, only less so. All the girls who swooned at his feet years ago have moved on to other idols and not been replaced. As a sign of the obscurity that French bicycle racers have fallen into in their nonwinning ways, Virenque was the only one ranked in a recent poll of the top thirty national athletes, finishing in 12th place. He was most highly thought of by men aged 50 to 64.

And, in a poll of eighty-nine French riders in the First Division by the newspaper *L'Equipe* this year, he received only 7 of 83 votes cast for the leader of the country's riders. The winner, with 39, was Laurent Brochard.

One reason for his low standing is his role in the Festina Affair.

Another is this frenzy to win mountain points. Kings do not usually pick through the trash.

One king of the mountains who never did is Lucien Van Impe, 58, the Belgian who won the Tour in 1976 and formerly shared the record of six overall climbing triumphs with Federico Bahamontes, the Spanish "Eagle of Toledo," and Virenque.

Normally the most placid of men, Van Impe, who now follows the Tour as a driver for Belgian television, can be caustic about Virenque.

"He's a good climber, but not a true climber like Charly Gaul, Bahamontes, and Pantani," Van Impe said in an interview during the Tour, naming some great climbers other than himself. "Virenque has already won six times, so he's got the record with us and that makes him a king of the mountains. But a champion? I don't think so.

"A true climber wins everywhere," he added. "All the great climbs, he's there. The Galibier, the Aubisque, the Tourmalet, no matter where—he's the first man over the great climbs. Virenque, he gets his points on second-, third-, and fourth-category climbs. I don't think Virenque is a pure climber. He's all alone in the mountains. I had to sprint to the top with the greatest Spaniards and Colombians glued to my back.

"Every year, Virenque pulls off an exploit," Van Impe said. "Congratulations. But, in my time, he wouldn't have been in any photograph of climbers going over the top. If he wins that seventh jersey, Federico and I will be disappointed. I like a rider like him, a rider who can climb like him. But for me, there's a difference between a climber and a true climber. Virenque can win seven, eight times, but that won't make him a true climber."

From Spain, Bahamontes was equally dismissive and even harsher.

Virenque responded: "The true climber, it's me—somebody who rides alone and wins the stage. I don't sprint on the peaks because I reach them alone. It's sad that these guys say that about me. It's just jealousy."

This was the third time he had announced his retirement. The first was when he was expelled from the Tour with the Festina team. The second was when he was convicted of doping and suspended.

Certainly Virenque will keep his word this time. He has a new job and a four-year contract as a public relations officer for a pharmaceuticals company. By his lights, he's at the top.

THE BARD AT THE WORLD'S

2004

Are the bicycle road world championships, which will be held in Romeo and Juliet's hometown of Verona, important?

The answer is "not at all" or "extremely," depending on who is speaking.

First, as Cole Porter advised, brush up your Shakespeare.

"There is no world without Verona walls, / But purgatory, torture, hell itself," exclaimed Romeo, lanterne rouge in the love department, on hearing of his banishment to Mantua.

Tell that to Lance Armstrong, who is home in Texas, hanging out.

Armstrong won the road race in 1993, at the age of 21, has been back only once, and not at all after he began winning the Tour de France, in 1999.

Wherefore are thou in Texas, Armstrong?

The world's, as they are known, are conducted too late in the year, he says. It's a long season, starting toward the end of February or the beginning of March, and by this time people want to be at home, taking their children to school, flipping burgers on the grill, and sucking down a beer before it gets too cold to stay mellow outdoors.

"Do you bite your thumb at us, sir?" asked Abraham, servant to Montague. "I do bite my thumb, sir," responded Sampson, servant to Capulet.

Many riders do, too.

When Armstrong won in Oslo, the championship road race was staged in August, in the full heat of the season. Since then, it and the championship time trial have been moved to the tag end of the riders' year, when only the two "Races of the Falling Leaves"—Paris-Tours in France and the

Tour of Lombardy in Italy—still dot the major European calendar. The season is already over, some riders insist.

"But old folks," complained Juliet, "many feign as they were dead; / Unwieldy, slow, heavy and pale as lead."

One of them is Thomas Voeckler, the revelation of the last Tour de France.

"I know that it's almost a duty to show my French national championship jersey at the world's," he says. "But, in my head, I can't do it."

"Everything that's happened to me this season is perhaps too much for me to handle," he told *L'Equipe*, "and I feel that I wouldn't honor my selection if I accepted and went in this state."

Other riders have bigger concerns than the road race or the time trial. "My wife is going to have a boy in November," the French rider Sylvain Chavanel told *L'Equipe*, "and I'm too occupied with that to go to the world's."

Besides, he said, the world's have lost luster in a year of the Olympics, in which he did compete. "To skip the world's doesn't bother me any more than skipping any other race," Chavenel said.

Even more indifferent is Stéphane Goubert, who rejected a possible invitation to come to Italy by saying: "Does the French team have a leader who deserves to have riders working for him? I don't think so."

Ouch, that hurt Laurent Brochard, the leader of the French team and a winner of the world's road race in 1997. Like Mercutio, Romeo's buddy, he could say of this wound: "'Tis not so deep as a well, nor so wide as a church door; but 'tis enough, 'twill serve."

What Brochard did say is: "I'm unable to understand some riders. The jersey of the French team deserves respect even if, it's true, it's not always easy to keep going at the end of the season. But it's no big thing to ride for eight more days.

"In any case," he told *L'Equipe*, "just the words 'world championships' are enough to motivate me."

Brochard is not alone. In the words of Capulet: "Go, sirrah, trudge about / Through fair Verona; find those persons out / Whose names are written there, and to them say, / My house and welcome on their pleasure stay."

Start with, of course, the host Italians. Better yet, start with the host Italian who comes from a suburb of Verona. That would be Damiano Cunego, the 23-year-old winner of the Giro d'Italia in June, who was born and still lives within shouting distance of Juliet's balcony, a major tourist attraction.

"And, to say truth, Verona brags of him / To be a virtuous and well-govern'd youth," according to Capulet. "I would not for the wealth of all this town / Here in my house do him disparagement."

Cunego, who won the junior world championship road race in Verona in 1999, will share the leadership of the Italian team with Paolo Bettini, who won the Olympic road race in Athens.

Their main rivals seem to be the Spaniards, headed by Igor Astarloa, the reigning world champion, and Oscar Freire, the winner in 1999 and 2001.

Belgium, headed by Tom Boonen, should also be a factor in the 265.5-kilometer road race, which includes eighteen climbs of the Torricelle hill. In 1999, when it was climbed sixteen times, the hill weeded the 200-man field down to 49 at the finish, with only 9 of them in contention for the victory.

As for the time trial, it will cover 46.75 kilometers, starting on the shores of Lake Garda outside Verona.

Favorites include Australia's Michael Rogers, who became world champion after David Millar, a Scot, had to forfeit his title because of doping. Also highly rated are Fabian Cancellara, a Swiss; José Ivan Gutiérrez, a Spaniard; and Michael Rich, a German.

But Jan Ullrich, who won the title on virtually the same course in 1999, said that he would not compete in the time trial because of a stomach problem. He added that he did not know whether he would be able to enter the road race. "I can't eat anything without being sick," Ullrich said on his Web site. "I don't know whether it's food poisoning or a virus."

The German, a former two-time world champion and Tour de France and Olympic victor, has had a disastrous year—fourth in the Tour, far out of the money in both Olympic races.

Or, as Juliet wailed: "Is there no pity sitting in the clouds that sees into the bottom of my grief?"

MORE OF THE SAME

2004

By now, after what seems like her millionth bicycle race, she is usually described as "the ageless Jeannie Longo."

Look again. Look closer.

Her face is lined, and those are wrinkles around her eyes.

She is not ageless—who is?—but she is a woman who carries her years well.

La Longo will be 46 on October 31, 2004, which means that she was twice as old as many other competitors in the elite women's world championship road race in Verona, Italy.

On the other hand, she had probably three times as many world championship gold medals as the rest of the 118-woman field combined.

Longo-Ciprelli, to give the Frenchwoman her married name, has won thirteen golds on the track and on the road and in the time trial.

There does not seem to be a major race or challenge in which she has not triumphed.

The Olympic Games? Gold on the road and silver in the time trial in 1996.

The Women's Tour de France? In 1987.

The hour record on the track? A handful of times, both at altitude and at sea level.

Her summary on her Web site, which does not seem to have been updated in two years, lists forty-seven French titles in every discipline imaginable.

Longo made headlines this year when she did not win her annual national championship in the time trial.

In the century-old annals of the sport, nobody—male, female, or changeling—has competed at so high a level at so elevated an age. Since a brief fling at retirement, which ended with a victory in the world championship time trial in 1997, she has shown no sign of getting off her bicycle.

In a mellow mood a few years ago, she said that she would keep riding as long as it was enjoyable. Nobody has dared ask the notoriously prickly Longo since then if she was considering retirement.

Her image has softened, though.

A few years ago, when the world's were also held in Verona, she was regarded with concealed amusement, even ridicule: a daffy older sister trying to disguise her 40 years with a skirt too short and lipstick too bright.

Now she is considered a grande dame, proof that, with an iron will and nonstop training, age can be irrelevant.

So the enjoyment continues, even if her triumphs are no longer recorded at major international events.

In one week in late July and early August, she finished first six times, all of them speed records, in climbing races in the Alps. The week before that, she won four climbs in the Alps in record times.

But in the Olympics in Athens, she finished 14th in the time trial and 10th in the road race. In this Verona world championships, she got off to a humdrum start by finishing in 15th place in the 34-woman time trial.

Longo attributed her problem to a bad position on her bicycle, which blocked her shoulders. That seemed an unlikely explanation for somebody who has been racing since 1979.

Her husband and trainer, Patrice Ciprelli, offered an even shakier reason. It wasn't her fault, he said, but his choice of her bicycle for the race against the clock.

Neither of them mentioned age. She promised to do better in the women's road race. "In my head, it's unthinkable that I can lose," she said. "It's a survival instinct."

Moments before the road race, Longo was in a familiar mood, rebuffing a photographer and snubbing a reporter.

When the French squad was called to the start line, she was nowhere in sight—as always, not an integral part of the national team. Instead she was alone in the crowd of riders at the back.

That was pretty much her road race too. Longo rarely rose above 20th or 30th place in the peloton and finished 21st, 1 minute, 7 seconds behind the winner, Judith Arndt of Germany.

Arndt had a splendid world championships: first place in the road race, second in the time trial.

She also finished second in the Olympic road race, flashing the infamous finger at the German selectors who left a friend of hers off the team.

In her results and demeanor, she resembles La Longo of an earlier era. The parallels end there, since Arndt is just 28 years old.

THE NEXT LANCE?

2004

While every other rider in the 200-man field came to the bicycling road world championships in Verona, Italy, with hopes of winning or at least shining, Tom Danielson, a 26-year-old American often described as the next Lance Armstrong, brought more modest ambitions.

"These are my first world championships," he said, "so I really don't have any goals other than being here to learn. To learn and be good in the future."

Those words—"learn," "good," and "future"—pepper his conversation. A big talent who won twenty-two races mainly in the United States in 2002 and 2003, he is just completing his first year as a member of a European team, Fassa Bortolo from Italy.

It has not been an easy year. Danielson described it tactfully in an interview as "a different year for me."

He is an acclaimed climber and a former mountain bike star who took to the road only three years ago. What he lacks, he acknowledged, are the elements of road racing that are not part of mountain biking, such as tactics, bicycle-handling skills in a pack, and especially time-trial experience.

He did not get that this season because his team used him strangely. Although he was scheduled to ride the Giro d'Italia in May and then the Vuelta a España in September, he was not entered in either three-week mountainous course, studded with races against the clock.

Instead he has spent his time mostly in flat one-day races with no climbing and no time trialing.

"They knew my situation, everyone knew my experience—there's no secret there," he said. "I was ready to do a big tour. Maybe I wouldn't have done that well, but I need the experience, I need to get in there to be ready to do it next year or the year after.

"Climbing is sort of what I was born to do, but I want to become a good stage racer, so I must be good at time trialing."

The world's, as they are known, may be an extravagantly high-level classroom to study needed skills, Danielson agreed. Still, why not try to learn from the finest?

Speaking in the warm-up area before the time trial, he said, "These guys are the best in the world, theoretically, and I'm not a time trialist. I'm trying to become one. If I do a top-20 time trial, I'll be more than happy."

Although he missed his goal, finishing 35th in the 46-man race, he seemed satisfied afterward. Nobody ever said school was easy. His goals in the road race are equally modest.

"It's the first time for me in the world's, so I have no idea what to expect," he said. "It's 265 kilometers and it's going to be a big battle against the one-day specialists. Whatever my role is in the team, I'll do that.

"If I'm in the front, fine. If I'm not, no problem—I'll be ready for a great season next year."

First, he will be making some changes in his life. After the world's, he will return home to Colorado, where he attended, and raced for, Fort Lewis College, and to Connecticut, where he was born and his family lives. He will be married, and he will move from a town near Bologna to Girona in Spain. "I'm joining the posse," he said about the move to Girona, which is home to many riders, especially those who race for Armstrong's U.S. Postal Service team, which will be sponsored next year by Discovery Channel. Danielson has been released from the second year of his Italian contract and will ride in a Discovery jersey next year.

"The advantages are endless," he said. "First of all, the team's infrastructure: It has the best rider in cycling's history—Lance Armstrong: six Tours de France, world championship, blah, blah, blah, it goes on forever," an appraisal that may startle fans of Eddy Merckx, the Belgian who is usually considered to be the sport's finest.

Danielson may never have heard of Merckx, who hung up his bicycle thirty years ago, but he certainly knows about Armstrong.

"I need to be on a team with a mentor I can learn from," Danielson said. "Some people say, 'Oh you have to work for someone,' but I'd be more than happy to blow my eyes out on every single climb for him because I'd know I'm learning and becoming better for the future.

"I'm not ready to be a contender in these big races yet. I need to learn. And to learn with someone who's been your idol your entire life is priceless, it's unreal.

"Another big reason is that the team is made for, it's sculpted around, stage races. They have the right directors, the right staff, the right riders, and that's what I need to get to the next level."

Danielson began to attract the label of "the next Armstrong" when he won the Tour de Langkawi, a multiday race in Malaysia with a major climb, as a member of the Saturn team. The prediction intensified this year when he won the Mount Evans Hill Climb in Colorado, knocking an astronomical 4 minutes, 10 seconds off the record set twelve years ago.

Danielson rejects the comparison: "Who he is, he's Lance Armstrong, he'll always be Lance Armstrong, and there will never be another Lance Armstrong. Obviously my physique and my talents are much different than his." They are about the same height, 5 feet 10 inches, or 1.77 meters, but Danielson, at 132 pounds, or 61 kilograms, is 30 pounds lighter.

"Of course I want to become like him," he said. "But who he is—his mentality, how he understands things, how he trains—will always be his trademark.

"I don't know where I can go in this sport, and every day I'm just going to take everything I can off the wonderful people around me and go as far as I can. I'll have my ears open and my eyes open, ready to absorb everything.

"Whether I achieve the highest things or come close, knowing that I tried my hardest, did the best things I could, I'll be happy."

Likeable, isn't he? Sweet, even. When a fan came over and asked him to autograph a T-shirt, Danielson asked his name. Then he began to write: "To Filippo." Instead of simply signing his name, he added, "Good luck and see you on the road. Tom Danielson."

THE LOST HERO

2004

The *Gazzetta dello Sport,* the Italian daily sports newspaper, got it precisely right in its headline about the death of Marco Pantani, the wayward champion of bicycle racing: "Lost Hero, We Adored You."

Pantani, found dead at age 34 in an Italian hotel, was surely lost, surely a hero, and surely adored.

Even the order of those words in importance is correct—lost does come first.

He had not ridden in a race for almost a year, and then only after a year of near inactivity. He checked into a clinic for two weeks to treat depression last year and emerged to grow fat, adding about 20 kilograms, or 44 pounds, to the 60 kilograms he used to carry when he was climbing mountains like a rocket.

"Forget about Pantani the cyclist," he advised his fans in a rare interview last autumn. As the new season started, he belonged to no team.

Increasingly withdrawn, he spent part of the winter traveling in South America, shedding some weight and thinking about a return to the sport.

"For him, it's all or nothing," Pantani's father Paolo told *procycling,* the British magazine. "For that reason, I'm pessimistic" about any comeback, he said.

Father and son were close and spent Christmas together. Pantani had no wife or children and, at least in recent times, few intimate friends.

But "hero" certainly fits, too.

When he won the Giro d'Italia and the Tour de France back to back in 1998—the first Italian to win the Tour in thirty-three years—he became a major star in his country.

Just a year later, he began his descent. On the next-to-last day of the Giro, Pantani was wearing the leader's pink jersey again when drug inspectors visited him.

He was found to have an abnormally high reading of red blood cells—an indication, if not proof, of the use of illegal performance-enhancing drugs. On the spot, he was ousted from the Giro.

On the mighty peak of the Gavia, 2,621 meters (8,650 feet) high, and a major climb in the Giro, a crowd estimated at two hundred thousand waited vainly the next day to cheer for Pantani. When the word of his disqualification spread, a great sense of anger and sadness swept the fans, the French sports newspaper *L'Equipe* reported.

"For me, it's the end of a dream," said a man identified as Francesco, 65. "He restored a sense of pride to Italy. But that's over now. He tricked us, and I can't forgive him."

Sure he could, and did.

The *tifosi*—the highly enthusiastic Italian fans—forgave everything done by Elefantino, or Dumbo, the nickname Pantani carried for years because of his big ears. He preferred to be called Il Pirata, the Pirate, and wore a gold earring with a bandana perched on his shaven head. He did have style, plus bounce and a big smile.

Lately, the past was closing in. He was accused in a handful of doping cases other than the one in the 1999 Giro. He was found not guilty on technicalities but suspended once for six months. Another charge was pending in court.

In his words and manner, signs of depression were evident even before he entered the clinic. For years he had been quarreling with rival riders and team officials, in contrast to his popularity with them during his strong years.

The Italian police scheduled an autopsy into Pantani's death. Sedatives were found near his bed and "some thoughts" had been written on hotel stationery, the police said.

They were not a farewell note, said a magistrate in the Adriatic city of Rimini, adding that the sedatives were not illegal.

Pantani had been a guest at the hotel for five days but reportedly was seen only at breakfast.

Among the riders paying tribute to Pantani was Miguel Indurain, the Spaniard who won the Tour five times in the 1990s.

In the Spanish sports daily *Marca,* he described Pantani as a "tragic genius."

"Apart from his undeniable quality as a rider, he got people hooked on the sport," Indurain said. "There may be riders who have achieved more than him, but they never succeeded in drawing in the fans as he did."

Referring to the failed test in the Giro, Indurain added, "It ended up complicating his whole life, and he was never able to get over it. He was never the same again."

Pantani took part in five Tours de France, winning in 1998 and finishing third in 1994 and 1997. He won eight daily stages, all in the Alps and Pyrenees.

His last Tour was in 2000, when he won two stages, including the one up Mont Ventoux.

In the Giro, he was second in 1994 in addition to his victory. He won eight stages there, too, all in the mountains.

The abiding image of Pantani dates to the 1998 Tour de France. The race had been ripped by the Festina Affair, in which the team of that name had been ousted for doping, and by subsequent police raids and riders' strikes.

The race had finished its next-to-last day, a time trial at Disneyland outside Paris, and Pantani, a notoriously weak time trialer, had survived his final challenge.

Elefantino—Dumbo at Disneyland!—bounded into a hotel elevator full of other riders. Shaking every hand in sight, hearing the praise for him on all sides, he wore a smile as broad as the moon. At just 28 years old, he was king.

The next year, his world fell apart forever.

A LOVE STORY

2004

This is a love story, and so it includes trace elements of rejection, threats, humiliation, and compromise—the usual—but, above all, love.

Pepe Quilès has nothing but love for bicycle racing: fierce, possessive love. Why else would his Kelme sports shoe company have sponsored a Spanish team for twenty-five years, an eternity in the sport?

Other sponsors flit by. Where are Fiat, Peugeot, Brooklyn Chewing Gum, Flandria, ADR? Where are Bianchi, Renault, La Vie Claire, Polti, Russlotto, Kwantum, Café de Colombia, Mapei, and Raleigh? Gone, all gone. Like a rock, Kelme holds; its nearest rival in continuous sponsorship is the Lotto team from Belgium, founded in 1984, four years after Kelme.

The Spaniards are a medium-budget team that Quilès has never let become part of the bidding wars for champions. Instead, Kelme has relied on discovering young talent in Spain and sometimes Colombia, nurturing those riders and then, alas, watching them leave for better-funded teams.

In the past few years alone, Roberto Heras won the Vuelta a España in 2000 and was bought out of his Kelme contract by U.S. Postal Service to help Lance Armstrong win the Tour de France. José Rubiera went with him. Aitor Gonzalez won the Vuelta in 2002 and immediately moved to Fassa Bortolo in Italy. Santiago Botero jumped from Kelme to Telekom in Germany two years ago. Oscar Sevilla left this winter for T-Mobile in Germany.

All except Rubiera are Tour de France contenders. Not to worry, Quilès says, we have other arrows in our quiver. We have been competing for a quarter-century, and there have always been other riders, other future champions.

The young Otxoa brothers, Javier and Ricardo, might have been among them until a car plowed into them during a training ride near Málaga in February 2001, half a year after Javier Otxoa won the Tour de France mountain stage up to Hautacam ahead of Armstrong.

The crash killed Ricardo Otxoa and left Javier in a nine-week coma. He now competes in the European Paralympic Championships, where he won gold, silver, and bronze last summer.

Now, with the loss of the promising Sevilla, Kelme will be led by Alejandro Valverde. Only 23 years old, he recorded seven victories last season and finished second in the world championship road race in Canada. Valverde is a hot property and both Saeco in Italy and the new Liberty Seguros team in Spain, formerly ONCE, have inquired about his availability. Valverde is under contract through 2007 and reportedly has a buyout clause of €2.5 million, or more than $3 million

No deal, says Quilès, even if he must be tempted.

Team Kelme is broke or so close to it that last year it was months behind in paying its riders their salaries.

There are tax bills owed in Spain and financial guarantees that did not satisfy the International Cycling Union, the overseers of the sport. Last year's fiasco with Team Coast, which defaulted on rider salaries and then folded, forced the federation to tighten its rules about money up front.

In December, Kelme failed to post those salary guarantees. Quilès was warned that, absent the money, his team would be dropped from the First Division, the big leagues of classics and major tours, into the obscure Second Division.

He was outraged at the thought of small races for a team so long a major player, a cradle of champions, a winner of two Vueltas in the past four years—Kelme, which placed a rider on the Tour de France podium as recently as 1999, when Fernando Escartin was third.

Quilès fought: threats, stamped feet, slammed doors, appeals for reconciliation—the usual. It's tough when love goes wrong.

Officials in Valencia, the team's base, wanted to help, offering €1.8 million and accepting a role in the Second Division.

Again Quilès balked. "He wants to keep a budget of €3.3 million, which seems far too much for a Second Division team," explained a Valencia official.

The compromise was reached two weeks ago. Down, down, down into the Second Division with such unknowns as Lokomotiv of Russia, eD system-ZVVZ of the Czech Republic, Team Wiesenhof of Germany, and Miche of Italy goes Kelme.

Even its name is changed. The team will be Comunidad Valenciana-Kelme.

For Valverde, the Second Division will be a barren place, depriving him of the major races' points he needs to move up in the rankings.

For Quilès, it will be worse. The big time is over, and he is a big-time kind of guy. The name is Kelme, not Comunidad Valenciana-Kelme.

What happens next in this shadow world? If Quilès finds it any solace, Ralph Waldo Emerson, yellow jersey of the Tour of Transcendentalism, insisted that love can cure all things.

SPILLING THE BEANS

2004

Until a week ago, Jesus Manzano was a 25-year-old former professional bicycle racer who was remembered, if at all, for two rare episodes.

The first occurred in the seventh stage of the 2003 Tour de France, a climb in the Alps from Lyon to Morzine under heavy heat. Manzano, who rode for the Kelme team from his native Spain, was heading uphill on a breakaway when his bicycle began to zigzag and he suddenly crumpled to the road. After emergency medical treatment, he was hospitalized.

While riders often drop out of the Tour in the mountains, they usually glide to the side of the road and dismount or simply fail to start the next day. Though dramatic, Manzano's collapse went unremarked because he was such an obscure rider: In his fourth year as a professional with Kelme, he had recorded only two stage victories, the first in the Tour of the Rioja in 2001 and the second in the Tour of Catalonia in 2003.

Two months after the Tour de France, toward the end of the three-week Vuelta a España, he made another bit of news. After team officials said they had found a woman in his hotel room during the night, Manzano was pulled from the race and sent home.

Kelme officials decided at the end of the last season not to renew his contract.

Part of the reason was financial. The team, now in its twenty-fifth year and by far the longest-lasting in the sport, has had money problems the last few years and has been unable to pay its riders on time. That instability caused the International Cycling Union, which oversees the sport, to drop Kelme this season from the First Division to the Second, where invitations to major races like the Tour de France and Vuelta are difficult to procure.

Another reason not to rehire Manzano was his record, both personal, as in the hotel incident, and professional, as in his sparse victories. He was just a hewer of wood and bearer of water for Kelme, and the cycling world is full of similar riders. Usually, when their careers are over, they go home, find another job, and tell their buddies about life in the sport. Not Manzano. He has been telling the world.

In a series of articles last week in the Madrid sports newspaper *As,* Manzano charged Kelme officials and doctors with systematic use of illegal performance-enhancing drugs and blood packing, or transfusing blood into riders to increase the red corpuscles that carry oxygen to muscles. This practice, which has been outlawed since the U.S. bicycle team used it to dominate the 1984 Olympics in Los Angeles, can also serve to dilute the concentration of drugs in a rider's blood.

Manzano's account is chillingly detailed. He has demonstrated how to inject EPO, an artificial hormone that increases red corpuscles, and how to beat the tests that detect it. He reported that he almost died on a train after being given drugs for racing. These charges are dynamite in a sport where doping is usually regarded as an individual, not a team, practice.

An exception was the Festina Affair, which nearly scuttled the 1998 Tour de France amid riders' protests over police drug raids. After the nine-man Festina squad was ousted from the race when a team car was found to be packed with illegal drugs, most of the riders admitted doping in a program organized by team officials.

Although the sport has since avoided any scandal on that scale, the Cofidis team in France was investigated in February by the narcotics police, who have accused three riders and arrested a team masseur.

In addition to France, police raids and charges have also marked professional racing in Italy and Belgium in the last few years, but Manzano's account of widespread drug use is a first for Spain.

He charged that team doctors twice extracted 500 milliliters of blood from each rider days before the start of the Tour last July, that the plastic pouches of blood were not marked by name and that they were not refrigerated. He had to pay €3,000, or $3,600, for this treatment, he said.

"It's like an open bar when it comes to growth hormones, and you get injected with EPO almost every day," he said in *As.* "If it wasn't for EPO, I don't think the average speed at major tours would be 41 kilometers an hour," or 25 miles an hour.

He also described how easy it is to fool drug inspectors when they visit a team's hotel during a race to test the riders' hematocrit levels, or the relation of red corpuscles to white. A level above 50 percent means an instant suspension of two weeks.

"You get around half an hour after the testers turn up," he said, because team officials "send down the riders with low levels first. The rest of the cyclists who have higher levels are given blood plasma and glucose products and then do the inspections—these can lower your hematocrit level by four points."

In his first article, Manzano said that before the seventh stage of the Tour he was injected with "something I'd never taken before" and phoned his girlfriend to say, "Get ready, because according to what I've been told, I'm going to ride well today."

Instead, he collapsed.

"My hands had gone to sleep," he said, "and I started feeling nauseated. I felt very warm but had cold sweats. I began to shake. I went on for 500 meters, and after that I don't remember anything."

His accusations mirror those of a French rider, Philippe Gaumont, who was fired by the Cofidis team last month after he admitted to the police that he had used performance-enhancing drugs and supplied those drugs to other riders. In an interview with *Le Monde,* a French newspaper, two weeks ago, Gaumont discussed what he described as the many illegal products and practices in use and explained why the riders' standard defense—that they have never failed a drug test—can be invalid.

"Above all," he said, "there are products that can't be detected, like human growth hormone, which riders use whenever they want. For cortisone or steroids, it's enough to have a doctor's prescription for therapeutic reasons and so turn an inspector's positive finding into a negative one."

Why Gaumont broke the sport's law of silence is a mystery. For Manzano, however, the reasons are clear: money and revenge.

Unemployed and having said that he did not have enough money to pay his rent, he was reported to have been paid by *As* for his story.

He admits he is angry with his former team.

"Kelme owes me money, about a month's wages and some expenses," he said. "An eye for an eye and a tooth for a tooth."

Can his allegations be believed? Kelme officials have called them lies, but the organizers of the Tour de France feel otherwise. The Tour has withdrawn the wildcard invitation it was saving for Kelme, once it got its financial affairs in order.

Speaking of Manzano, the Tour's director, Jean-Marie Leblanc, told *L'Equipe* newspaper: "We can't imagine that just by himself he's done all that he describes. There had to be complicity, passive or active, by team officials or doctors. I don't think this fellow can have invented all of this.

"We organizers have the duty to tell that team we don't want to see it again," he said. "For us, the Kelme team is finished. There is no more Kelme."

NO HERO OF LABOR

2004

On the May Day holiday, Jan Ullrich joined the multitude, celebrating the dignity of labor by abstaining from it.

As some 150 other workers of the world united to whiz around Frankfurt in the Henniger Turm race, Ullrich was loosening his chains at home, possibly with a weisswurst or two and a slice or three of nüsseltorte. He seems to be off his diet of lettuce leaves, hold the dressing.

Says who? Eddy Merckx, for one.

Merckx, the greatest rider of all time, had some harsh words about Ullrich in the German newspaper *Bild am Sonntag* a few weeks ago: "It seems Jan once again hasn't worked hard enough and is carrying too much weight."

That stung.

"It isn't fat, it's muscle," insisted the 29-year-old German, presumably thumping his breadbasket. "I trained a lot in the winter and built up muscle mass," he told *Bild*.

He did admit, though, that he was 2 or 3 kilograms, or 4.5 to 6.5 pounds, over his desired weight for the Tour de France, about 75 kilograms.

Not to worry, he said, although Ullrich's weight problems are as inevitable a sign of spring as the blooming of forsythia. Since his Tour victory in 1997, he has started nearly every season pudgy, not to say bloated.

He has paid the price, too: five times he has finished second in the Tour, including three times in four years behind Lance Armstrong. The exception was 2002, when Ullrich was injured and then suspended by his Deutsche Telekom team for various infractions.

Back he came last year in the colors of the troubled Coast team, which could not pay its riders and suspended operations before it was rescued by Bianchi. Ullrich brushed off this turmoil and his year away from the sport by finishing second, a little over a minute behind Armstrong in a Tour that was not decided until Ullrich crashed in a time trial on the next-to-last day of the race.

In 2004 he returned to Telekom, now known as T-Mobile, and pledged that at long last his head was right. He understood, he said, that he had squandered his prodigious talent.

Yes, he is the reigning Olympic road race champion and has been the world time-trial champion, and yes, he has won the Vuelta a España and the world amateur road-race championship in addition to that Tour victory in 1997. But his reputation is based on those five second places in the Tour: so close, so many times, to greatness.

It was going to be different this year, he promised. He was watching his weight and devoting his time to training. He was happy to accept the responsibility of leading a powerful team, he said, and he was awaiting the shootout with Armstrong in July.

So here it is May, nine weeks before the Tour starts in Belgium, and Ullrich is floundering. Hobbled, as he often is, by illness at the start of the season, he has consistently been far behind in the races he could finish. Lately he has been unable to finish, dropping out of the Amstel Gold Race and the Flèche Wallonne and now, as in the Henniger Turm and Liège-Bastogne-Liège the weekend before, not even starting.

What's gone wrong?

On his Web page, www.janullrich.de, he has dropped his insistence that he's doing great ("Ich bin voll im Plan!"). Instead, he states blandly, "I have changed my preparation program for the Tour de France."

Discussing the dropouts in Frankfurt and Liège, he said, "My fitness isn't such that I would have a chance to finish well. The two race cancellations don't influence my chances at the Tour de France. I have a lot of kilometers of training in my legs. But I still don't have the toughness to ride—like in the beginning of the Flèche Wallonne—at 55 kilometers an hour."

Auf Wiedersehen, Jan.

A HANDS-ON JOB

2004

Jan Ullrich's collapse in the two Tour de France stages in the Pyrenees surprised everybody, not least Birgit Krohme.

"He's in good shape, better than last year," Krohme said only days before the German leader of the T-Mobile team lost at least two and a half minutes on each day in the mountains. In 2003 he finished second in the Tour to Lance Armstrong by just sixty-one seconds.

Krohme should know about his shape, since she is Ullrich's personal physiotherapist, and for two to three hours each day, seven days a week, most months of the year, she kneads, pummels, and massages his body.

"It's not only massage," she said in an interview. "We do complete physical therapy."

A 32-year-old German with a doctor's degree in homeopathic medicine who studied both in Germany and the United States, Krohme denied that Ullrich had any problems now. "No, not really," she said. "But after what he does on a bike, you have to make it global, the whole body structure."

Ullrich, the Tour winner in 1997 and five times the runner-up, had problems with his right knee for a few years, which is how he met Krohme.

In March 2001 she was working with the German national mountain biking team at a training camp in South Africa when Ullrich, also in South Africa to train, was recommended to her. "He had an overly large bone in his knee, and the tendon was rubbing on it," she remembered.

They worked together for three weeks, interrupted by a hospital stay in Germany for the rider, then parted company, and she went to Cairo to teach physiotherapy, anatomy, and sports medicine at the military university there.

In that same year, 2002, he was suspended by his Telekom team for various infractions, including the use of recreational drugs. He also had an operation on his knee.

"We had no contact for a year," Krohme said. "Then my cell phone rang, and this voice said, 'Hi, Birgit, I'm Jan. Do you remember? I want to restart my career.

"'I've had surgery on my knee, they've taken care of that bone, and I need a full-time physical therapist, and I hope you'll do it.'"

She agreed and began working with him when he joined the Coast team last year, then switched to Bianchi for the Tour. When he rejoined Telekom, now called T-Mobile, in 2004, she came with him as a team employee.

"I massage only Jan, but I'm available for chiropractic help to anybody in the team," she said.

Krohme also serves as Ullrich's nutritionist, but not as his dietitian. He is notoriously prone to grow far overweight during the off-season, and Krohme sounded indignant when she was asked if she was responsible for keeping him at the roughly 77 kilograms, or 170 pounds, that is his best riding weight.

"No, no, no, no," she replied. "This is not true. He has a dietitian. I'm only there during a race so that if I see there is a change, not in his weight but in his physical condition, I say, 'Focus more on this, focus more on that.'"

Surprisingly for a man who is believed to train in the off-season on Black Forest cake, Ullrich is spartan at the dinner table during the Tour, she said.

"He eats mainly the things he likes," she reported, "a lot of vegetables, salads, and special stuff." Uh oh, special stuff. Like whipped cream on his Black Forest cake?

"Never," she said. "We have a cook with us, and if Jan says, 'Tonight, spinach,' he gets spinach, and he's happy."

But Ullrich as Popeye is not what comes to mind when he shows up each spring, as he did in 2004, bulging in his jersey.

"If he wants to have cake December 1, fine, I'll give it to him," she said. "If he wants to have it July 1, I would say, 'Jan, maybe this is not the best thing'—and then I would eat it."

As part of her duties to keep him from becoming stylishly stout, she prepares the bag of food that Ullrich snatches in the feed zone of a daily stage as he whizzes past her. "Mostly the usual food," she said. "He may want a different sports bar or different drink than the rest of the team."

Krohme learned her trade by studying physical therapy for three years in Germany, doing a one-year internship at a German hospital, and then going to the United States.

"My focus was high-performing athletes," she said, "and where are the best athletes coming from? America."

She went first to Montana, polishing her English there because family friends lived near Missoula, and studied at the Northern Rockies Rehabilitation Center with a knee specialist.

"They do knee surgery, and twenty-four hours later they send you home, and your insurance doesn't have to pay so much. This for me was the strangest thing on the planet. We in Germany do the surgery and are careful not to move the patient for a week."

She went next to Manhattan and studied at Lenox Hill Hospital. "I was not legalized, so I couldn't take exams," she said. "But they let me watch surgery on knees. That was the best that ever happened because in Germany you're not allowed to go in the operating room without big connections. So I saw anatomy, and not from a book."

Returning to Germany, she worked at the Olympic Sports Place in Stuttgart for four years with the men's national gymnastic and mountain bike teams, which led to her meeting with Ullrich.

"We'll stick together to the end of his career," she said, adding that she would accompany him to the Olympic Games next month and the bicycling world championship this autumn.

Ullrich praises her work highly. "She's great," he said, "and great to work with. She's helped me a lot, a very fine worker."

As for her place on the T-Mobile team, Walter Godefroot, its manager, said of Krohme, "She's the first woman with us, and there are no problems even if, personally, I prefer women when they stay at home."

Wait till Krohme gets her hands on him, on or off the massage table.

LIFTING A CUP OF CHEER

2004

Let's go bar-hopping in western Belgium with the Tour of Flanders, a race that broke millions of hearts and ended with a collective groan. A lot of beer was downed en route.

First stop: The town of Gistel, 27 kilometers into the 257-kilometer classic, one of the five so-called monuments of one-day races. The weather when the race left its start in picturesque Bruges was windy and cold with the threat of rain—typically Belgian.

Unlike the center of Bruges, rich in medieval Flamand architecture, Gistel is not picturesque. At its best, which it was not when the sun hid behind a thundercloud, it is plain.

Gistel, however, is a monument all its own. The town is home to two champions, Johan Museeuw, the current king of the classics, and Sylvère Maes, winner of the Tour de France in 1936 and 1939.

Museeuw, now 38, has won the Tour of Flanders three times, tying the record, and was making a final attempt before he retires to win it a fourth time.

He is nicknamed the Lion of Flanders after the local flag, yellow with a black heraldic lion. Maes, nickname uncertain, has been dead for years but long ran the Café Tourmalet, named for his Tour stage victory over that peak in the Pyrenees.

Although the Café Tourmalet seems to be a jolly place, strewn with bicycles, photographs of the former proprietor in racing garb, and jerseys from Museeuw's collection, the first stop on the itinerary was actually outside its doors at a stand labeled Bierhandel—Drink Market. Soft drinks were available but, even at 10:40 a.m., everybody preferred beer.

Crushed plastic cups littered the ground on which stood two 30-something men, each sporting a club racing jersey.

Since they declined to give their names—"Why should we?" one asked reasonably—they may be labeled knowledgeable sources who spoke on the condition of anonymity.

"We're here to see Museeuw, of course," the first source said. "This is the last time he'll be in a Tour of Flanders. One more victory and the record is his alone. Also, we're here to see the race itself."

"What he says goes for me," the second source confirmed.

Just then the race swept through town, where immense crowds swelled into the street and were swept back by motorcycle policemen, only to return to their places when the police sped down the road.

A twenty-man early breakaway was being chased by a ten-man group, followed three minutes later by the main pack, including Museeuw.

As he pedaled through town, past his father's garage and his own home, past hundreds of yellow flags with black lions rampant, the sun emerged from its dark cloud and flooded the road with light. It was surely a sign.

"Maybe," a knowledgeable source said. "Museeuw's not so young any more and he's been having back troubles. This may not be his day."

"Correct," another source said.

Second stop: The fifth of eighteen climbs, the Oude Kwaremont hill, 2,200 meters long with a maximum gradient of 11 percent. More specifically, In 'tPalet, the Palette Inn, decorated with etchings and paintings.

The drinking room in the front and the dining room in the back were packed at 2 p.m., even though the menu was limited to two regional specialties, grilled cheese sandwiches and spaghetti with meat sauce. Also beer.

Much beer. Most patrons preferred a brand called, like the hill, Oude Kwaremont, a dark, somewhat sweet brew. In a corner, watching a televised account of the race like everybody else, two old men had chosen a lunch of a bottle of Chablis wine and cigars.

"Of course Museeuw," said one of them, speaking on condition of anonymity. "Who else?" asked the second, requesting the same privacy.

The race approached, with the two breakaway groups holding fast and the pack, including Museeuw, still three minutes behind.

Nearly everybody poured out of the inn to watch the riders climb the hill outside and to flap their Flanders flags, but the two old men lingered over the Chablis dregs.

"He'll catch them," the first source said. "Certainly," Source B chipped in.

Third stop: The next-to-last climb, the dreaded Muur, or Wall, officially the Kapelmuur, just 825 meters long but with a maximum gradient of 20 percent. Riders have been known to walk their bicycles uphill here.

Near the top, alongside the road, sits 'tHemelryck, the Paradise, tavern.

It is always packed for the Tour of Flanders, as is a tent erected especially for the race over a deck outside. The tavern and the tent both feature big television sets.

Why stand in the cold wind and occasional rain, jostling with thousands of others for a view, when Paradise and its refreshments beckon?

About 4 p.m., when the race usually passes, the sun is far gone over the yardarm and there's nothing to do except watch the riders on television and drink beer.

"Museeuw isn't that far back," said an unshaven fellow who identified himself as Albert II, King of the Belgians, but was almost certainly an impostor.

"Not...that...far...back," said his consort, definitely not Queen Paola.

Museeuw was still in the chasing group, less than a minute behind three unsung leaders: Steffen Wesemann, a German with the T-Mobile team; Leif Hoste, a Belgian with Lotto; and Dave Bruylandts, a Belgian with Chocolade Jacques.

They were half a minute ahead with 15 kilometers to go and their chasers included not only Museeuw but also Peter Van Petegem, the Belgian who won Flanders last year; Paolo Bettini, the Italian who won the ten-race World Cup classics series; George Hincapie, the American who won the Three Days of De Panne race a few days before; Frank Vandenbroucke, the Belgian who finished second in Flanders last year; and Michael Boogerd, a Dutchman who always rides well here.

In other words, all the favorites were chasing three minor riders.

Chase them they did, unsuccessfully, all the way to the finish.

If Museeuw, the Lion of Flanders, could not win his final Tour of Flanders, all that the crowd under yellow flags wished was that another Lion—Hoste, from Kortrjik, or Bruylandts, from Lier—could.

In the final sprint, they couldn't. When Bruylandts attacked and opened a small gap, he was quickly caught by his two companions. Wesemann then took the lead and finished a clear-cut first.

A German. No Museeuw. No Lions. A groan shook 'tHemelryck, the same groan that certainly shook Café Tourmalet, Bierhandel, and In 'tPalet.

Flags large and small were hurled to the floor in anger. Ten seconds later, it was time to drown all sorrows.

Waiter!

THE LION RETIRES

2004

His back aches. His power has waned. Training rides in the sleet and winds of Belgium are less a pleasure, more a chore. A confusing drug charge bedevils him. He will turn 39 in October. For Johan Museeuw, it's time to retire.

He will after the minor Grand Prix de l'Escaut, also known as the Schelderprijs Vlaanderen, in Museeuw's native Flanders. In any language—Flemish, French, English—he is the Lion of Flanders, the winner of 101 races, and he wants to end his seventeen-year career as a professional racer before his home fans.

Museeuw would have liked to go out by a bigger door, but what would have been his twelfth victory in a World Cup classic eluded him.

Fifteenth in the Tour of Flanders nearly two weeks ago, fifth then in Paris-Roubaix—for any other rider, that would have been a fine week's work. For Museeuw, it was a letdown. Another victory in the Tour of Flanders would have been his fourth, setting a record; another victory in Paris-Roubaix would also have been his fourth, tying the record.

Although he had a shot at winning both races, things went wrong.

In Flanders, the problem was tactics. His Quick Step teammates were unsure whom to support among their handful of potential winners, and over the last few hills Museeuw was left adrift. Paris-Roubaix was different. His teammates were dedicated to Museeuw in his last hurrah.

Tom Boonen, the 23-year-old Belgian who finished third in Paris-Roubaix two years ago and has become Museeuw's protégé, spoke for the team when he told the newspaper *Het Nieuwsblad* how he wanted the race to conclude: "Johan wins his final Paris-Roubaix. A fourth time. Again, completely alone, against the wind."

It nearly happened that way, too. With about seven of the race's 260 kilometers to go, on the next-to-last of twenty-six cobblestoned sections, Museeuw was in a group of five with a secure lead over what was left of the field. The four others were minor riders, not the caliber to worry the Lion of Flanders. He looked comfortable.

But those cobblestones challenge not only riders but also their bicycles.

If a rider crashes or gets a flat early in the nearly seven-hour race, teammates can help lead him back to the front. Late in the race, however, time simply runs out: A rider with a mechanical problem will lose unrecoverable seconds on the leaders.

That is what happened to Museeuw in the group of five.

His rear tire punctured and, in the fifteen or so seconds it took to replace it and push him back into the race, the four others were gone, uncatchable.

"I was sure I'd win," he said after he finished 17 seconds behind the winner. "The four others looked spent. In the final sprint, I wouldn't have had any trouble. My fourth victory was so close and then I heard the 'psitt' of the puncture.

"Beforehand, I had a funny feeling, I thought that for my last Paris-Roubaix, luck would be with me. That would have been too good to be true."

Once across the finish line, he retreated to his team bus and admitted that he wept for half an hour.

This was his fifteenth Paris-Roubaix and he has finished all but one. In 1998 he crashed and injured a knee, which because of inept medical treatment nearly turned gangrenous and left him in a coma for three weeks.

Two years later he won Paris-Roubaix for a second time.

He won Flanders in 1993, 1995, and 1998, and Paris-Roubaix in 1996, 2000, and 2002. His other classics victories included the Amstel Gold Race, the Championship of Zurich, and Paris-Tours. He was twice champion of Belgium, in 1992 and 1996, twice winner of the World Cup series, in 1995 and 1996, and once world road-race champion, again in 1996.

If he was king of the one-day races, he was not dominant in long stage races.

As a second-year professional in 1989 with the ADR team, he helped Greg LeMond finish first in the Tour de France, a race in which Museeuw, never a contender, won two daily stages in 1990 and wore the yellow jersey for three days in 1994 and two days in 1993.

"He's had a fabulous career," said Sean Kelly, the king of the classics in the 1980s and, like Museeuw, a man known for his toughness and dedication.

"When he came to the professionals, he wasn't a big star on the amateur scene but he developed to be a great rider," Kelly said in an interview before the Tour of Flanders. "He's put in a lot of hard work, a lot of sacrifice to get the results he has. He's been the greatest classics rider over the last fifteen years.

"In the classics, he's probably been greater than I was because he's concentrated everything on them for his season. When I was doing the classics, I was also doing Paris-Nice and two or three other stage races."

The Irishman won the weeklong Paris-Nice an astounding seven successive times and the ten-day Tour of Switzerland twice.

"I think Museeuw could have won those also," Kelly said, "but then maybe he wouldn't have won all the classics he did."

He turned to what he described as one of Museeuw's strengths, "your commitment to be training and resting."

"All the big riders have it for a moment, but do they keep it going on for five years, seven years?

"That's the difficult one to do, to carry on for a number of years. When you get fame and fortune, it's difficult to keep working at it."

Museeuw has certainly kept working at it. He originally planned to retire last year after the Tour of Flanders and Paris-Roubaix but fell sick beforehand and struggled in those races.

Back he came for one more year of training and racing, determined to go out with a splash.

"What's most important to me is that, at my age," he told the newspaper *L'Equipe*, "I've remained at such a high level as a rider. Above all, I want to avoid the image of a Johan Museeuw in decline.

"When you've won as many races as I have, you can't allow yourself to retire as anything but a great champion."

On that reckoning, Museeuw has no worries.

LONG ODDS

2004

When Lance Armstrong sets off on a three-week, 3,390-kilometer quest to cross one of the final frontiers in sports, he will be competing against not simply twenty teams of nine riders each but also the forces of age and history.

Can he do it, win a sixth Tour de France? Since the race began in 1903, only four other riders have won five times, and none were successful when trying for a sixth victory. Of those four, only one recorded five consecutive victories, as Armstrong did last year.

That is the lesson of history. The lesson of age is equally daunting: None of the four won the Tour past the age of 31 and Armstrong, the Texan who leads the U.S. Postal Service team, will have to break the record as a 32-year-old.

He acknowledges that with age, strength fades. An athlete realizes this earlier than most—the football loses its spiral, the one-bounce peg from center field begins arriving in a sputter. It is a natural occurrence that not all the will in the world can overcome.

"Some might say I'm exiting my peak years," he admitted during the winter.

He also knows that most of his major rivals are younger than he is.

Although Tyler Hamilton, the American leader of the Phonak team from Switzerland, is 33, Iban Mayo, the Spanish leader of the Euskaltel team from Spain, is 26; Roberto Heras, the Spanish leader of Liberty Seguros from Spain, is 30; and Ivan Basso, the Italian leader of CSC from Denmark, is 26.

Armstrong's archrival, Jan Ullrich, the German leader of T-Mobile and the man Armstrong says he constantly thinks about, will be present and looks fit. The winner of the Tour in 1997 and five times a finisher in second place, three times to Armstrong, Ullrich is just 30 and showed his form recently by winning the weeklong Tour of Switzerland.

"He has several things going for him," Armstrong said of Ullrich. "He has, first of all, a great team, he has the motivation of wanting to win again—he's won before and wants to get it back. He'll be tough to beat. He's entering his peak years for an athlete in our sport."

These names of contenders were all furnished by Armstrong in an interview at his home in Spain early in the season.

"I think Mayo will be good," he said then. "The course suits him. I think Ivan Basso is going to have a good Tour. Yeah. I'm quite sure about that. I think he's got new motivation, new morale.

"Tyler will have a good Tour," he continued. "I don't know about Roberto, but the Tour this year suits the climbers," and Heras is one of the best.

Big Tex, as Armstrong sometimes jokingly refers to himself, is right that the course suits climbers.

Starting in Liège, Belgium, the Tour will meander westward on flat countryside in Belgium and France through July 11, 2004, with a team time trial over 64.5 kilometers on July 7 a highlight. After the first of two rest days on July 12, the riders will encounter hills on the next three days in the Massif Central.

On July 16 and 17, the race goes into the Pyrenees for demanding stages that finish at altitude, meaning that there will be no descent after the final climb for a rider to recoup lost time.

After another flat stage on July 18 and another rest day on July 19, the Alps arrive.

"The last week looks really tough, the toughest we have ever done," Armstrong said. "It will be much better to have a stronger second half than a strong first half."

As an appetizer, the stage on July 20 will include five testing climbs. The next day is the main course: an unprecedented individual time trial up the 15.5 kilometers and twenty-one hairpin curves that lead to Alpe d'Huez.

"That could be the deciding moment," Armstrong said. "It will be a big moment. But the stages before are very hard. There are incredible mountains, you'll have a lot of selection there."

It gets no easier after Alpe d'Huez, with two more mountain stages on July 22 and 23 and a 60-kilometer individual time trial on July 24 before the Tour reaches its finale in Paris on July 25.

"A tough Tour, a very tough Tour," Armstrong said in summation. But then, no Tour is easy and he has won five consecutively since his remarkable comeback from the testicular cancer that invaded his body in 1996.

To repeat the question, can he do what no one has done before and make it six?

Jacques Anquetil, the first to win five Tours, did not try for another after his last victory in 1964. Following his fifth victory, Eddy Merckx finished second in 1975 when a French fan injured him with a punch in the liver during a major climb. Bernard Hinault was second in his final year, 1986, when his teammate, Greg LeMond, was overwhelming.

Finally, Miguel Indurain, who also won five Tours consecutively, collapsed in the rain and cold in 1996, finishing 11th and retiring at the end of the season.

As Indurain knows, the weather can be a big factor. An oppressively hot July is predicted and Armstrong does not enjoy heavy heat.

Last year he prevailed over Ullrich by 1 minute, 1 second, his smallest margin of victory by at least four minutes, and admitted afterward that "I was just not happy with my performance."

"Maybe I took the race too much for granted," he said at a news conference in Brussels in December. "Maybe I was a little too comfortable with success.

"It was a tough year emotionally, physically, and psychologically. You can't win forever. You get older, bad luck, somebody comes along. The argument can be made that we've already seen that curve start."

Armstrong has had strong but not dominant performances thus far in 2004. Sometimes he has struggled one day and been a master the next. Unlike other years, he has not left his rivals believing that he cannot be beaten.

On the plus side, his Postal Service team seems to be as powerful as ever and certainly as dedicated as usual to his victory.

"We have a very experienced team and more than anything else, we have a very committed team," he said when the lineup was announced.

"They know what it takes to win the Tour and they want to do that again." Armstrong has finished his customarily thorough preparations, scouting the major climbs and time-trial courses, especially Alpe d'Huez, which he has ascended this spring for days at a time.

As history and age conspire against him, Armstrong replied simply, "I'm ready."

Don't bet against him.

LOOKING FOR THAT BIG VICTORY

2004

Everybody in the small world of bicycle racing has seen the photograph of George Hincapie, covered in dust, sitting slumped in a cubicle, holding his head in his hands, after the 2002 Paris-Roubaix race. In black and white, a bit grainy, the photograph sums up that fearful race over cobblestones and the toll it takes on riders.

Hincapie has seen the picture, of course, even though he was surprised to learn that it was voted French sports photograph of the year.

He agrees that it caught the moment.

"I was devastated," the 30-year-old American rider for the U.S. Postal Service team said in an interview in Girona, his base in Spain for the season. "The picture got it right.

"When I was sitting there, I was so tired I was shaking. I sat there for about thirty minutes. I could not change clothes, I was just shaking."

Putting words to the photograph, Hincapie discussed his emptiness after finishing sixth for the second time.

"I felt so good in that race and it just went away with little mistakes: I didn't eat, I didn't stay warm when it was freezing cold, I had no jacket on, I just lost all my energy. When I was sitting there, I had nothing left."

How this happened to Hincapie—a professional since the age of 20, a man who has finished seven of the eight Tours de France he has ridden and who is one of Postal Service's main hopes in the Tour of Flanders and Paris-Roubaix—offers a primer on how punishing these one-day classics are.

"There was a breakaway and we started chasing," he remembered as he sat over a coffee in a restaurant after a training ride with his team leader, neighbor, and friend, Lance Armstrong.

"It was 45, 50 degrees and the temperature changed to pretty warm," Hincapie said of that Paris-Roubaix race, "so we took our jackets off, left them at the team car. And I felt so good that I wasn't eating enough.

"Then the temperature dropped to 33 or 34, a big change, but at that point we were at the front, chasing, so I didn't want to tell the team to go back and get jackets and more food. I thought 'This is it, this is the time.'

"But there were still 150 kilometers to go," or a little less than half the race.

"So we kept going and the guys, one by one, they got dropped and before you knew it there were just four of us left chasing the breakaway and I was wasting all this energy and not eating and being cold. By the time we caught them, I thought, 'Oh, no, I have nothing left.'" And he didn't. In the finale onto the velodrome track in Roubaix, he could not overtake the five riders ahead of him.

How could the experienced Hincapie have let this happen?

"Paris-Roubaix is . . ." he started to explain and stopped. "There's so much going on, so. . . ."

Another pause.

"Yeah, it was stupid," he said. "But you learn. I learned."

He could not benefit last year, when viral and parasitic infections scrubbed his early season.

"You can get it anywhere—bad water, bad food," he said.

"I was cured by just rest and a lot of herbal remedies."

Perhaps because his season started late, he had an especially strong Tour de France, helping Armstrong to victory for the fifth successive year. Hincapie is usually the fellow at the front of the Postal Service train as it moves up early in the mountains, setting a rapid pace to prevent attacks and tire Armstrong's rivals.

"The last few years I've been doing a lot more training in the mountains," he said. "I'm not a climber by any means, but I do my job there now."

It's in the early classics that Hincapie sheds his job of support rider and becomes a team leader.

"If I'm healthy, Flanders and Paris-Roubaix are definitely my style of race. There's not so many guys left at the end, it's a race of attrition, a kind of survival race, everybody has just a little fuel left in their tank. That's my style."

In the past, his style has been somewhat cramped because Postal Service is built for the Tour, not the classics, where strong teammates, Hincapie said, are equally vital.

"They help at the beginning and at the end, when there are only ten, twenty, thirty guys left" of the nearly two hundred who start the race.

"People are attacking and typically are attacking just to make you work more.

"So if you have some teammates with you, they can do that work. Instead of somebody softening you up, you soften them up, and save yourself for close to the line.

"Also, they can give you their wheels if you flat, shelter you from the wind, things you need."

As far as tactics go, both races are similar, he explained.

"Flanders is definitely a race of attrition, of extreme concentration. At the beginning especially, you always have to battle for position, not be too far back before the hills and the cobblestone sections. Paris-Roubaix is the same but no hills and a lot more cobblestones.

"At the end of Flanders, you have to think about conserving energy for the last two or three climbs when the group goes from thirty guys to five."

There are eighteen short but steep and narrow climbs.

As for the bad weather that often marks both races, Hincapie shrugged. "I don't like bad weather but it doesn't affect my performance," he said.

"A lot of guys wake up and they see it's pouring rain or snowing and then half the field is pretty much done, not a factor anymore.

"But for me, I wake up and see it's raining and I don't like it but I know I'll perform just as well. That's because I grew up in New York. I trained in the snow and the rain and raced in Central Park in snow and rain all the time. It's just something I'm used to."

He lives now in the off-season in Greenville, South Carolina, which he described as "a great place: good roads for training, good restaurants, good climate, and nice people."

Hincapie's highest placing in Flanders was fourth in 2002. He has finished Paris-Roubaix in fourth place twice and sixth place twice. His biggest victories include the U.S. national championship in 1998, the San Francisco Grand Prix in 2001, and the semi-classic Ghent-Wevelgem race in Belgium, also in 2001.

Looking back on his career, he noted one of the high points: "Being part of a five-time Tour de France winning team. I never thought that would happen."

He also admitted to a disappointment. "I would have loved to have won a World Cup race by now and it's been nagging at me."

Then he brightened. "I'll give it a couple of more shots," Hincapie said. "Starting soon."

AT HOME

2004

When Lance Armstrong announced that he would ride in a new bicycle race in Colorado, the buzz started: After years of infrequent appearances in American races, Armstrong will race in the Tour of Georgia in April 2004, then in the Rocky Mountain Classic in Colorado in September and, a week later, in the T-Mobile Classic in San Francisco.

Was this, fans wondered, a farewell tour for Armstrong on native soil before he retired? Sitting in his home in Girona, Spain, as that question was put to him, Armstrong said, "I really don't know."

Like many questions in his life now, the answer is shrouded in what he describes as "circumstances," both sporting and personal.

"I'm not planning a farewell tour, but it could be a farewell tour," he admitted. "It depends on how the Tour de France goes, how I feel after the Tour, how our search goes for a new title sponsor for this program."

The U.S. Postal Service has sponsored his team since late 1996 and its contract expires this year.

"We don't know yet if they'll continue," he said. "They haven't decided. This will be close to ten years of sponsorship, which is a long run in this sport."

In that time the Postal Service has seen the team rise from mediocrity to support Armstrong in victories in the last five Tours de France. The attendant glory has wiped out the service's identification with "going postal," or showing up for work enraged and with a gun.

But critics wonder why the U.S. Postal Service pays $6 million to $7 million a year for a team of nearly forty riders, officials, doctors, mechanics, and masseurs who spend most of the season at European races. Why not, instead, lower the cost of a stamp? In response, Postal Service officials in Washington cite worker morale—the identification that the average postal worker makes with Armstrong and his teammates as they sweep to victory, year after year, in the world's most publicized bicycle race. We're all world-beaters, this reasoning goes.

"I think we have the best team in the world. I think we provide more for a sponsor than any other team because the Tour de France is clearly so big,"

Armstrong said as he sat in the dining room of his spacious apartment, furnished in baronial style.

"Consider the last three Tours, and we've been an incredibly dominant team. The team, the support riders, have been better than most people who know cycling can remember in a long time."

That reflects on the sponsor, he said.

If the U.S. Postal Service does not extend for at least a year and if another sponsor cannot be found, he continued, his future in the sport is doubtful.

Referring to a secondary sponsor based in Belgium, Armstrong said, "Berry Floor will step up, but they're not the size of company to take over the whole program. That will have a serious effect on whether I continue. I don't foresee switching programs, switching directors, switching everything."

He has raced in the red, white, and blue colors of the Postal Service team since 1998, the beginning of his comeback two years after a diagnosis of testicular cancer that had spread to his brain and lungs. In 1999, the former specialist in one-day races astonished bicycle fans by dominating the three-week Tour de France in the first of five successive victories.

What does he think of his chances of winning it a record sixth time? None of the four other riders who have won five Tours—Jacques Anquetil, Eddy Merckx, Bernard Hinault, and Miguel Indurain—did it past the age of 31.

"I like my chances," he said. "Last year there was some bad luck, but there was some poor planning, poor preparation, and, of course, circumstances."

Personal circumstances?—meaning his then-impending divorce and his separation from his twin daughters and son—or sporting circumstances?

"All of the above," Armstrong said quickly. Then he thought about it.

"More sporting circumstances," he decided. "Crashes, distractions, equipment issues.

"But mostly, I was too confident. Even with all this stuff going on, I was still sure I was going to succeed. I won't be that confident again. That Tour humbled me. I didn't feel the bullet, but I heard it. I heard it well."

His margin of victory in the 2003 Tour was barely above a minute, or five minutes less than usual.

For someone who acknowledged dodging bullets, he looked and sounded relaxed. Armstrong had spent part of the day in a training ride on the roads near Girona, a pretty city in Catalonia, about 80 kilometers, or 50 miles, north of Barcelona, and was fresh from a massage in one of the apartment's four bedrooms.

Baronial, indeed. The furniture in the main rooms is antique and massive, his garden includes a grotto with a fountain and a portico with four columns from a nearby castle, while pride of place is given to a small chapel with a fifteenth-century painting of the crucifixion of Jesus.

"I've never gone in there and done just much other than show it off," acknowledged Armstrong, who leans more to an inner morality than to organized religion.

He shares his home and an adjacent apartment that he owns with his masseur; with a friend from Texas who handles some business dealings; and with Armstrong's companion, Sheryl Crow, the folk-rock singer who booms onstage and speaks in a whisper off it.

She uses one room as a workplace and said she had written four songs this winter in Girona. Three guitars were ranged against a wall along with computer equipment. "Basically is like a little recording studio. It's really simple," she said.

Crow pointed to a MIDI digital electronic keyboard.

"It has the capability of doing some pretty sticky film scoring. Clearly the sounds aren't going to be like a professional orchestra," she said, "but you can pump up live guitar and bass and plug directly in and put a little demo track together."

Because they met last autumn after his marriage dissolved, she has not yet seen him in the Tour de France, she said. She seems not to be much of a bicycle racing nut, a fact that landed Armstrong in a mini-controversy.

"We were at a Los Angeles Lakers basketball game," he remembered, "and some journalist spotted us and asked Sheryl, 'How are you on a bike?' And she said, 'I don't ride a bike, I'm just looking for the Krispy Kreme stand.' Just a joke but that started it."

Suddenly the racing Web sites were flooded with complaints by fans that Armstrong should not be neglecting his training by wolfing down doughnuts and staying up late at basketball games. When the couple were photographed at a movie premiere, the complaints increased.

"The doughnut thing started as a joke and got carried away," Armstrong said. "The Internet is a haven for people with no face and no name. So we can say, we can do, we can act however we want on it."

Life in the spotlight with a celebrity like Crow is a new dimension, he agreed.

"But the only thing I have to do is stay focused on my job, train, show up ready to win the Tour de France. And I'm doing that. I mean, if you can go to a late-night movie every night and still win the Tour de France, who cares? If I can drink a twelve-pack every night and still win the Tour de France, who cares? I don't care.

"Now, would I do that? Absolutely not. But the bottom line is winning the Tour. From a sporting perspective, doing something in December or January," the off-season, "has no bearing."

"I don't even like Krispy Kremes," Armstrong protested. "I don't eat them. I like apple fritters."

Turning back to business, he predicted that "it will be a tough Tour."

"Ullrich will be tough, his team will be tough," he said. Armstrong was referring to Jan Ullrich, the German who finished second last year for the fifth time, and the T-Mobile, formerly Telekom, team.

"The Tour this year suits the climbers," he continued, "because of the addition of the uphill time trial and the subtraction of a long flat time trial."

In addition, the rules for the team time trial have been changed to limit losses for those, unlike Armstrong, with weak teams.

"I think Mayo will be good," he said, referring to Iban Mayo, a Basque climber with Euskaltel who lost three and a half minutes in the team time trial last year.

"The uphill time trial will help him and the new team time trial rules—which are very hard to understand and even harder to believe—will help teams like that."

The rules were changed, he explained, "just to keep the race tighter. But I disagree. Don't do it. Let's just have a road stage if you want to keep it tight.

"Tyler will have a good Tour and Vino has certainly looked good so far," he went on, referring to Tyler Hamilton, the American who was fourth last year, and Alexandre Vinokourov, the Kazakh who was third.

"I don't know about Roberto," referring to a former teammate and current rival Roberto Heras, a Spaniard.

"Ivan Basso is going to have a good Tour. I'm quite sure about that."

Basso, an Italian, was 11th last year when he rode for the Fassa Bortolo team in his homeland. Now he has joined CSC in Denmark.

"I think he's got new motivation, new morale with CSC," Armstrong said. "They will do a very good team time trial, so even with the new rules, with him in CSC as against him in Fassa Bortolo, you still could be talking about two minutes gained."

In all, he thought, perhaps ten riders could be considered contenders.

First among them is, of course, the defending champion. His morale is strong, he said, especially because he would shortly be returning to his home in Austin, Texas, after a French race to see his three children for the first time in nearly two months.

"Life's good," he said, "it's very good. The only tough thing is missing the kids and I'll see them pretty soon. The situation is a temporary one, of being separated from them months at a time," instead of having them live with him in Girona during the season as they used to do.

"When I retire eventually, my time with them will be much more consistent, much more predictable."

That will have a bearing on when he retires, he agreed: "Of course. Definitely." Until then, he is following his usual schedule of racing and training, with the emphasis on training in daily rides in the countryside around Girona.

"You have easier days, recovery days, long days," he said. A long day is six or seven hours, a short day two or two and a half hours.

Few riders over the age of 30 are as devoted to training as Armstrong is.

"Absolutely," he said when asked if he preferred training to racing.

"Especially if you're at home. It's good to be home. Racing is switching hotels every night. You're in a different place and you don't know what the roads will be like, what the meals will be like. Whereas at home, I love being here, I'm comfortable here, I like the town to walk around in. It's a home. It's not a house," he said firmly, "it's a home."

AN ITALIAN DRAMA

2004

The most endearingly theatrical of people, Italians adore high drama wherever they find it. That may be in politics, opera, cuisine, dodging tax collectors, or even bicycle racing.

Even bicycle racing: The theft of a small monument to Marco Pantani in the Italian mountains he climbed so brilliantly has been a national calamity. Rewards for the plaque's return have been posted, a replacement has already been ordered, and the police are pursuing the perps with almost the same assiduity they showed in hounding Pantani himself.

He died in February, barricaded in his room in a cheap hotel, of a cocaine overdose at the age of 34.

Not Puccini—think *Tosca*—nor even the Verdi of *La Traviata* could have done honor to his funeral.

Twenty thousand people, weeping and moaning, attended in his home town, and six pallbearers carried his coffin from the church to the cemetery, 2 kilometers, or a little over a mile, away.

"They spoke not a word," testified a Belgian reporter who walked behind the coffin. "No words at all, not even a grunt. All that wailing behind them, and they marched to the cemetery silently."

Maybe, then, not *Tosca*. No elephants, scratch *Aida*. Which leaves what?

Cue in the muffled drums from *La Forza del Destino,* the force of destiny, where the leading characters, or so the music encyclopedias attest, "have no control over circumstances."

That certainly fits Pantani, the winner of the 1998 Giro d'Italia and Tour de France and a rider who was ousted on drug charges from the 1999 Giro on its next-to-last day while he held a commanding lead. He never recovered from that disgrace.

Another rider it may fit is Davide Rebellin, 33, an Italian who won three one-day classics in a week in April, vaulted into the lead of the World Cup series, and then watched his universe disintegrate.

After he was not selected for the national team at the Olympic Games in Athens in August, Rebellin deduced that he would also be passed over for the world championship road race in Verona, Italy. Blocking his way was his assumed reluctance to work as a support rider for Paolo Bettini, 30, the Italian who won the Olympic road race.

So Rebellin applied for Argentine citizenship, which was granted but not definitively enough to get him into the world championships. The passport he needed to ride as the one-man Argentine team did not arrive in time to qualify him.

Worse, a week later, while he held a six-point lead over Bettini in the World Cup standings, Rebellin finished thirteenth in the Paris-Tours race, gaining 13 points. Bettini finished sixth, gaining 32 points and moving into the lead, 340 to 327.

They will duke it out in the finale of the ten-race World Cup of one-day classics, the Tour of Lombardy in Italy.

Verdi would have had a field day, lacking only a soprano.

In this corner, Rebellin—bland, inarticulate, and, like Pantani, a suspect in a doping case or two. A consistent high finisher over the years, he was rarely a winner until that golden week in April as the leader of the Gerolsteiner team from Germany in the Amstel Gold Race, the Flèche Wallonne, and Liège-Bastogne-Liège.

In the other corner, Bettini—well-spoken, engaging, maybe not a Hollywood guy when it comes to looks but clean, never a suspicion of illegal performance-enhancing drugs or other shenanigans. Forget that accusation that he tried to buy the world championship in Canada in 2003; everybody denied it, including the Spanish rider who first reported it in his native language to his national press and then said he had been misquoted.

Bettini, who rides for Quick Step from Belgium, has won the World Cup the last two years. Although he has yet to win a classic this year, he has come close.

He has a habit of beating on his handlebars with his right fist when he is nipped at the finish line and so clanged his way through August, second in the Hew Cyclassic Hamburg (thump), second in the Clásica San Sebastián (thump), and second in the Championship of Zurich (thump).

As the favorite in the world championship road race—and here evolves the high drama so beloved in The Boot—he withdrew after injuring his right knee more than halfway through.

While he struggled through two more laps, the national team dared not attack and leave him behind, thus setting up a sprint finish that was won by Oscar Freire, a Spaniard.

How Bettini hurt himself is uncertain. On television, he said he hit his knee on the door of a team car after a wheel change on his bicycle because of a flat.

Hours later, he said he hit the knee on his handlebar.

The Italian team coach, Franco Ballerini, said Bettini's foot had slipped out of the pedal and his knee had hit first the car door and then the handlebar.

This confusion ripened into controversy when Francesco Moser, a champion of the 1980s, insisted that Bettini had faked an injury because he was having a bad day and needed an excuse to quit the race.

Moser's credentials as an impartial witness are blighted by his family ties to a rider who was left off the Italian team because of his assumed reluctance to work for Bettini. No, not Rebellin, but Gilberto Simoni, another man with no control over circumstances.

Or perhaps he does have a bit of control: Simoni is hinting that he will also exchange his Italian citizenship for an Argentine, or Austrian, one and ride in the next world championships.

So the storm rages. Was Bettini hurt or dogging it? Can Rebellin make up his World Cup deficit in the final race? Who took Pantani's monument?

The answer to at least the second question should be known soon.

Unless, that is, Freire wins the Tour of Lombardy and Bettini and Rebellin both finish lower than 25th. In that case, the Spaniard, now in third place in the overall standings after he finished third in Paris-Tours, would leapfrog into first place as the season ended.

Wouldn't all these plots, innuendoes, and rivalries make a gorgeous opera? Music, maestro, please.

MAN OF THE YEAR

2004

A new generation emerged this year in professional bicycle racing, led by Damiano Cunego, an Italian who, at age 22 in the spring of 2004, had registered his biggest victories in the world championship junior road race in 1999 and a third-tier race in China last year.

Then Cunego won the Giro d'Italia in June and, now 23, finished the season in October with a victory in the esteemed Tour of Lombardy classic. He climbs, he sprints, he is single-minded, and he ranks No. 1 in the computerized rolls of the sport.

In Spain, but only in Spain, the skies were lit up by Alejandro Valverde, barely 24 and condemned to miss most big races because his Communidad Valenciana team, formerly Kelme, was banned outside its homeland amid suspicions about doping and questionable finances. Now that Valverde has moved to the strong Iles Balears team for the 2005 season, he will be an international star.

So will Tom Boonen, 24, the Belgian who emerged as a top sprinter, and Michael Rogers, not quite 25, the Australian who has been world champion in the time trial the past two years. Honorable mention goes to Fabian Cancellera, 23, a Swiss prologue specialist; Yaroslav Popovych, 24, a Ukrainian all-arounder; and Thomas Voeckler, 25, the Frenchman who led the Tour de France for ten days.

The older guard did well this year, too. Davide Rebellin, 33, an Italian, won three classics in a week in May; Paolo Bettini, going on 31 and another Italian, won the World Cup and the Olympic road race; and Roberto Heras, 30, a Spaniard, finished first in the Vuelta a España for the second successive year.

Another graybeard, Lance Armstrong, won his sixth consecutive Tour de France at age 33.

The Tour remains the pinnacle of the sport, and Armstrong gave his all, metaphorically, to break the record of five victories.

However, bicycle racing's man of the year, Emile Brichard, gave his all, literally, to the Tour.

If Cunego, Valverde, Boonen, Rogers, and others are the young guard, Brichard was definitely the old guard. He was 104 years old.

When the Tour began its centennial edition in Liège, Belgium, Brichard was the oldest former participant. The record books showed that in 1926, he was a member of the Alcyon team in the race.

There was not much more for the records to show, since Brichard dropped out during the first stage—373 kilometers from Evian to Mulhouse—and never again participated in the Tour. He spent the rest of his working days as a miner.

Still, the race organizers decided, he was the oldest participant, and he was Belgian, living not far from Liège. Race officials descended on his home and, possibly waking him from a nap, lavished him with honors.

In bicycle-mad Belgium, this was a big story, and the voracious national press leaped on it when Brichard also turned out to be the oldest living Belgian veteran of World War I.

Dozens of reporters and television crews visited Brichard over the next few days as the Tour meandered through the French-speaking part of Belgium. He told his story over and over again, and the excitement of his newfound glory was, alas, too much for his ancient heart.

The Tour had moved into France when word came that Brichard had died. Because the race's collective mind was on the mountains ahead, not the flatlands of Belgium behind, no memorial service seems to have been held.

Let's do it now: Hail and farewell, old-timer.

AFTER THE SCANDAL

2005

Meet the revamped Cofidis bicycle team—now, back racing after its mammoth drug scandal, as clean as a hound's tooth.

Cleaner, insists François Migraine. He is president of the Cofidis company, the team's sponsor, as well as the head of its sports organization and an admitted bicycle racing nut, so he ought to know, right?

Wrong. After he had to suspend all team racing for a month last year to try to unravel the scandal, Migraine confessed that he had never suspected a thing, really had little to do with the riders and, in general, didn't like most of them anyway. So he might not be the best authority on the team's state of health this season.

But riders and other team officials also insisted that those bad old days are long gone. They spoke in Paris at the Cofidis presentation, where nobody needed a Jacques Derrida decoder ring to fathom the event's subtexts.

One was that Cofidis, a company that supplies credit by telephone, is pleased to continue as a sponsor in the sport for a ninth year, a long time in racing, and probably for three years afterward. Business is booming, Migraine announced, with expansion into Eastern Europe.

This growth may have something to do with the drug scandal, which became widely known as the Cofidis Affair. When a similar scandal enveloped the Festina team in 1998, sales of the sponsor's watches soared each month that the name Festina appeared in headlines. Who remembered why there was so much free advertising?

Another subtext was the site of the presentation. Instead of the nightclub-cum-auditorium of the Cofidis unveiling last year, this one was held in the headquarters of the French Olympic Committee. Gone were the potted palms, replaced by photographs of French winners of gold, silver, and bronze medals in the Olympic Games.

"A symbolic site," Migraine called it in his opening remarks, citing the Olympic spirit as he alluded to the Cofidis Affair. It involved the importation, distribution, and use of illegal performance-enhancing drugs and eventually cost more than half a dozen riders and officials their jobs.

He was staying in the sport, he said, because he loved it, "even if love often makes you suffer."

Admitting that he had lacked vigilance before, he said, "What does a victory represent when it was gained through doping? I prefer a rider who behaves loyally even if he doesn't win. Stolen victories mean nothing to me."

What went unmentioned was the relative humility of the occasion. In a change from the previous year's glitz, when the riders arrived on stage on bicycles amid thumping music, this time they simply strolled down the aisle to polite applause. The Cofidis management also shunned its previous chest-beating about its three world champions.

Last year they were David Millar in the time trial, Igor Astarloa in the road race, and Laurent Gané in the keirin and sprint on the track. As the Cofidis Affair exploded, Astarloa, who was not a suspect, fled to an Italian team, and Millar, the Cofidis leader, was arrested and confessed to using the forbidden drug EPO. He was stripped of his world championship and banned from the sport for two years.

Gané was not involved in the scandal and remains. He, Mickaël Bourgain, and Arnaud Tournant, all Cofidis riders, wore rainbow-striped jerseys because they won the team sprint for France at the world championships. But, now that Migraine understands that pride goeth before destruction, they were introduced chastely.

At a buffet lunch afterward—finger food instead of the seared foie gras and asparagus risotto of yesteryear—some riders talked about the Cofidis Affair. All of them had something positive to say.

"It could have gone either way—destroyed the team or made it stronger," said Matthew White, 30, an Australian. "Look at our results at the end of the year: We turned into a great team and a lot closer team."

Those results included seventeen victories on the road, among them two stages in the Tour de France, and a gold medal for Stuart O'Grady on the track in the Olympics.

O'Grady, 31 and an Australian, admitted that the month the team was forced to skip all races had been difficult.

"It was like sitting out with a broken collarbone—you don't have any form, it's something completely out of your control," he said. "In the end, it came down to a business decision, and I think they did the right one.

"It would have been easy to sit back, throw in the towel and say the season's stopped," he added. "That would have been a pretty good excuse to get lame results, but I used it the opposite way.

"The best way to show everyone what we're capable of was to come out all guns firing and win bike races." In addition to his gold medal, he won a stage in the Tour and the Hew Cyclassic Hamburg, a World Cup race.

A newcomer to the team, Nicolas Roche, 20, who has dual French-Irish citizenship, was similarly upbeat.

Asked if the Cofidis Affair had affected his thinking about joining the team, he said: "It didn't bother me at all. They did a very good comeback, they showed power, and it seemed a much better team afterward. Maybe it was even good for the team because it showed they wanted to change things. They had to change things."

Migraine cautiously agrees. "Is this a new start for the team?" he was asked before the presentation. "I hope so," he replied. "One can only hope so."

Or, as he said in his speech later, "I know that we're doing the maximum to protect against doping, but I can't be 100 percent certain it will work."

WHO'S OBSESSED?

2005

Obsession? What obsession? asks Andrea Tafi, who has not spent longer than twenty-four hours a day and no more than seven days a week all year thinking about the coming Paris-Roubaix race.

Early in February, when everybody else was racing in southern France, Italy, and Spain, Tafi and three of his Saunier Duval teammates were in northern France, checking out changes in the traditional Paris-Roubaix course and testing their new bicycles for the 260-kilometer race over nearly 55 kilometers of cobblestones.

You call that frigid five-hour inspection an obsession? Tafi doesn't. He calls it preparation, careful preparation.

"To win Paris-Roubaix, I need the right bike," the Italian, who will turn 39 next month, explained in an interview before the Tour of Flanders.

"So we tested the bicycle on the cobblestones and it wasn't just right. Scott, the manufacturer, they've done everything I asked to change the bicycle. Now it's just right.

"I also wanted to check the state of the cobblestones. I don't think they're so dangerous."

So he has indeed been thinking about this one race all year?

"Yes," he replied quickly and enthusiastically. "Even longer.

"This race is for me something special. When I won the Tour of Flanders, it was a great feeling, a very nice race, but Paris-Roubaix is special.

"Milan-San Remo was important for me, Tirreno-Adriatico was important, the Tour of Flanders will be important for me, every day is important. But Paris-Roubaix is the most important.

"Paris-Roubaix, my heart is in this race."

The affable Tafi, a great favorite of Italian fans, has won Paris-Roubaix, so this is not a case of a rider at the end of his career yearning for the big victory that has eluded him.

Not many big victories have, in fact. After he spent years as a support rider for leaders of the powerhouse Mapei team, he blossomed in the sport's venerated classics in 1996, when he won the Tour of Lombardy.

He also finished third that year in Paris-Roubaix and second there in 1998.

That year he also won the Italian national championship, enabling him to fulfill a boyhood dream of winning Paris-Roubaix, as he did in 1999, with that champion's jersey on, just as his boyhood idol, Francesco Moser, did in 1980.

In 2000, Tafi finished first in another great classic, Paris-Tours, followed by his victory in Flanders in 2002.

Since then, with advanced age and the breakup of the Mapei team three years ago, victories have been harder to come by. He finished 69th, more than eleven minutes behind, in the Tour of Flanders this year.

His best results in the last two years, while he rode for CSC from Denmark, were fifth place in Paris-Roubaix in 2003 and 43rd in that race last year. If he had won or come close to winning last year, he said in the interview, he planned to retire immediately on a high note.

"But last year, when I finished Paris-Roubaix, I didn't feel so good," he continued. "I struggled, too many problems. I didn't even have good training.

"When I finished, I thought, 'This is not the way to stop. This is not a good feeling. I want one more Paris-Roubaix, but with good conditions.'"

Thus far, he added, conditions have been fine.

"My form is OK," he said. "My team is working for me all the time. They're working to make me a winner. For me, second or third is not important."

As he knows from the days when he was a support rider himself, it is difficult to win Paris-Roubaix without strong teammates to shelter the leader from the wind, keeping him near the front of the big field for the first 97 kilometers until the cobblestones start, and then be ready to offer him a wheel or even a bicycle if he has a flat on those stones.

"In this race you can be strong, but you need luck," Tafi said. "No crashes, no punctures. Bad luck changes everything."

Luck is often a factor in Paris-Roubaix, which is nicknamed "the hell of the North" because of its cobblestones. In rainy weather, the dirt between them turns to mud; in sunny weather, it turns to choking dust. In any weather, the stones pound the riders.

The most demanding stretch, the 2.4-kilometer-long Arenberg forest, has been dropped from this year's race because its brutish stones, which have caused many crashes and injuries, are judged to be in too dangerous a condition.

That does not please Tafi, who is almost alone in his objection.

"That sector was a symbol," he told the French magazine *Vélo* this winter. "By dropping the Arenberg, they're removing the magic from the race, they're diminishing the myth. The beauty of Paris-Roubaix, its legend, comes from its difficulty.

"Without the Arenberg, the race will be totally different, especially for team strategy. If you're going to remove the most difficult stretches, you might as well hold the race on a highway."

In the interview, Tafi smiled when he was reminded of those words. The tougher, the better, he said. Paris-Roubaix is a race of difficulties, strength, and luck.

But good luck or bad, he continued, the race will be his finale in Europe. Next comes the business world. He has been fixing up an old mill in his native Tuscany as a hotel for cyclotourists.

"I'm leaving racing but I'll keep riding my bike and, with the hotel, I'll stay in the world of cycling," he said.

He has no regrets, he insisted. As one of the oldest riders in the pack, he accepts that his career is over.

"Probably," he tacked on as a disclaimer. "Maybe I'll ride in the Tour of Georgia. Scott, the people who made my bike right for this race, are an American company. So if I go to Georgia, I go for Scott.

"Maybe I'll go to Georgia as the winner of Paris-Roubaix.

"I hope so," he said dreamily. "I hope so."

A RELIC OF A RACE

2005

Like the beret, the accordion, and a game of boules on a vacant lot, the small-time bicycle race seems to be vanishing from French life.

The big races are doing fine, especially now that the new ProTour requires the twenty top teams to participate in them. There should be enough leftovers from this banquet table to nourish mid-level races.

But at the bottom, those races that almost no major riders pay attention to outside the home country, the pickings are slim. The Midi Libre died a few years ago, returned zombielike under another name for a year, and then perished forever. Just last week, the Across Morbihan race in bicycle-mad Brittany was canceled because sponsorship money has dried up.

What's a race organizer to do?

Ask the people who put on a race that starts in Magnanville, 55 kilometers northwest of Paris and ends in Vimoutiers, a town of 4,800 in deepest Normandy. Magnanville-Vimoutiers? It doesn't sing.

So they changed the first name to Paris, as in such races as Paris-Tours, Paris-Nice, and Paris-Roubaix, none of which starts in Paris either.

Then, for Vimoutiers, they substituted a nearby speck—a church, a cemetery, a farm, a monument, and a tourist center—with a name known around the world: Camembert.

The monument, a pillar of gray stone, is dedicated to Madame Harel, 1761-1812, "who invented Camembert." The tourist center exists presumably to inform the hordes who arrive to view cows and milkmaids, curds and whey, that the speck is as good as it gets shrinewise. Anybody wanting to see the cheese actually being produced can be directed to the many factories and artisans in places, like Vimoutiers, with less-evocative names.

As a race, Paris-Camembert was called Paris-Vimoutiers when it was founded in 1906. For some reason lost to memory, the race was not run again until 1934, when it was still Paris-Vimoutiers.

In the early 1940s, it became Paris-Camembert, then switched back and forth with the original moniker until recent years, when the Camembert Lepetit manufacturing company signed on as primary sponsor and started to pay the bills. The organizers were delighted to say "cheese."

That's the first step in race survival: Find a rich, long-term sponsor.

The second step is to get lucky in the calendar: Paris-Camembert is always staged on the Tuesday after Easter Sunday, which means that it ends a four-day festival in Vimoutiers that includes a donkey show, shooting galleries, numerous rides for children, and food stalls with dangerous looking sausages. Who wouldn't turn out for a bicycle race after that excitement?

The Tuesday after Easter usually coincides, too, with the spring series of classics, thus allowing a rider to limber up in racing conditions for a demanding one-day haul on the following Sunday.

This year the race precedes the Tour of Flanders and that is why Lance Armstrong showed up for Paris-Camembert.

"It's a fine ride for him before Flanders," said Sean Yates, a directeur sportif with Armstrong's Discovery Channel team. "We're not going to win the thing, but we have a reasonable chance, I think," Yates judged beforehand.

He was right on both counts. Armstrong, Discovery Channel's top finisher, placed 24th in the field of 120 and was in contention for most of the 90 final hilly kilometers of the 200-kilometer race.

The American winner of the last six Tours de France likes this race and had ridden in it three times before since his comeback from cancer in 1998, finishing as high as second in 2000.

"It's a demanding race with a finish for the strongest guys," he explained a few years ago. "It's the kind of effort that gives you a good idea of your form." That is a question with an uncertain answer for Armstrong right now.

A third key to a race's survival is to put on a good show: Spend money on police protection of the roads, get the fans to turn out at the start and finish, and select a good course to guarantee competition.

Check, check, and check.

On a raw day with frequent drizzles, a large contingent of volunteers and motorcycle gendarmes kept the roads clear from the start in verdant flatlands through the seven short but steep climbs near the finish.

The fans did turn out in good numbers and better humor, especially at the start, where many put a reassuring arm around the shoulders of young riders from nearly unknown teams as they waited their turn to be introduced.

There in Magnanville, the mood was definitely "family." Five geezers riding bicycles and wearing jerseys from Verneuil, many kilometers away, offered advice to anybody who would listen, explaining, however, that they did not actually race any longer.

"Just cyclotourists," they said. "At our age, easy, easy."

Finally, the competition was intense.

"It's a nice little race," said Yates, who rode it many times a decade or two ago. An Englishman, he was one of the best descenders in the sport and served finally as Armstrong's mentor and the road captain for Motorola.

"It's tough," he said, "with a beautiful finishing circuit." That was the hills past sheep and cattle farms. "It's a good opportunity for guys with good legs to shine.

"Obviously the French are up for it—it's an opportunity to win a home race."

The French were up for it, with Laurent Brochard of the Bouygues Télécom team bolting away on the final climb and holding his seven-second lead on the 10-kilometer downhill to the finish.

The last secret of race survival: Give great prizes, like the winner's weight in Camembert. Actually, the winner got €3,147 (more than $4,000), a trophy, a bouquet, a magnum of apple cider, another regional specialty, and a box of three cheeses.

Two were Camemberts and one was a Brie, also manufactured by Lepetit, the sponsor. Coming next year: Paris-Camembert-Brie.

ASLEEP AT THE WHEEL

2005

Every once in a while, Franck Bouyer dozes on the job. Who doesn't? As anybody who participates in the workplace knows, it can be a soporific experience. Papers pile up, inane questions are asked, the room is overheated, and the most beguiling e-mails are the frequent Nigerian get-rich-quick schemes. ("Esteemed Sir, Your benefactor, the governor of Kano state, has left you his fortune in oil and diamonds. We shall be pleased to send it to you immediately after you remit $10,000 to cover handling and postage.")

Under these circumstances, whose eyelids wouldn't become heavy? Who wouldn't answer the Sandman's call?

Hold on, Bouyer says, that isn't the way it happens to me. He is not bored at work or plain tired, he explains—he's sick.

Bouyer, a 30-year-old Frenchman, has narcolepsy, a sleep disorder marked by recurring, unpredictable episodes of sleep during normal waking hours and disturbed sleep at night. He was diagnosed with this genetic disease in the autumn of 2003.

Against his will, he can nod off at any moment, which is a distressing situation since Bouyer is a professional bicycle racer and he works on the open road amid a pack of other men on bicycles. Let one of them drift into dreamland and swerve and the result can be a mass crash and broken bones.

It has not happened that way yet, he says, but he has fallen asleep while out training alone.

"One time, I found myself in the courtyard of a farm, woken up by a barking dog without knowing how I got there.

"Another time, out training with the team between the Flèche Wallonne and Liège-Bastogne-Liège, my eyes closed as we rode along and I had to go off alone when we reached the sprints." That's the point when a team forms a tightly linked chain and any bumping of wheels can bring everybody down.

Bouyer was speaking last October to the newspaper *L'Equipe*, trying to explain why he needed to take the drug Modiodal to control his disease.

His doctors say that his prescription of two to four 100-milligram pills a day will enable him to stay awake and alert while holding down a job.

The problem is that Modiodal's prime component is modafinal, which is banned in Bouyer's job. As a type of amphetamine, it is on the list of drugs prohibited by the International Cycling Union because they enhance performance.

Until his medical troubles began, Bouyer was a well-regarded team rider. Since he turned professional in 1994 and joined the first of six French teams, he has won the Tour of the Vendée and the Tour of Limousin, both secondary French races. He has finished, far back, five Tours de France.

His best year was 2003, when he finished 2nd in Chôlet-Pays de Loire, 3rd in the Etoile de Besseges, and 50th in Paris-Nice. Just as he seemed to be approaching his prime, he learned that he had narcolepsy.

Through the doctor for his Brioches la Boulangère team, Bouyer applied last spring for an exemption from the ban on the medicine he uses.

"It's obvious that Franck is sick and must take his medicine," said the doctor, Pierre-Yves Mathé, who noted that he had insisted on the prescription even though Bouyer was reluctant because "he thought he would be looked upon as a doper."

Mathé was speaking after the three-man medical commission of the World Anti-Doping Agency refused Bouyer's request for an exemption. The ruling said that there was no risk he would fall asleep while racing because physical activity is a stimulant. Besides, it added, there was no guarantee that Modiodal would not enhance his performance.

The team doctor was aghast. He pointed out that the French doctor who had tested the team at the start of the year had refused to authorize Bouyer's license unless he did take the drug.

"We're caught between two contradictions," he said. "On the one hand, he won't get his license to race unless he takes the drug; on the other, he can't race if he takes the drug."

Bouyer was puzzled.

"They're talking about enhanced performances, but what they don't take into account is that, without my medicine, I wake up at 3 o'clock in the night because my sleep is so disturbed. What consequences does that have on my performance?

"In my sport," he continued, "they allow racers who have failed three drug tests to continue but they shove aside somebody who's really sick."

Although he has remained with the team, now sponsored by Bouygues Télécom, Bouyer has not raced since last May as he awaited the medical commission's decision. Now he is taking legal action.

On the sidelines, at least, he is widely supported. Just before the start of the Tour of the Haut Var in France, all the riders paused for a minute to show their solidarity with Bouyer.

At the headquarters of the Bouygues Télécom team, officials said they were acting through their doctor and lawyer to help him too.

"He remains, of course, a member of the team even if he cannot race now," one official said.

As for Bouyer himself, repeated attempts to contact him at home failed. Perhaps he was taking a nap.

THE NEW KING

2005

Public relations officials for a bicycle team are not usually allowed to be among the first to clamber onto the stage at the end of a race and congratulate a winner. But, since the PR guy was Johan Museeuw, nobody blocked him at the Paris-Roubaix race.

Museeuw knew the way to the stage, of course. Among his eleven victories in the great classics before he retired last April were three triumphs in Paris-Roubaix. He knew where the steps are and where the winner stands, toweling the grime from his face before he reappears in public to lift his trophy, a cobblestone, overhead.

Tom Boonen, the 24-year-old Belgian who had just won the race with a strong sprint, seemed happy, if not surprised, to see Museeuw and embrace him. They were teammates until Museeuw retired, and people are always saying that they were mentor and student.

That isn't true, Boonen says in a polite way. Accessible and exuberant, he strives to be bluntly honest. If he had not won the Tour of Flanders and Paris-Roubaix on successive weekends and thus stamped himself as the next great rider on the cobblestones, Boonen might be regarded as naive for saying unguardedly what he feels.

So he praises Museeuw as a great champion while noting that he rarely gave any advice to the younger rider. In a series of interviews after the euphoria of the Flanders victory, Boonen even set the record straight on why he bought his way out of the U.S. Postal Service team three years ago:

It was not to ride with, and learn from, Museeuw, but because Postal tended to stop racing once Lance Armstrong won the Tour de France every July.

"There were no big races for me after the Tour," he said. "That was unacceptable for a rider as ambitious as I am." His Quick Step team concentrates on the classics, which continue all autumn.

Although Museeuw did publicly anoint him as his successor after Boonen finished third in Paris-Roubaix in 2002, "I didn't pay it too much attention. I was too happy on the podium in Roubaix to think about the future."

His own hero, Boonen continues, is not Museeuw but Miguel Indurain, the Spaniard who won the Tour de France five times a decade ago. "He impressed me a lot," Boonen tells interviewers. "I loved the way he rode, he was intelligent and perfect on his bike. He had a certain class."

Boonen has never met or spoken with Indurain. He did, however, share training camps, meals, races, and downtime with Museeuw.

"All his details, all his gestures had their importance," Boonen says. "Unintentionally, he guided me." The key word is the first one.

Museeuw, now 40 years old, is as closed as Boonen is open. While not exactly suspicious of reporters while he raced, he was always wary.

A favorite anecdote about him concerned the meeting he had one December with a reporter and a photographer. Museeuw consented to be photographed at home on the condition that no questions would be asked.

As the photo shoot proceeded, the reporter asked idly, "'What are you hoping to get for Christmas, Johan?"

Museeuw bristled. Glaring at the reporter, he said, "No questions, I told you."

The Belgians took him to their heart. He was the tough man they all aspire to be, the rider who crashed in Paris-Roubaix in 1998 and injured a knee that, because of inept medical treatment, nearly turned gangrenous and left him in a coma for three weeks. Two years later, he won the race for a second time.

In his final attempt, in 2004, he was poised for victory when his rear wheel punctured near the end of the long race and he finished fifth, seventeen seconds behind the winner. In his team bus afterward, he wept.

Nobody seems to hold it against him that in October, six months after he retired, he was suspended from all direct involvement in the sport for two years because of a doping conviction, which he is appealing. He is not allowed to serve as Quick Step's assistant directeur sportif, a job he wanted, but he rides in a car with guests of the team, telling them about the race. Museeuw wears a Quick Step sweater.

"He works for the sponsor, not the team," explains Patrick Léfevère, Quick Step's manager and Museeuw's friend. "You don't need a license to work for the sponsor."

Saying this, Léfevère barely resists a wink. He is not the sort of person to abandon his former star. He does resist, however, any comparison of Museeuw and Boonen—he knows who leads his team now.

Like Léfevère, the Belgians have taken Boonen to their heart. He is the joyous winner, the kid they all aspire to be.

As a rider, Boonen resembles Museeuw far more than Indurain. Museeuw was the king of one-day races, twice the winner of the World Cup series, twice champion of Belgium, and once, in 1996, world road-race champion. Indurain, like Armstrong, mainly made winning the Tour de France look easy.

Will Boonen aim for the grand Tours? Not to hear him tell it. His ambitions for the rest of this year, he said, are to claim the green points jersey in the Tour de France, where he won two sprints last year, the last of them on the Champs-Elysées as the race concluded.

Then comes the world championship road race in Madrid in late September, with perhaps a few classics before that. He will skip the hilly classics, including Liège-Bastogne-Liège in a couple of weeks because, at 80 kilograms, or 176 pounds, he finds long climbs too demanding.

While Indurain weighed the same and always got his big carcass over the Tour's mountains at the front, Boonen would have to sacrifice his sprint and lucidity over the cobblestones to train to emulate the Spaniard.

For now, at least, he seems content to remain the wunderkind of the cobblestones and a few more flat classics.

The new Indurain? No, not now. The new Museeuw? Not him either.

"I'm not like anybody but me," Boonen says. "I don't want to limit myself to races in Belgium. My goal is to be known throughout Europe."

LIFE AFTER LANCE

2005

Yes, Johan Bruyneel said confidently, there will be life after Lance.

Definitely, said Bruyneel, a 40-year-old Belgian and the directeur sportif of the Discovery Channel team. He was speaking in an interview before the Dauphiné Libéré race pushed out of Aix les Bains, a thermal resort on the doorstep to the Alps and a fun city for anybody suffering from arthritis or wearing a truss.

Bruyneel and Lance Armstrong have been together since 1999, when the Texan began his streak of six consecutive victories in the Tour de France. Now Armstrong is in his last race before the Tour, after which he will retire, just short of his 34th birthday.

When a colossus like Armstrong leaves the sport, his team flounders while seeking a replacement. Usually nobody of great talent is willing to be second banana to the leader for years while being groomed to succeed him.

This dire prospect should be especially true for Discovery Channel, formerly U.S. Postal Service, which is dedicated during the Tour de France to Armstrong's victory: Everybody rides only for him. No teammate has won a daily Tour stage during his reign while he has won many.

Not to worry, Bruyneel insisted. He and Armstrong are exceedingly close, often conferring intercontinentally on the phone several times a day during the off-season, and the retirement, announced in April, was no surprise. The succession is assured.

"After Lance, there is no American leader for the moment who can replace him," Bruyneel said. "Either we will find him in the future or in the meantime we will have some other leaders."

He named Yaroslav Popovych, a 25-year-old Ukrainian, a former world champion in the under-23 age group of riders, a third-place finisher in the Giro d'Italia two years ago, and the recent winner of the demanding Tour of Catalonia; and Paolo Savoldelli, 32, an Italian who unexpectedly won the Giro this year.

"Maybe Azevedo too, with a bit more freedom," Bruyneel said, referring to José Azevedo, 31, a Portuguese who joined the team last year and finished fifth in the Tour as Armstrong's main support rider in the highest mountains.

"We'll look for some new guys also," Bruyneel added.

He dismissed the suggestion that his team, so closely identified with the red, white, and blue because of its days with U.S. Postal Service as the sponsor, might seem askew with a leader who does not speak English.

"Our new sponsor insisted on the wideness of the team, not having the focus on an American team, and that really helps us a lot," he said. "They have been insisting, for example, on our taking a Japanese rider," who turned out to be Fumiyuki Beppu, 22.

"They really like the fact that we are so international," Bruyneel said. "That's the philosophy of their company too. Of course we're an American team because we're an American-based company and we're still going to be looking for the best possible American riders."

Of the twenty-eight riders on the roster, seven are Americans, with the majority of them riding primarily in U.S. races.

Bruyneel was in a relaxed and affable mood, and well he should have been. Now in his seventh year as a team director, he has seen his riders win eight major Tours, an unprecedented feat. In addition to Armstrong's six triumphs and Savoldelli's victory, Roberto Heras, a Spaniard who has since left, won the Vuelta a España in 2003.

A month before the Tour de France sets out with Armstrong the favorite, this has already been a splendid season for Discovery Channel.

"We've won four stage races so far with four different riders, not Lance," Bruyneel pointed out.

"We won Three Days of De Panne with Stijn Devolder, we won the Tour of Georgia with Tom Danielson, Catalonia with Popovych, and the Giro with Savoldelli. We're going to do it without Lance in the future and we've shown already that we can do it. If you name those four races—De Panne, Georgia, Catalonia, and the Giro—it's something a lot of teams would be happy with for their whole season."

Most of the credit for the versatility of his riders belongs to Bruyneel, who is known for his ability to spot talent.

He explained: "There have been a few people who say, 'Where the hell did you find this guy?' It's just an instinct. But I always try to have a lot of information. I do, let's say, a private investigation."

Savoldelli, for example, was recruited after he spent two unsuccessful years with the T-Mobile team in Germany. Danielson languished last season, badly used, with Fassa Bortolo in Italy.

Bruyneel's major protégé, however, is Armstrong, who was a strong one-day rider before he was stricken with cancer in 1996 and whom Bruyneel encouraged late in 1998, the Texan's comeback year, to think bigger, to think Tour de France.

"I raced with him," said the Belgian, who turned professional in 1987 and concluded his career as a rider in 1998. He briefly wore the yellow jersey in the Tour in 1993, finishing seventh, and won two stages in that race over the years. He won a stage in the Vuelta and finished third there in 1995. Among his other victories were the Tour de l'Avenir and the Grand Prix des Nations.

"I was successful at certain times," Bruyneel said. "I didn't have the engine, I wasn't a really big engine to be there all the time, but I could pick my moments. Every year I could pull off a big victory or something that was big. That was my strength."

Smiling pleasurably at those memories, he paused as Armstrong walked by on his way to a warmup ride and exchanged greetings.

"When he was young, I saw a lot of talent there," Bruyneel said of the old days.

"When you see that and he doesn't really take 100 percent advantage of his talent, you try to figure out a way to convince him how to do it. If the guy believes in it, it's not so difficult.

"The key is that you have to have an athlete who believes in what you say. I tried to convince him and I could convince him—that was the key."

NOT MUCH OF A NUMBER

2005

The number is not really that important, Lance Armstrong concedes. Seven would be nowhere near as big as six.

Six was monumental. When Armstrong, the 33-year-old American leader of the Discovery Channel team, won his sixth Tour de France last year, he broke the record he shared with other giants of bicycle racing.

Jacques Anquetil, Eddy Merckx, Bernard Hinault, Miguel Indurain, and Armstrong had all recorded five victories in the century-old Tour, and Indurain and Armstrong had recorded them consecutively.

The record fell when Armstrong cruised into Paris on July 25, 2004, an easy winner by more than six minutes. Now, as this year's Tour de France opens, he stands alone, and everybody, including Armstrong, acknowledges that a seventh victory, while satisfying, would be merely icing on the cake.

"The number seven is different," he has said in a series of farewell news conferences. "It doesn't hold the cachet that six did, but that's not important. This one is more for me, a personal goal" before he retires at the end of this Tour de France.

With that end in sight, Armstrong says that he is relaxed.

"I was nervous last year because I was up against a demon" in going for a sixth victory. "Now I'm not chasing history, I'm not chasing the legend, I'm not chasing the record. I'm just here to have a nice time and try to win again.

"Athletes can't play at the highest level forever," he admits. "So much of it is about timing and figuring out how long the body can continue to do what it does.

"This year felt like the right time to stop and based on what I can tell, I'm ready to go out at or near the top."

"The top" is Armstrong's obsession. For years he has built his season around only the Tour de France, knowing that victory in the world's biggest, toughest, and richest bicycle race is to be at the top.

Will he be there when the Tour completes its three-week clockwise journey covering 3,608 kilometers around France?

He looks as fit as ever despite a crash during a recent training ride. Armstrong says he has dropped the final couple of pounds he carried in the Dauphiné Libéré race a month ago.

His team, he insists, is better than ever and, as always, singlemindedly dedicated to his victory. His motivation is obvious.

"Still, it's the Tour, the roads are open, anything can happen," he notes. Only glancingly does he mention two factors working against him. One is that he will face an exceptionally strong field of rivals and the other is his age.

Since the Tour de France began in 1903, just six men have won it at the age of 33 or beyond. Armstrong will turn 34 in September.

Nevertheless, he talks mainly about victory. Asked if there had been any change from last year to this, he answered, "The most obvious change is that I haven't won a race to date."

What really drives him, he acknowledges, is not so much winning as not losing. Time and again he has said that his ultimate motivation is the fear of losing.

It is useless to argue with him that although a bicycle race has a winner, it cannot have "losers," since that would involve farcical numbers of everybody else in the race. In his reckoning, to finish second is to lose.

Therefore the desire to win his final race is compelling.

"I would love to go out on the top," he said. "I'm not interested in going out on my back."

In addition to the challenge, the Texan is bound by his contract with the new sponsor, Discovery Channel, to ride one final Tour de France, either this year or next. There will not be a next year, he insists.

"I'm excited about the Tour because I'm ready and I'm excited about what comes after," he says. "I like to think I'm approaching the race with complete balance."

He minimizes the effect his pending retirement will have on his rivals. A major one, Jan Ullrich of the T-Mobile team from Germany, has said that his goal is to win a Tour with Armstrong present.

Ullrich won the race in 1997, while Armstrong was recuperating from cancer, and has finished second five times, three of them behind Armstrong. This will be his last chance to unseat the American.

"My goal is obviously to win the Tour de France again," the German said at a news conference.

"And, above all, to beat Armstrong. I really can't conceive of a victory without beating the guy who's been the best for six years. This is my last chance to race against him and that's an extra motivation."

That should have come as news to Armstrong.

"I don't like to think I'm throwing down the gauntlet" in announcing his retirement, he insisted. "I've simply said this is my last Tour and whether that adds motivation for the others, I don't know."

He does not sound particularly concerned, either.

A NEW FAN

2005

Lance Armstrong is not the only person who will retire from racing at the end of this Tour de France. Sheryl Crow, the rock star and Armstrong's companion for the past year and a half, will also stop accompanying him to races, following his progress on the road in a team car, and generally behaving like what she describes as a fan.

"I hang out by the team bus like a groupie," she joked with a few reporters recently—while hanging out by the team bus. "I'm a big fan of these guys," she said, referring to the Discovery Channel team that Armstrong leads.

Crow has become a darling of French television, which delights in showing her giving Armstrong a thumbs-up before a stage or a kiss and a hug after it. During the team time trial, she gained split-screen status with Discovery Channel as it crossed the finish line.

Why not? She is vivacious and photogenic, and French television is obsessed with celebrities, even those whom nobody recognizes. By now, on the other hand, everybody recognizes Crow.

She has a unique perspective on the sport, which heretofore banned wives and female friends from the inner sanctum, except during family visits on rest days in long races.

As a performer herself, Crow is experienced in dealing with the media and far too savvy to be indiscreet. But she is also articulate and enthusiastic about her life with the team and willing to discuss her feelings, up to a point.

"I'm not sure I've ever met such great young men, with their interesting stories, each and every one of them," she said. "Great people. And there's great healthy competition. To me, it's just a beautiful sport. It's the greatest sport.

"I think the dedication that these guys show on a daily basis, the way they exercise mind over body, drive themselves past the point of pain, and experience that kind of anguish—to be part of a successful team is for me a beautiful ballet."

Crow, who has taken up bicycle riding to stay fit, admitted that she did not know anything about racing until recently. "When I met Lance, I didn't even know it was a team sport," she said.

"It's been an interesting time, the last year and a half," she added. "I've gotten to be in the position of a support person, which for me is a luxury, since my life has been ego-driven. It's all been about me and my career, and this has been a very good opportunity to be a support person to somebody I really love and admire a lot."

As a singer and composer, she has won Grammy awards and had platinum-selling albums. With Armstrong's retirement, she said, "My life is going to change a lot. I'm going back to working on my music, but I'll still be there for Lance when he decides what he wants to do with the second part of his life."

And that will be? "I'm sure he's going to be extremely involved in his cancer foundation and in the cancer community at large. I know that's going to be his main focus, but there are lots of other things, especially Discovery Channel.

"I think the biggest part will be spending time with his kids," she said. Armstrong has three young children, a son and twin daughters, from a marriage that ended in divorce.

She deflected a question about whether the two of them would miss the Tour de France next year, saying: "I know we'll be back. He's part owner of the Discovery Channel team, he's definitely invested in the team emotionally and wants to be as much a part of it as he can."

The next question was whether Armstrong seemed more relaxed now than he did last year when he was attempting to set the record of six Tour victories.

"Lance Armstrong relaxed?" she said in mock wonder. "I doubt it. Highly. I don't know that I would ever use the words 'relaxed' and 'Lance Armstrong' in the same sentence.

"He's very dedicated, he's been focused in his training, and I believe he's maybe more motivated this year than he was last year. He was motivated last year because he was making history, and this year he definitely wants to go out on top. I don't think he wants to go home not in the yellow jersey.

"He's very aware this is his last race, and he wants to be able to remember these moments. He's experiencing every bit of it. Every day he's getting closer to retirement, and it's a bittersweet feeling."

IN OTHERS' EYES

2005

When it comes to discussing his legacy, Lance Armstrong wants no part of the job.

"An individual can never dictate his legacy," he says. "That's not my job. I'll let other people write on the tombstone."

Some of those "other people" were asked in interviews about Armstrong, who won his seventh consecutive Tour de France nearly nine years after he learned he had cancer.

His accomplishments were generally, but not always, regarded as broader than the Tour victories.

Frankie Andreu, an American who finished nine Tours, two of them as Armstrong's teammate, before he retired in 2000: "Lance is the greatest American rider and the greatest Tour de France rider ever. Lance, he's past being a cycling person—he's moved to that superstar, rock star status, which I think benefits the sport."

Odessa Gunn, a Canadian who rode for Timex Cannondale for two years and "a barrage of little teams" before she retired in 2000: "He brought the sport to the mainstream and gave it the recognition it deserves in the United States."

Erik Breukink, the Dutch director of the Rabobank team and a rider a decade ago: "He's one of the best riders in history, like Merckx, like Hinault, like Indurain. To win the Tour seven times is something special." He referred to Eddy Merckx, the Belgian champion, Bernard Hinault, a Frenchman, and Miguel Indurain, a Spaniard, all of whom, with Jacques Anquetil, a Frenchman, won the Tour five times.

Hinault himself, who retired in 1986: "He's dominated for seven years. He's a professional down to his fingertips. He's the champion of his generation, the last ten years."

Jacques Augendre, a French historian of the sport who is attending his 53rd Tour: "Lance Armstrong deserves his victory, all his victories, because he's the most motivated, the strongest, the hardest worker, the most conscientious rider. And he deserves his popularity in France because he's done what nobody ever did before—two victories more than anybody else. Bravo, Armstrong."

Alex Stieda, a Canadian rider in the 1980s with Motorola and the first North American to wear the yellow jersey, in 1986, before he retired in 1992: "Lance has done so much for road racing, really raised the level of the sport in North America. People always thought of cycling as a third-tier sport, maybe even fourth tier, and Lance has shown people that 'Hey, you can have fun riding your bike. Road cycling is a legitimate activity, not just a sport, it's something you can do.'"

José Miguel Echavarria, a Spaniard who directed Indurain during his five victories in the 1990s: "I think we're going to have to wait a while for an answer about Armstrong's legacy. We're still under the effect of his domination of the Tour, his perfect domination.

"You can't compare him to Indurain, you can't compare them any more than you can compare painters. Each one was an artist. Armstrong was the superspecialist of the Tour. Merckx won everything, Indurain also won the Giro d'Italia, but Armstrong concentrated only on the Tour."

Jean Luc Vandenbroucke, a top Belgian rider in the 1980s and a former team director: "Obviously Armstrong's made a place for himself in the record books and the history of the Tour de France. But only in the Tour de France.

"The problem was that, as an American, he did not have the same vision of bicycle racing as European riders do. In the United States, I believe people are interested only in the Tour de France. Our culture is different.

"I'm very happy to see riders who compete all season and win different races, the classics, the monuments of the sport. Armstrong doesn't do that.

"So his legacy lies in the Tour de France only."

Jogi Müller, a Swiss who raced more than a decade ago, retiring in 1994, and is now head of media relations in Europe for Armstrong's team: "Lance's legacy will be understood better in years to come. What he brought to cycling is his history. What he lived through, having cancer, I think he showed the community of cancer survivors that you have to believe in yourself. You have to work and you have to believe and be strong.

"When he was trying to come back, in 1998, I said, 'The guy has cancer, what are the odds he can come back, getting only to a professional level, we're not talking about winning the Tour de France?' A million to one?

"His biggest achievement has to do with life, with dedication, with professionalism, with believing in yourself."

THE FRENCH DISCONNECTION

2005

Alexandre Vinokourov really dissed the French when he chose a new bicycle team, but if you can't kick a man when he's down, when can you kick him?

That the French are down, if not quite out, is indisputable.

French riders—as distinct from riders for French teams, which are stocked with foreigners—scored one victory in the twenty-one daily stages of the Tour de France. Add four second places and one third place, and the honor roll is complete.

The highest ranked Frenchman when the race ended was Christophe Moreau of the Crédit Agricole team, in 11th place overall. Next came Laurent Brochard of Bouygues Télécom in 28th.

Brochard is 37 years old and Moreau, whose performance so disappointed his team officials that they told him to find a new employer for next year, is 34.

It gets worse: No Frenchman made it into the top 10 in the points competition and only two—Moreau, fourth, and Brochard, eighth—ranked among the climbers. In team performance, the top French finisher among the twenty-one entries was Crédit Agricole, in 4th place, with AG2R next, in 10th place.

Dismayingly for the future, in the standings of the best riders under the age of 26, only one Frenchman, Jérôme Pineau of Bouygues, in fifth place, made it into the top 15.

No Frenchman has won the Tour since Bernard Hinault in 1985, and none has stood on the final three-step victory podium in Paris since Richard Virenque was second in 1997. As a sign of general weakness and reliance on foreigners, the French had just 30 riders in the 189-man field this year, their lowest number since 1963.

The trough of national ambition in this Tour might have been the sixth stage, when Christophe Mengin of the fdj.com team led the race into Nancy and then crashed on the final turn over roads that he travels nearly every day on training rides from his home in an adjacent village.

Or perhaps it was the thirteenth stage, into Montpellier, when Sylvain Chavanel of Cofidis overtook the last member of a long breakaway, Chris

Horner, an American with Saunier Duval, and refused to work with him in the sprint to the line as the pack closed in on both of them.

They were the prince and the pauper: Chavanel is the highest-paid French rider, getting about €800,000, or $980,000, a year, and Horner earns beans and bacon from his Spanish team. Thus Chavanel acted as if it was his due that the American should work for him rather than cooperate with him.

Horner refused the bait.

"If I led him out, he'd just come around me at the end and win," he said. "Second place is the same as last place."

In fact, he finished 10th in a mass sprint and Chavanel was 16th, complaining later about Horner's attitude.

About his own obstinacy, he said nothing. It comes with the territory when a pampered rider with few results mistakes himself for a star because the French firmament is so dark.

So it was understandable that Vinokourov, a 31-year-old Kazakh with T-Mobile who finished fifth in this Tour after winning two stages, rejected hiring offers from both Crédit Agricole and AG2R and signed instead with Liberty Seguros in Spain.

His goal, after all, is to win the Tour de France in the next two years. Neither French team, he explained, could enable him to do that. The reasons that they cannot are illuminating about the national racing scene.

Crédit Agricole, he said, has goals too modest—it was content that its Norwegian sprinter, Thor Hushovd, captured the green points jersey. "I don't think you can ride for both the points jersey and the yellow jersey" of the overall leader, he said.

As for AG2R, it simply does not have the talent. "With them, I could win Paris-Nice, the Dauphiné Libéré, or even a big classic, but not the Tour," he said.

Too bad, he added, because he likes and respects AG2R's director, Vincent Lavenu, with whom Vinokourov started his professional career in 1998.

The Kazakh was a whizbang from the start with what was then the Casino team, winning the Four Days of Dunkirk, the Tour of the Oise, and the Circuit des Mines in 1998, and the Tour of Valencia and the Dauphiné in 1999.

The next year he moved to the German team Telekom, a black hole for foreigners. (Among those who have clambered out after no individual success with Telekom or its successor, T-Mobile, and gone on to shine in big races this year are Bobby Julich, an American; Santiago Botero, a Colombian; Paolo Savoldelli, an Italian; and Cadel Evans, an Australian.)

While Vinokourov won prestigious classics like Liège-Bastogne-Liège this year and finished third in the 2003 Tour, in that race he was at the service of Jan Ullrich, the German leader.

Vinokourov joined Telekom for more money, a lot more money, than Lavenu could pay then. He can't pay it now either. With a budget of about €4 million a year, he has less than half the disposable income of T-Mobile or Liberty Seguros, Vinokourov's new team, which is sponsored by an American insurance company.

This was a squandered opportunity for AG2R's sponsors, a French insurance company. Although the team is not part of the ProTour, a twenty-entry organization that guarantees participation in all the big races, a spot will open next season with the breakup of Fassa Bortolo from Italy. Fassa's hopes of finding a new sponsor ended when one of its riders, Dario Frigo, an Italian, was jailed during the Tour on doping suspicions.

A few million euros more and AG2R could have signed Vinokourov and a handful of strong support riders, forcing its way into the ProTour. Instead it has signed the lackluster Moreau on the cheap and will have to continue to rely on wild cards, like the one that allowed it into the Tour de France.

"It's a shame," Vinokourov said. "Three years from now, maybe I'll return to Lavenu to finish my career and help teach young riders. He's the guy who gave me confidence at the start of my career and I'll never forget that."

Goals too modest, talent too sparse, and sponsors too pinchpenny—all of this is familiar in French racing. Autopsy reports on the corpse have been unvarying for a decade.

Equally predictable were the doping suspicions raised by Jean Pitallier, the president of the French Cycling Federation, in an interview with Agence France-Presse.

Noting that French riders had questioned the performance of several unnamed foreign teams, Pitallier said: "I support them. I ask if other countries apply measures as strict as the ones in France. The climate of suspicion that reigns is very disagreeable since bicycle racing is without doubt the sport with the most drug tests. But everybody knows the limits of the classic tests."

He concluded, "French riders are not as bad as everybody says."

Tell that, please, to Vinokourov.

THE DEBATE OVER DRUGS

2005

Since the French sports newspaper *L'Equipe* published its front-page banner headline "The Armstrong Lie," much that is misleading, malicious, unfair, and just plain dumb has been said on both sides of the debate. That it is a debate is unquestionable. Dick Pound, chairman of the World Anti-Doping Agency, or WADA, is not the only person who has remarked that this is a case study in "he said, she said"—accusations and denials by both sides, with neither having real proof.

These are some of the facts: The French national antidoping laboratory tested urine samples taken from riders in the 1999 Tour de France, the first of seven that Lance Armstrong won, in an effort to refine its detection methods for the banned drug EPO. The original test, developed at the laboratory, was introduced in 2000 at the Olympic Games in Sydney and in 2001 in the sport of bicycle racing.

When a rider gives a urine sample in a race, it is divided into two, the A and the B. If the A sample proves positive, the B sample must confirm the finding for the result to be conclusive. In the new tests, which began late last year, there were no A samples, since they had been used in developing the test six years ago.

In their work, the laboratory technicians had flasks marked with six-digit identification numbers, but not with names. Forms filled out by the riders carried both their names and the six digits, but they were not furnished to the laboratory. Instead, they were filed with the International Cycling Union, which governs the sport, and with the French sports authorities.

A reporter for *L'Equipe* heard about the new tests and managed, presumably through the cycling union, to get the forms with names and numbers.

When the laboratory gave its report to the World Anti-Doping Agency in late August, the reporter immediately obtained a copy, compared the numbers of the samples that allegedly showed the use of EPO, or erythropoietin, with the forms identifying the riders, and published the results.

In six cases, the donor of the tainted urine specimen was said to be Armstrong. In six other cases, the rider or riders were not identified.

Armstrong vigorously denies the charge, calling it unfair and malicious.

He has a strong point: The fact that only the B sample was tested invalidates the result.

In addition, as he said, "A guy in a Parisian laboratory opens up your sample, you know, Jean-François so-and-so, and he tests it—nobody's there to observe, no protocol was followed."

Again, he has a strong point. Dr. Christiane Ayotte, director of the Doping Control Laboratory at the National Institute of Scientific Research in Montreal, told the magazine *VeloNews:* "This whole thing is a breach of the WADA code. We are supposed to work confidentially until such time that we can confirm a result."

On his Web site and in later statements, Armstrong charged that "the paper even admits in its own article that the science in question here is faulty and that I have no way to defend myself." Although *L'Equipe* did not quite admit that the test was flawed, investigation has shown that some scientific researchers consider it less than decisive.

Although many people felt that disclosing the results a month after Armstrong retired was unfair and a violation of his privacy, Armstrong has been misleading.

While his standard defense—that he is the most frequently tested athlete in the world—is true, the fact that he has never failed a drug test is irrelevant. Richard Virenque, the French king of the Tour de France's mountains, never failed a drug test but finally admitted in court that he had long used illegal performance-enhancing drugs. David Millar, the Briton who won the world time-trial championship in 2003 and passed a drug test immediately afterward, later admitted that he had used EPO before that race.

The analogy here is the person who says he has never been caught cheating on his taxes. That does not necessarily mean he has never cheated; it means he has never been caught. On the other hand—a clause that marks this case countless times—perhaps he never has cheated.

Armstrong further said, in an international television interview, that the accusations against him might be based on tense U.S.-French relations. "If we consider the landscape between Americans and the French right now, obviously relations are strained," he said.

"Once I had a French teammate and he said to me, 'Look, Lance, the French don't like winners,'" he continued.

There it was, red meat for the American public, 72 percent of which, polls show, stand behind him. He is, after all, an iconic figure in American life, bigger than a sports champion, a hero even to people who have never seen a bicycle race—a truly inspirational figure who overcame cancer to win the toughest endurance test in the world not once but seven consecutive times.

Who are you going to believe?

Bill Luckett of Stephenson, Virginia, has no doubts. He wrote in a letter published in *L'Equipe*, "I find it unbelievable that you're trying to tarnish Lance's reputation in this way. I ask you to withdraw your horrible accusations about the lies of this great athlete who has brought much publicity to France."

(Sébastian R., a Frenchman, took a more European view: "Whether Lance was doped or not, it doesn't matter, since everybody does it.")

Gerard Bisceglia, chief executive of American cycling's governing body, USA Cycling, also leaped to the defense. "Lance Armstrong is one of the most tested athletes in the history of sport and he has come up clean every single time," he said.

"This kind of years-ago testing of a single sample with new technology is completely without credibility," he added, not explaining how he would know that so quickly. In a later statement, he rowed back and said his organization would await developments.

Further foolishness centered on attacks on *L'Equipe* itself.

An Associated Press article from New York said the newspaper had long attacked Armstrong, which is not true. The critical newspaper is Le Monde. *L'Equipe*'s coverage of the Tour champion often verges on fawning.

But that was brushed off on a Web site by Sean Cridland of Jemez Springs, New Mexico.

"*L'Equipe* is and always has been the sporting equivalent of the *National Enquirer*," he wrote in part. "Its content has always been suspect as a source of facts. Just ask any athlete who has ever been a subject of its articles, foreign or French."

Anybody who does just ask will probably get a testimonial to the newspaper's honesty and veracity.

But in its rush to judgment in the Armstrong case, *L'Equipe* seems unconvincing in stating that it has found a smoking gun.

THE TALK OF THE TOWN

2003

The Tour de France is over, the riders gone to other races. In la France profonde, deep in the countryside, the Tour will not be over for ages.

In the village of Souel, in the southern department of the Tarn, for example, the Tour's visit on July 18 will stir the same memories years from now that any flypast of the race does in similar villages around the country. Stop at one of these places and ask if the Tour has ever come by; people recall the occasion decades later.

Since the routes change from year to year, the race does not often re-trace its flight on such back roads as where the D922 meets the D25, both one lane each way, a kilometer outside Souel, population 580.

At that crossroads, amid fields of wheat and grapevines, villagers turned out on a hot and windy day to watch a 47-kilometer individual time trial. The 167 riders still in the race sped by two minutes apart, the woo-woo-woo of their rear disc wheels barely audible over the villagers' applause and cheers. It was a Friday, a workday on the farm, but that meant nothing.

"The grapes will have to look after themselves today," said Monsieur Yvan, whose output goes into Gaillac, a sturdy table wine. He was there with his wife and their son, a man in his early twenties who works on the family farm.

"This is a big day," the son said. "Not much happens here."

That was not quite true.

On a nearby telephone pole, a poster advertised an August full of attractions in Souel. On the 10th, there would be a competition in petanque, a game played with metal balls tossed at a target. On the 14th, a dance was scheduled with Coco Malko as the star attraction. On the 15th, a full day included a fishing contest, a Mass, and a laying of flowers at a Monument to the Dead (presumably of both world wars), and a tournament in belote, a card game.

For those villagers game for more, an outdoor dinner dance was planned with Serenade offering music to go with the meal of foie gras, preserved duck, cheese, pie, fruit, and coffee. The price was €17, about $19, and reservations could be made by phone.

But those good times were weeks away when Madame Yvan stood on hay bales piled on a trailer behind the family's tractor. Prudently, she remained under an umbrella against the sun as she waved red streamers at each passing rider.

A gendarme guarded the crossroads, making sure that no cars cut across the Tour's route. Dozens of cars were parked on the D922 while their drivers watched the race and cheered. Anything rated a cheer, even the arrival of a police car for an officer to give a bottle of water to the gendarme.

The loudest cheers, though, were reserved for French riders.

"Naturally," Monsieur Yvan explained. His own favorite is Laurent Jalabert, now retired. "Any other Frenchman too," he said.

Just then, 26 kilometers into the race against the clock, one of those French riders, David Moncoutié of the Cofidis team, came down the road with a motorcycle policeman ahead of him and a team car behind him. Also behind him, just barely, was Michael Rogers, an Australian with the Quick Step team, who had his own police escort and team car.

They whooshed past Souel, where the only question was "Who started first?" Had Moncoutié started two minutes ahead of Rogers and been caught, or, as Monsieur Yvan, his wife, his son, and their neighbors hoped, had Rogers started first and been caught?

A list of the starting order was produced. It broke many hearts: Moncoutié was the laggard.

"There are a lot of others in the Tour," somebody muttered, meaning Frenchmen.

Before the stage was over, spectators had more to remember. Seven riders were penalized for riding too closely behind an opponent and thus using his slipstream to ease their labors. The most blatant of those seven, Unai Extebarria, a Colombian with the Euskaltel team, rode that illegal way for 13 kilometers, or almost a quarter of the time trial, including his stretch past Souel. At that point, he was so close to his rival that they seemed to be riding a bicycle built for two.

Extebarria was fined 100 Swiss francs, or $74, and penalized 5 minutes, 51 seconds.

Added to his already slow speed, that was enough to disqualify him for failing to finish within the time limit.

Won't that give the villagers something to talk about for years?

MOSTLY DOPING

2005

Andre, who is Belgian and one of the most helpful and knowledgeable bicycle writers around is also softspoken, so when he has something to say, people listen.

During the world championships in Madrid, he had this to say: "Four more days."

He said it almost wistfully, and he obviously meant more than that the worlds, as they are known, would end on Sunday. In fact, he meant that his world would end then.

His old world, he explained. In four days he was retiring. He covered his first world championships in 1973 in Barcelona and now, with a kind of Spanish symmetry, he was winding it up in Madrid.

But he doesn't look or act old and weary. Why retire?

"Too much that's not bicycle racing," he explained. "Now what I write about is mostly doping and politics."

Instead he has a swell idea: He and his 12-year-old granddaughter will sit down and plan books for children her age to read. She'll give the story line, and he'll do the writing.

"Anything except doping and politics," he said.

So, and luckily for him, Andre was thinking about fairy godmothers and frog princes, or whatever 12-year-old girls are reading now, when Belgian prosecutors announced that Johan Museeuw had been officially charged with possession of illegal performance-enhancing drugs and was suspected of being part of a ring of drug traffickers.

Six other riders, a veterinarian, a masseur, and two couriers were also charged, Belgian newspapers reported. The public prosecutor's office in the city of Kortrijk said Museeuw would appear before a grand jury that will decide whether there is enough evidence to refer him to a criminal court.

The case dates to 2003, when the Belgian police searched twenty homes, including Museeuw's in the town of Gistel in the heart of Flanders in western Belgium. After he retired from racing in 2004, Museeuw was banned from the sport for two years by the Belgian bicycling federation and has been unable to serve as a directeur sportif with his former team, Quick Step.

Andre, who knows everything, knew all about this case maybe even before it became public. He talked about it a couple of years ago, and he sounded solemn, even morose.

Museeuw, remember, was the Lion of Flanders, the winner of 101 races, including 11 major classics. Three victories in the Tour of Flanders, three in Paris-Roubaix, one each in Paris-Tours, the Amstel Gold Race and the Championship of Zurich. Twice he was champion of Belgium, in 1992 and 1996, twice winner of the World Cup series, in 1995 and 1996, and once world road race champion, in 1996.

Was he tough? In 1998, he crashed in Paris-Roubaix and ripped up a knee. Because of inept treatment by doctors, the wound nearly turned gangrenous and left him in a coma for three weeks. Two years later, he finished first over the cobblestones of Paris-Roubaix.

He was a hero not simply in Flanders but also throughout Belgium— the hard man, the survivor, the winner.

Andre thought Museeuw was a fraud.

He cited intercepted telephone calls and police findings. It is doubtful that he could write about this ahead of judicial action, but he knew his stuff, Andre did. He is not a man to exaggerate.

So now he is writing books with his granddaughter. He is no longer writing about drug scandals in the sport in France, Italy, Spain, the United States, and Belgium.

Have a happy retirement, Andre. Let all your words concern heroic nurses, brave firemen, dedicated teachers, or whatever 12-year-old girls dream about.

All of us, your friends and former colleagues, sincerely hope your stories will have nothing but happy endings. Of corruption, not a word.

OBSCURE OBJECT OF DESIRE

2002

The bicycle race was leaving the hotel in Shah Alam, Malaysia, heading a few dozen kilometers away for the start of the next stage, but one journalist was staying behind. The race was going to Klang—then to places he imagined as Bang and Boom—and he was leaving the hotel to go home later in the morning. Duty called, another duty entirely. This was not the first time he had left a race early, and each time the feeling was the same: He felt abandoned. The hotel lobby had been full of luggage, none of it his, and then the cars and buses had been packed and driven away. Riders, officials, support crew, journalist friends from Europe and Asia—Tommy the Irishman, Daniel from Belgium, Lillo from Italy, the Malaysian woman he always addressed politely as "Granny"—all gone.

The bicycle storage room was empty. The noise that surrounds a race crowd had died and he could clearly hear a recorded muezzin calling the faithful to the Blue Mosque across a field.

Now the last car was leaving. It carried the commissaires, the judges, and they were in no rush, knowing that no race can start without them. Behind them the lobby was filling with a different bunch. Businessmen awaited contacts, a wedding reception for a couple named Yeoh and Marie was being set up, and tourists headed to the pool.

The race would return to the hotel in a week for its finale in nearby Kuala Lumpur, so not all its traces had disappeared. Posters were left on the lobby walls, the waitresses in the lounge continued to wear the race's T-shirt, and the display of bicycles hanging from overhead railings was still in place.

Most of the bicycles were up to the minute, either all-terrain models with alloy frames, shock absorbers, and twenty-one-gear automatic shifting, or sleek titanium road models with aerodynamic styling. Signs from what Malaysians call a basikal store gave their prices at around 450 ringgit ($125).

Much more expensive was the ancient machine sitting in the middle of the lobby on a stand, surrounded by small spotlights and pots of yellow and violet orchids. "Raleigh Gentleman Old Style," said its sign, with a price of 2,250 ringgit.

Before the race left town, there were so many riders to talk to that he had hardly glanced at the bicycle. "I used to have one of those," he had remarked to a team official as they walked past the stand. "It was called an English racer."

"Shows how old you are," the official said.

With everybody gone and nobody to interview, he took the time to inspect the bicycle. The saddle was a Brooks, he remembered, with a tool kit hanging behind it. He looked and there was the small Brooks label. The brakes were made by Sturmey Archer, he thought. And there was another small label, Sturmey Archer.

He remembered the big light in front, the bell on the handlebars, the luggage rack behind the saddle, and the red reflector on the mudguard. He remembered the decal that said "Raleigh, Nottingham, England" and the one that said the bicycle was made of steel. And there, on the down tube, were the decals.

He also remembered then that he had never had a Raleigh. Never. Memory plays tricks. He had desperately wanted an English racer and had pleaded with his father for months. But Raleighs were expensive. What he was given instead was an ancient bicycle used by a distant cousin when he competed in six-day races.

That bicycle was far too large for a boy and its color was repulsive. What must have been a flashy yellow had turned over the years into a shade resembling yesterday's scrambled eggs. The stiff saddle hurt too. He remembered that, now that he was remembering.

Once he was given the yellow clunker, he resumed pleading for an English racer. A couple of birthdays later he was given a new bicycle, not a dashing Raleigh but a mundane Schwinn, and a woman's model at that. The idea, it was explained to him, was that when he outgrew it he could pass it along to his younger sister.

So many years ago, he thought with a grudging smile. Only now that the race was gone, and his friends with it, there was nobody to share the joke with.

INDEX

ABOUT THE AUTHOR

Samuel Abt, a news editor for the *International Herald Tribune*, has covered bicycle racing for 30 years. He has written 10 books about the sport, including the acclaimed *Breakaway: On the Road with the Tour de France, LeMond,* and *Off to the Races.* He is the only American to have been awarded the medal of the Tour de France for distinguished service to the race.